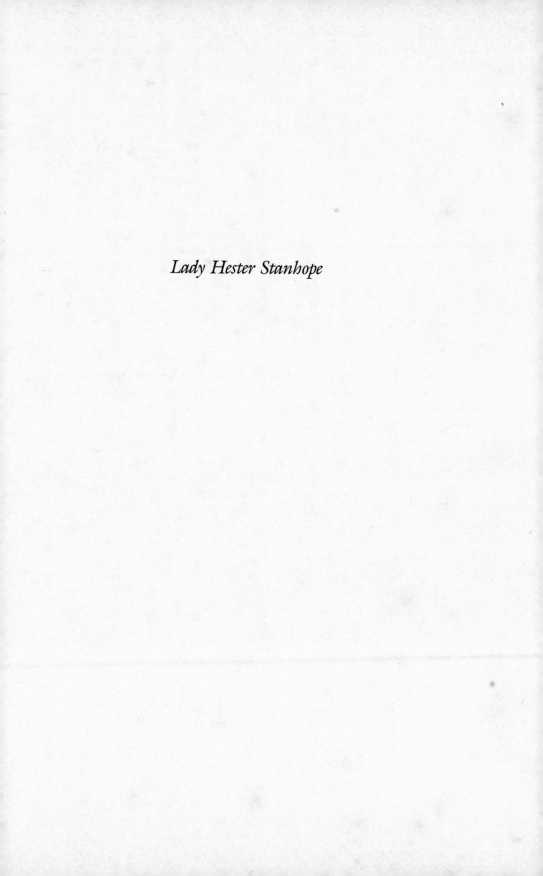

Lady Hester Stanhope

If those who have had experience of my character cannot give me credit for honour, disinterestedness and integrity without statement to prove I am neither mad nor unprincipled, I must content myself with the flattering hope that strangers will be more just to my present conduct as well as to my memory.

> By foreign hands her humble grave adorn'd;
> By strangers honour'd and by strangers mourned.

Lady Hester Stanhope

Lady Hester Stanhope

Queen of the Desert

———

by
Virginia Childs

———

Weidenfeld & Nicolson
London

For my father, David Howarth, with best love and thanks

Published in Great Britain in 1990 by
George Weidenfeld & Nicolson Limited
91 Clapham High St, SW4 7TA

British Library Cataloguing in Publication Data
(applied for)

ISBN 0 297 81017 0

Printed and bound in Great Britain by
The Bath Press, Avon

Contents

Contents

Illustrations

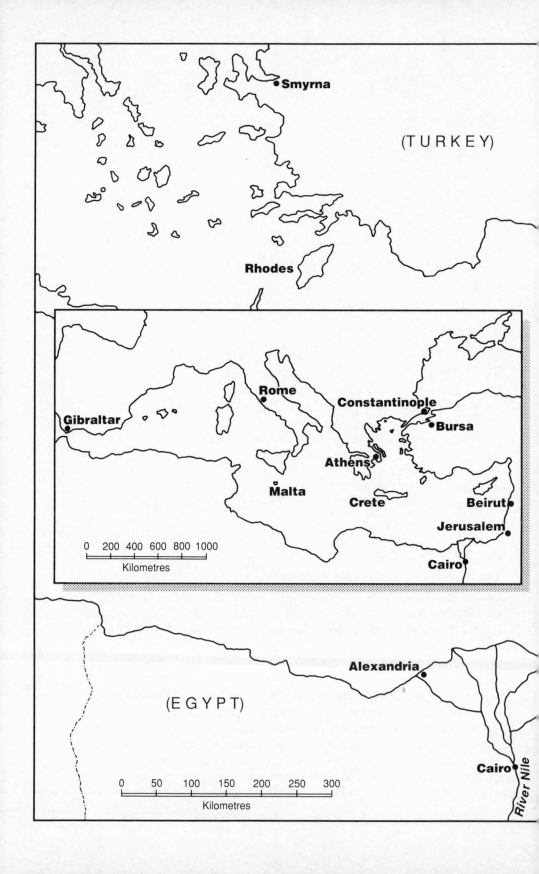

OTTOMAN EMPIRE

------- INDICATES PRESENT-DAY BORDERS ONLY

Taurus Mountains

Adana

Aleppo

(SYRIA)

Latakia

Hamah

Cyprus

Palmyra

Tripoli

Druse Mountains

(LEBANON)

Baalbec

Beirut

Sayda

MEDITERRANEAN SEA

Djoun

Damascus

Meshmushy

(IRAQ)

Acre

Jaffa

Amman

Jerusalem

Ascalon

rt Said

(SAUDI ARABIA)

(ISRAEL)

River Jordan

(JORDAN)

Chronology

12 March	1776	Lady Hester Stanhope born at Chevening.
	1780	Lady Hester's mother dies.
	1800	Lady Hester leaves Chevening to live at Burton Pynsent with grandmother.
	1801	Lady Hester rescues Philip, Lord Mahon from Chevening.
September	1802	Lady Hester journeys to Europe.
3 April	1803	Grandmother dies.
May	1803	Napoleonic War precipitates Lady Hester's return to England. Now homeless. She moves in with Pitt at Walmer Castle.
	1804	Pitt made Prime Minister again.
23 January	1806	Pitt dies. Lady Hester homeless.
	1809	John Moore and Charles Stanhope killed in action at Corunna.
10 February	1810	Lady Hester leaves England.
11 March	1810	Arrival at Gibraltar. Meets Michael Bruce.
April	1810	Lady Hester leaves for Malta. Joined by Michael Bruce.
June	1810	Writes memorable letter to Craufurd Bruce.
August	1810	Arrives in Athens. Meets Lord Byron.
September	1810	Arrived in Constantinople.
	1811	Michael proposes marriage.
June	1811	Trip to Brusa.
October	1811	Leaves Constantinople for Alexandria. Shipwreck. Landfall at Rhodes.
11 February	1812	Arrival in Alexandria.
May	1812	Departure for Jaffa.
Summer	1812	Visits to Jerusalem, Acre and Druse mountains.
October	1812	Entry into Damascus.
20 March	1813	Departure for Palmyra. Crowned 'Queen of the Desert'.

Chronology

End April	1813	Triumphant return to Hamah.
		Epidemic of plague.
May	1813	Departure for Latakia.
13 October	1813	Michael Bruce leaves for England.
November	1813	Lady Hester ill with plague.
January	1814	Departure for Mar Elias.
	1814	Michael volunteers financial help, then reneges.
17 March	1815	Departure for treasure hunt at Ascalon.
November	1815	M. Boutin's murder.
Spring	1816	Visit from Bankes and Buckingham.
January	1817	Dr Meryon leaves for England.
		Final severance with Michael Bruce.
	1817	Lady Hester's father dies.
		Lady Hester quarrels with brother Philip.
		Captain Lousteneau arrives.
		Captain Lousteneau dies.
		Lady Hester moves to Djoun.
	1825	Visit from Captain Yorke.
		Civil war in Lebanon.
		Brother James's suicide.
	1827	Meryon's return to Lebanon stopped by bad weather and pirates.
October	1827	Battle of Navarino.
		Djoun full of refugees.
		Lady Hester and Miss Williams contract yellow fever.
		Miss Williams dies.
	1830	Meryon returns to Lebanon with wife.
April	1831	Meryon and wife leave.
	1832	Ibrahim Pasha of Egypt invades Lebanon.
		Djoun becomes stronghold against him.
September	1832	Visit from French poet Lamartine.
	1835	Visit from Kinglake.
	1837	Ibrahim Pasha imposes conscription in Syria and Lebanon. Djoun filled with refugees again.
		Bedu and Druse uprising against occupation.
		Dr Meryon returns with wife and daughter.
January	1838	Letter from Colonel Campbell informing Lady Hester of confiscation of pension.
February	1838	Lady Hester resigns British citizenship and pension in letter to Queen Victoria.
Spring	1838	Visit from Prince Pückler-Muskau.
		Lady Hester has Djoun walled up.
August	1838	Dr Meryon leaves for England.
23 June	1839	Lady Hester dies.

Acknowledgements

Driving past the tiny village of Chevening one day with my father, I asked him to suggest a suitable subject for a biography. 'A woman,' I said, 'and one who lived a couple of centuries ago.' He thought for a long time before suggesting Lady Hester as a suitable candidate, but as soon as I started my research I was utterly hooked. Not only had she evidently led an extraordinary life, but we were joined by a series of coincidences. When we drove past Chevening that day we did not know that she had been born and brought up there. An even closer link was that my husband and I had been married in Chevening church, and both our sons were christened there. We had also recently returned from living in the Middle East for five years, and Lady Hester lived almost half her life in Syria and Lebanon. It was fascinating, and so was she.

My first thanks, therefore, must go to my father, David Howarth, not only for his suggestion, but also for his pride in my carrying on what is perhaps becoming the family tradition of writing. Secondly I would like to thank my brother Stephen, who despite his own busy writing schedule, was always generous with his time in answering my questions.

David Roberts, of Weidenfeld and Nicolson, must be thanked not only for his bravery in taking me on, but also for his enthusiasm, which was most heartening. Allegra Huston has also been most encouraging and helpful.

During my research I have met with nothing but kindness from the people I badgered. I would particularly like to thank the Board of the

Acknowledgements

Trustees of the Chevening Estate for allowing me to be shown around Chevening House, and for permitting reproduction of various pictures. I also thank Coutts Bank, in particular Barbara Peters, for allowing me access to their archives, and Julian Saunders of the National Army Museum.

There are many others who deserve my thanks, but perhaps particularly my mother, Nanette McLean, for her encouragement, Jean Brown for her practical help, and of course my husband Michael and our two dear sons Daniel and Gregory for their loving support.

V.E.C.

Preface

On 23 June 1839 in a vast dilapidated monastery on top of a hill in Lebanon an old woman lay gravely ill. The room where she lay was filthy, bare of everything except a pallet bed, and she was quite alone. It was a scene of the utmost poverty and desolation, a dying that not even a beggar should have to endure. But this was Lady Hester Stanhope, who was descended from two of the most aristocratic families of the age, and whose brilliance, bravery and wit had earned her an extraordinary reputation.

As the niece of William Pitt, she had lived with him and acted as his hostess during his last, most glorious reign of office, and had become the toast of London society. After Pitt died she left England to travel in the East, where no European woman had ever before travelled alone, and she quickly gathered such power and reputation that not one Eastern leader had succeeded in standing against her. As a result of her daring expeditions into the desert and her friendship with the Bedouin Arabs, she became known as the Queen of the Desert, and people travelled great distances to meet her, to ask for her help and to receive her charity. Nearly thirty years later, she was deeply in debt and deserted by her family, her friends and her country. She resigned her British citizenship and walled herself in to her mountain home. Finally, as even her servants crept away, taking her last few possessions with them, she died.

CHAPTER ONE

Democracy Hall

Lady Hester Stanhope was born on 12 March 1776, the first child of one of the most illustrious marriages in the country. Her father was Charles, Viscount Mahon, son of the 2nd Lord Stanhope and heir to the richest estate in Kent. Her mother, also called Lady Hester, was the daughter of Lord Chatham, the 'Great Commoner', and sister of William Pitt the Younger. The marriage united two brilliant and distinguished families, but it was far more than just a superb alliance – it was a marriage of love.

Their first daughter, Hester, was soon joined by another, Griselda, and two years later a third, called Lucy. The stage seemed set for a happy family life. Charles was a man with a brilliant scientific mind of whom great things were expected, and his wife Hester was a loving and much-loved woman. 'A woman rarely to be met with,' a cousin wrote of her, 'wise, temperate, and prudent, by nature cheerful without levity, a warm friend and free from all the petty vices that attend little minds.'

Suddenly and tragically, everything changed. Hester, Lady Mahon, died from complications a few days after her youngest daughter was born. She was just twenty-five and the loss to the family was incalculable, especially, as it transpired, for the children. Not only were they now motherless, but Charles appeared half-crazed with grief. His family were greatly concerned about him and rallied round to help. His mother came to the family home at Chevening to look after the three little girls and keep an eye on her beloved son.

Given the apparent depth of Charles's grief, it is hard to explain how he recovered himself sufficiently to remarry within six months. It would be kind, perhaps, to guess that it was out of concern for his children, but if it was for their sake then he could scarcely have chosen a worse person to be their stepmother. Her name was Louisa Grenville and she was his wife's first cousin, but they could not have been less alike. Charles's mother described her as 'chilling', and she was indeed a cold, conventional woman who displayed no concern at all for Hester or her sisters.

After efficiently providing Charles with three sons, Philip, Charles and James, she devoted herself to her social life, which meant that the children scarcely ever saw her. She was so seldom at home that little Lucy said, in later years, that she thought she would not recognize her if she saw her walking down the street. Lord Mahon rapidly discovered that he had nothing in common with his second wife and they spent very little time together. Neither did Lady Mahon's neglect of their children mean that Charles spent more time with them: they were left very much to their own devices. Perhaps the loss of his first wife and the disappointment of his second were even greater blows to him than they had appeared to be, for it became evident that his brilliance was tainted with a streak of instability. However, although they scarcely ever saw him, Charles exerted a powerful influence on the lives of all his children, an influence they would have been far happier without.

He was a man of extremes. Vastly gifted in many ways, he was also strangely lacking in more ordinary characteristics such as self-control and plain common sense. All his children except for Lady Hester lived in fear of him. There seemed to be no happy medium for them: they were either heartlessly punished for crimes they scarcely knew they had committed, or, more usually, totally ignored.

It was a childhood of inconsistencies, insecurities and a total lack of parental love.

Charles had always been an eccentric man, and, denied a loving family by the death of his first wife, he immersed himself in politics and his world of inventions. An education in Switzerland had given him strong republican ideas – strange tendencies for an aristocrat, and ones he found difficult to reconcile with his inherited wealth. In his early years as a Member of Parliament he frequently shocked the other members of the House with his frenzies and his wild enthusiasms, and his first appearance at Court was notable mainly for the fact that he refused to powder his black hair, as was the current fashion. In 1786 his father, Lord Stanhope, died and Charles took his place in the House of Lords, continuing to be controversial. He was particularly pleased on one occasion when he forced a division and found himself without a single supporter: he revelled in his 'glorious minority of one'.

Charles's true genius showed in his inventive imagination, and it was perhaps the greatest tragedy of his life that this was never fully acknowledged. His Stanhope printing press was the forerunner of almost all subsequent presses. He invented the first calculating machine long before Babbage, but perhaps most impressive of all was his steamship. His invention used the screw-propeller 'for navigating ships of the largest size without any wind and even against wind and waves', and it anticipated Fulton's paddle-box design by ten years. He worked on the design for twenty years, built models and tested them on the lake at Chevening, and in 1793 he offered his work to the Admiralty. In a staggering display of shortsightedness, both the design and the whole concept of steam power were rejected, and Stanhope dismissed as being madder than usual. He knew his invention was a good one, however, and told them so in the House of Lords. The first steamship crossed the Atlantic in 1818, only two years after his death.

These, then, were the projects on which Charles Stanhope focused his energies, to the great detriment of his personal life and his children. His political life became ever more extreme. As the years went by he became a self-professed Jacobin, and championed the French Revolution. From being a firm supporter of his brother-in-law, William Pitt, who was then Prime Minister, he became one of his most outspoken opponents. He had the Stanhope coat-of-arms removed from the gates of Chevening, renaming it Democracy Hall and himself, Citizen Stanhope. Many other fairly harmless displays of eccentricity provided the London satirists with plenty of material, but made an uncomfortable life for the children at home.

Although he was a champion of democracy and freedom for the people, he ruled his own household with ferocity. Unable to bring to terms his private wealth and his political ideas, he deprived his children of many of the comforts of life – and some of the necessities too.

The deprivations began in a small way. 'If any of us happened to look better than usual in a particular hat or frock,' Hester recalled, 'he was sure to have it put away the next day, and to have something coarse substituted in its place.' Sometimes he would make Hester go out on the common to tend the turkeys, and as the boys grew older he decided that they should have no formal education at all. Instead he apprenticed them to work with the local blacksmith and shoemaker. His relatives and society in general thought he was quite mad, but no one could do anything to change his mind. Life at Chevening became very dour, but Hester's natural high spirits kept her cheerful and optimistic despite everything. She was the only one of the six children who was able to influence her father. 'I could always govern my father better than anybody,' she said in later life, 'because I could bear his oddities with more patience, and could joke him into things plain sense and argument would have failed in.' Her good humour was sorely stretched one day when, for some unknown reason, he held a knife to her throat. She was quite unafraid, however: 'I felt only pity for the hand that held the knife,' she remembered sadly.

Although Hester was only four when her mother died, her character had already emerged strongly. She was a gifted child: clever and imaginative, energetic and brave. She was also supremely self-confident and fond, as one cousin put it, of 'playing the empress-queen'. As she grew older she became fiercely devoted to her sisters and in particular to her little half-brothers. She showered them with love and bossed them about whilst they in their turn adored and obeyed her, usually without question. Lucy was the pretty one, a happy contented child, whilst Griselda was clever but discontented. Hester was very much the older sister: 'I . . . obtained and exercised, I can't tell how, a sort of command over them. They never came to see me when I was in my room without sending first to know whether I would see them,' she wrote in later life.

The children were all looked after by a series of French and Swiss governesses upon whom Hester waged 'eternal warfare'. One particular woman strapped them round with boards – 'they would have squeezed me to the size of a puny miss – a thing impossible!' Lady Hester exclaimed indignantly. Another tried to flatten her high instep, which also made Hester furious since she regarded an arched foot as a sign of aristocracy.

She was an independent and determined child with a quite remarkable tenacity. Once, when she was only seven or eight, the French ambassador to London called at Chevening. He was gorgeously dressed in the frills and furbelows, lace and diamonds of pre-revolutionary France and made a tremendous impression on the young Hester. She decided she had to go to France at the first opportunity, and the chance soon came on a visit to Hastings. 'I got into a boat one day unobserved,' she recalled, 'let loose the rope myself and off I went.' She was finally spotted bobbing happily out to sea, on her way to France, and was retrieved by a posse of irate and terrified governesses who had press-ganged a passing fisherman into the chase.

Hester was her father's favourite child, mainly because she was not afraid of him, and even he could see that she had extraordinary powers of perception and logic. Occasionally he would draw her into his study for philosophical discussions. Putting his feet up on the fender, he would listen intently to her arguments, sometimes interrupting to say that her reasoning was good, but 'the basis is bad.' Despite his neglect and cruelty, these little sessions helped her think for herself and have the courage of her convictions.

Although it is notoriously difficult to try to link character too closely with heredity, strong family characteristics could be seen to emerge time after time in both the Stanhope and the Pitt families. In every generation of both lines there seemed to be at least one truly outstanding person. In those days when women were obliged to be content with supporting roles, nearly all of the great achievers were men, naturally enough, but when Charles Stanhope and Hester Pitt married they combined so many powerful family traits in their firstborn child that she seemed destined for fame even though she was merely a female.

Much of the shortlived Pitt fortune had been made in India by the ruthless 'Diamond' Pitt, Lady Hester's great-great-grandfather, and it was said of his blood that it 'came all aflame from the East and flowed like burning lava to his remotest descendants with the exception of Chatham's children, but even then it blazed up again in Hester Stanhope'. Lady Hester had even more of the Pitt blood in her than she might have done, because she was doubly linked to the family. Her father's grandmother and her mother's grandfather were brother and sister: two of 'Diamond' Pitt's five children.

Many of the Pitt attributes flared up in her: pride, courage, shrewdness, outspokenness, extravagance and hatred of injustice and hypocrisy. Fearlessness came from the Stanhope side too, together with humour, good horsemanship and a sometimes violent temper. She also found from somewhere a thoughtfulness and an infinite kindness to those less fortunate than herself which, combined with her Pitt capacity to spend money, was to lead to her downfall.

Despite all the hardships at home, Hester grew into a tall, personable young girl. She was critical – or maybe realistic – about her looks. 'He is deceived if he thinks I am handsome,' she said of someone who had complimented her, 'for I know I am not. If you were to take every feature in my face, and put them one by one on the table there is not a single one that would bear attention. The only thing is that, put together and lighted up, they look well enough. It is a homogenous ugliness, and nothing more.'

Her feminine vanity would never allow her portrait to be painted so there is no authentic picture of her, but it seems that she judged her looks too harshly. Even though her family and friends agreed with her that she was not a beauty, they were unanimous in their verdict that she was vibrantly attractive. She was tall – nearly six foot – with dark blonde hair, a fine figure and regal posture. Her face was a perfect oval, with a high forehead, a firm chin, and the long, rather prominent Stanhope nose. Her eyes were blue but seemed to change colour according to her mood, and she had a gentle mouth and an unusually pale and flawless skin. This perhaps rather Madonna-like appearance was constantly enlivened by her wonderfully vivacious personality. She loved to tease people, especially if they were pompous; she was a superlative flirt and adored a good joke. She had never been taught to be prim or demure, and the constant animation of expression as she reacted with wit and intelligence or indignant outburst to what went on around her was a compellingly attractive combination.

Slowly Lady Hester began to get out into local society. Lord Stanhope kept a decent stable and encouraged his children to ride. Hester quickly became a superb rider and the talk of the district. She looked wonderful on a horse, brilliant and dashing, and she spent much of her time hunting and visiting friends in Sevenoaks. The countryside around Chevening was good riding land: the chalky hills of the North Downs rise behind the Chevening estate, whilst to the south lies the Weald of Kent. The Pilgrims Way follows its ancient route from west to east, and all around the area, Hester made friends amongst the local people. There were a great many soldiers and officers living in the area, and it was on horseback that she had one of her first little social triumphs, an occasion she recalled with a mixture of pleasure and pride over forty years later. She was riding home from a hunt one day in a pelting shower of rain when she caught sight of a local colonel and his groom. The groom's horse was particularly beautiful and she decided to have a closer look at it.

'I accordingly quickened my pace, and in going by gave a good look to the horse, then at the groom, then at the master who was on a sorry nag. The colonel eyed me as I passed and I, taking advantage of a low part in the hedge, put my horse to it, leaped over and disappeared in an instant.' This flirtatious display of good horsemanship impressed the colonel tremendously. Having found out who she was, he 'made such a fuss at the mess about my equestrian powers that nothing could be like it. I was the toast there every day.'

Lord Stanhope had decided that his children would never be a part of London society, but he reckoned without Lady Hester's determination. 'Nobody ever saw much of me until Lord Romney's review,' she recalled. The review was a grand occasion when George III, Queen Charlotte and all their Ministers and courtiers came down to Kent to mingle with the local gentry. Hester knew her father would not allow her to attend, but she was quite determined to go. 'I was obliged to play a trick on my father to get there,' she said unrepentantly. 'I pretended the day before that I wanted to pay a visit to the Misses Crumps ... and then went from their house to Lord Romney's.' She went entirely on her own, without even a maid, which must have required a colossal amount of nerve. Like an exotic butterfly that had burst out of its chrysalis, she was a glorious and unexpected success.

Lords, officers and courtiers crowded around her, curious at first merely to meet William Pitt's niece, but they stayed, entranced by her liveliness, her wit and her irreverent remarks. She was soon the centre of attention and she loved it. After a while the conversation and the laughter grew so loud that the King sent to see who was the cause of it all, and had Lady Hester presented to him. He too fell under the spell of her freshness and flirtatious charm and had her seated at the table next to his. At the end of the evening he announced he would take her away with him. 'My dear,' he said to the Queen, 'Lady Hester is going to ride bodkin with us. I am going to take her away from Democracy Hall.' The Queen was not amused, and observed with remarkable restraint that such a thing would be most inconvenient for Lady Hester since she did not have her maid with her. The idea was dropped, but Lady Hester had made a conquest of the King, and he never forgot her.

After this resounding success even Lord Stanhope was unable to keep his daughter out of society, and for the next few years the stultifying severity of life at Chevening was punctuated by the wonderful excitement of parties in London. Society life was brilliant and sophisticated. Glittering circles and cliques of dukes and duchesses, princes and politicians whirled and spun through the great houses of London. Fashionable stylish parties gave way to drunken debauches where the Prince of Wales and his friend George Brummel held court. The jaded palates of an over-stimulated and blasé *beau monde* were astounded by the freshness and unsophistication of the young woman from Chevening, but soon, like the King, they were won over by her wit and charm. She made her entrance into society under the protection of the Grenville family and her uncle William Pitt, who sometimes chaperoned her himself, but soon Hester had no need of help from anyone.

She was outspoken, she was fun and she possessed an unusual and wicked talent for mimicry that she used to the full to make people laugh and squirm. She began to make conquests and break hearts. One of her most unexpected admirers was Beau Brummel. Given Lady Hester's habit of ridiculing affectation, it was an unlikely alliance but one that is easily explained. 'You know, my dear Lady Hester,' he drawled to her one day, 'it is my folly that is the making of me. If I did not impertinently stare duchesses out of countenance and nod over my shoulder at a prince, I would be forgotten in a week, and if the world is so silly as to admire my absurdities, you and I may know better, but what does that signify?'

He understood himself well and by admitting to Hester that his foppery and affected ways were only a game, he gained her respect and friendship. Another bond between them was a healthy cynicism about many of the people they met, but whereas Brummel masked his feelings with mockery Lady Hester was sometimes too open in her contempt. She made enemies in London as well as friends, but her popularity and her impeccable connections provided a strong shield against them.

She possessed an extraordinary ability to judge people's characters quickly and accurately, an invaluable aid in the maelstrom of London society, and one that was to be useful to her all her life. She met and disliked the Prince of Wales and his slovenly wife Caroline, but was drawn into the circle of the Duke and Duchess of York with whom she became the best of friends. Another of the Princes, the Duke of Cumberland, named her his 'little bulldog' for her fearlessness and tenacity. She liked very few women that she met in London; indeed, she had a very low opinion of women generally. This situation had probably originated in her childhood when the only role model she had – her stepmother – had been a vain and shallow person and quite uninterested in forming relationships with her children. The only other females that Hester had known were her sisters, but they were weak and easily browbeaten, and although they inspired love in her they did not inspire respect. Exposure to female society in London did little to raise her opinion of her own sex: many of the women she met were afflicted with one of her pet dislikes – affectation. 'I hate affectation of all kinds,' she later admitted. 'I never could bear those ridiculous women who cannot step over a straw without expecting the man who is walking with them to offer his hand. I always said to the men "No, no; I have got legs of my own, don't trouble yourself."' Whilst in London she contrived to avoid or ignore most of the social butterflies, although she often managed to offend them as well. She did not suffer fools gladly whether they were male or female, and although she admired a few of the women she met, it was men to whom she turned for intellectual stimulation.

Soon she was able to go anywhere she liked, without a chaperon and confident of a rapturous reception. She had arrived on the social scene unsophisticated, inexperienced but irrepressible. Despite and because of that, London was soon at her feet.

Lucy and Griselda, Lady Hester's sisters, were not nearly so successful in breaking their father's hold over them. They were neither as brave nor as innately cheerful as their elder sister and, though Hester tried hard to help them, they had a miserable life at home. Lucy had had enough by the time she was sixteen, and escaped in the classic way by eloping with the local apothecary. Lord Stanhope was furious, but in view of his republican philosophies, could scarcely complain about her not making a grand marriage. After she left, life at Chevening became even more intolerable for Griselda and later the same year she left home as well, and went to live in a cottage at Walmer, lent to her by their uncle William Pitt. She, too, married shortly afterwards.

Finally even Hester could take no more of life at Chevening. She had managed to tolerate her father and his ferociously republican ideals for longer than most, but in 1800 she left home to live at Burton Pynsent in Somerset with her grandmother, Lady Chatham. She left behind her a cold and loveless childhood, and it would not have been surprising if Hester had sunk into grateful obscurity like her sisters, but the strength of character that was to see her through so many triumphs and crises in the future was by now too firmly established to allow that to happen.

Hester's one concern as she left her childhood home was for the welfare of her half-brothers Philip, Charles and James. They were nearly adults now, but were still totally dominated by their father. Shortly after she left she embarked on an extraordinary scheme to help Philip, the eldest of the boys, who had inherited the title of Lord Mahon when his father became 3rd Earl Stanhope. It was a plan that was as daring as it was compassionate, but although it was wholly successful it estranged her from her father for ever.

CHAPTER TWO

Happy to a degree

Lady Chatham, Lady Hester's grandmother, was a kind and loving person and she welcomed her granddaughter with open arms. Everyone knew what a hard life Hester had endured at Chevening, and if she was now a trifle hoydenish it was hardly surprising. Hester settled in to her new home very easily. The skills of horsemanship that she had learned at her father's stable were put to good use over the first few months. There was no horse too difficult for her to train or ride, and soon all her new neighbours were bringing her their problem mares to break in or cure of bad habits. The peace and tranquillity of the Somerset countryside and a normal family home were a new experience for Lady Hester and she became relaxed and happy, but it was a shortlived respite. She received a distraught letter from Philip in which all her worst fears for him were confirmed.

Since Hester had left, their father had been behaving in an increasingly harsh way to his sons, and towards Philip in particular. Philip had asked him somewhat forlornly if he could leave home to go to college somewhere, but the request was brutally rejected. He had slowly realized what his father's plans were: he wanted to sell Chevening and all the estates – to sell everything that was Philip's heritage. For this he needed his son's cooperation, and since he was unlikely to get it voluntarily, he was trying to gain complete ascendancy over him by bullying and threatening him. Philip's desperate cry for help galvanized Hester into activity. Extreme measures were called for. She wrote to Sir Francis Burdett, an old childhood friend, for money, to Francis Jackson, a more recent conquest, for a passport and letters of credit and introduction, and to Pitt and her cousins the Grenvilles for advice. Her plans were a total success. With the help of a sympathetic servant at Chevening, she spirited Philip away in the early months of 1801, and no one, least of all their father, had any idea where he had gone. Charles was outraged at having been thwarted. He wrote immediately to Pitt, to Burdett, to Griselda and Lucy, demanding to know where his son had gone, but with no result. The plan had been conceived and executed in utter secrecy, and the few people who were involved thought it perfectly justified and said nothing. Hester had been careful not to let her two younger half-brothers know anything about the plans, but even so she was worried about them. 'They will be flogged to death to make them confess what they are really ignorant of,' she wrote to Lord Haddington, but thankfully Charles managed to control himself when he realized the two young men were truly innocent of any part in the affair.

After Philip was safely out of the country, Hester wrote a letter to Lord Glastonbury, to be shown to all of the Grenville family. 'He is gone abroad,' she wrote of her brother, 'in order to be placed at a foreign university at Erlang, under the care of Professor Breyer, a man of great ability and most extensive knowledge.' Philip had been furnished with everything necessary for an extended trip abroad including letters of credit and introductions to local luminaries. One letter was addressed to the Margravine of Brandenburg-Bayreuth, who was, as Lady Hester explained, 'the best sort of woman in the world, and keeps a little court. Therefore Mahon will not only have information within his reach, but enjoy the best society of that place.' She had thought of everything and her brother was truly grateful. He wrote her an ecstatic letter telling her of his enrolment in the university and of his gratitude to her. 'His astonishment, his happiness and his gratitude to his friends, is expressed so naturally and with so much feeling it is quite delightful,' Hester wrote after she heard from him. 'Dear fellow! if he had been ten times my own brother I could not have been more anxious, more interested about him.... Charming, charming, incomparable Mahon!'

This daring rescue operation had required a huge amount of organization and attention to detail. It had also required imagination, tact and a great deal of nerve. Hester had forgotten nothing. She even wrote to her stepmother at Chevening, assuring her that her son was safe, and offering to forward any letters that she might care to write to him. It was a coup that earned her the respect and admiration of all who came to know about it, and she had good reason to feel proud of herself, but she was greatly relieved when Philip's escape was safely completed. The months of sustained effort and anxiety had taken their toll on her health, and she was told by her physician that she should forego indulging in the excesses of London society until late in spring.

Although depleted of her physical energies, she was much buoyed up in her spirits by the success of her plans for Mahon. They had, after all, been very ambitious and to have had them meet with such triumph and approval had been a huge boost for her self-confidence, not that she seemed to need it, usually.

One of the people who had given her encouragement was her uncle William Pitt. He and Hester had grown very fond of each other when he had acted as chaperon for his high-spirited niece. Hester's mother had been his favourite sister, and he never ceased to mourn her loss. He had shown kindness to Griselda by offering her accommodation when she could no longer stand life at Chevening, and Hester knew that she could turn to him for advice whenever she needed it. Although she did not want to impose on him too much, they both knew that Charles and James, Philip's two younger brothers, would have to be rescued from Chevening. They were in no particular danger, but their lives were a misery and they had no prospects at all. Lady Hester was greatly pleased when Pitt managed to arrange commissions for her two half-brothers, in the Army for Charles and the Navy for James. 'How instinct taught me to love this "Great Man",' she exulted in a letter to a friend, 'and if I had not kept sight of him at a distance, what would have become of us all?'

After the satisfaction of seeing her three half-brothers all happily placed, there was a short time when she was able to relax at Burton Pynsent and try to mend her beleaguered health. Although it was very quiet there, occasional excursions to fashionable Bath to take the waters provided plenty of scope for meeting her society friends. She started her practice of writing letters to friends further away, a habit she never stopped even when she became so old and sick that she could scarcely hold a pen.

It was during her months at Burton Pynsent that Lady Hester's name was first linked with a man. Thomas Pitt, Lord Camelford, was a cousin of hers descended from the older branch of the family, and heir to the estates of his ancestor 'Diamond' Pitt, the East India trader. Although a member of the aristocracy, he was quite unlike any of the other young Lords that Hester had met in London. Massively tall and well-built, he enjoyed a quite ferocious reputation in the drawing rooms of London, which made women less bold than Lady Hester draw aside with a delicious frisson of fear when he entered a room. It was said of him that he was mad, that he was a murderer and a spy.

Lord Camelford had chosen a career in the Navy but his unfortunate habit of challenging his superiors to duels did little to endear him to those in authority. The first real scandal erupted when he shot a fellow officer dead in St Kitts during a quarrel over a matter of precedence. The court-martial that followed decided that the officer's life had been lost in a mutiny, and Camelford was acquitted, but he continued to be controversial. The next débâcle came when, despite the European War, Camelford attempted to travel secretly to Paris to obtain some French charts. The mission was scuppered before it began, but led to an appearance before the Privy Council, who suspended his command. Outraged, Camelford resigned from the Navy, and took to roaming the taverns of London wearing his naval greatcoat and a 'monstrous large gold-laced cocked hat'.

Perhaps because she herself was not cast in the usual mould, Lady Hester was never frightened of this alarming man. She discovered that in many ways they were alike – both had 'Diamond' Pitt's blood flowing in their veins: neither could stand hypocrisy or injustice, both were always generous to the needy.

Gossip about their friendship spread like wildfire through the salons of London but there is no evidence that the relationship was serious or even romantic. They soon began to see less of each other and on hearing news in 1804 that Camelford had been shot in a duel and that there was no chance of his surviving, she reacted with equanimity. All who knew him guessed he would never make old bones. 'You know my opinion of him, I believe,' she wrote, 'therefore can judge if I am not likely to lament his untimely end. He had vices, but also great virtues, but they were not known to the world at large.'

By October Lady Hester was feeling much restored and decided to travel abroad the following spring with a Mr and Mrs Egerton. She hoped that Mahon might join them for a while. In a letter to her now much valued friend Francis Jackson she told him of her plans and of her unusual choice of travelling companions.

'You will, perhaps, wonder at my not having fixed upon more dashing persons for companions,' she wrote. 'In that case we must have all dashed away together; in the present case I shall have perfect liberty to act in all respects as is most pleasing to myself, and in so doing be certain of pleasing them. They want a companion and I want a nominal chaperon.'

She had always done as she had wanted, even within the restraints of childhood. Now she was a grown woman she saw no reason to change her ways, but was still willing for the time being to pay lip service to society's demands.

'Besides they are vastly good people,' she went on, 'she is very sensible, and he vastly good-natured, but vastly shy, and not brilliant; but, as I do not shine through the medium of another person's husband, that is of no consequence to me.' A little footnote at the end of this typically assured letter told of a recent jolly adventure: 'I have not room to tell you of the military honours I received at camp, and what a great General they think me. A whole regiment saluted me ... *eyes right*. Officers SWORDS DROPPED. Oh charming!' She was always happiest in the company of men, preferably those that were handsome, intelligent and half in love with her.

She started to prepare for her trip to the Continent. Travel in those days involved an almost inconceivable amount of preparation and organization. Carriages had to be ordered, servants engaged, advice taken as to the safest routes, and domestic affairs settled for the months to be spent away, so it was not until the late summer of 1802 that the little party was ready to leave. Bidding her elderly grandmother a loving farewell, Lady Hester set off for Dover. She had planned to stop on the way at Walmer Castle to say goodbye to Pitt, but when she arrived she found to her great dismay that he was seriously ill. Postponing all her plans she stayed to nurse him back to health, and it was not until the end of September that she was able to write to Mr Jackson 'the first thing I must say is that, thank God! he is quite recovered, and if he was to be ill, perhaps my having the opportunity of showing him I have talents as a nurse is better than his having had to nurse himself.' Pitt's physician was evidently an army man. 'The day is our own now,' he wrote of his patient's recovery, 'and the last battle proves that the mainsprings are good.'

Lady Hester loved her first journey abroad. She was never frightened of the dangerous roads, though they had 'two or three bad overturns', nor was she alarmed by numerous rumours of highway robbers. She revelled in the sense of freedom that travel brought, and was far more daring than her companions. She wrote from Turin of how she had crossed 'Mont Cenis'. 'I chose my own mule and muleteer,' she reported, 'and left the rest of the party to their frights and fears. The day was divine, and I enjoyed it very much. . . . I rode the whole way and my mule never made a false step.'

At Lyons they were joined by her 'incomparable' Mahon, and at first Hester was overjoyed to see him, but it soon became apparent that his months abroad had changed him. 'He thought no person's judgement equal to his own,' she reported sadly to Mr Jackson when she wrote from Naples, and 'his conduct disgusted me extremely.' Philip had finished his studies and was on his way home to England, where Pitt had appointed him Lieutenant-Governor of Dover Castle. He and Hester parted coolly at Florence in November, but within a few weeks she received an apologetic letter from him asking for her advice and instruction. 'I am pleased with this,' she said, 'as it proves to me he is rather changed since we parted.'

Since she had left Chevening and become more experienced in the ways of the world, her instinctively held ethical feelings about right and wrong had crystallized into firm convictions. Her beliefs were basically very sound. She insisted on loyalty, fair-mindedness and generosity, and despised pretension and hypocrisy. Whilst utterly convinced of her own unassailable superiority to many people, she was opposed to any idea of high birth conveying automatic supremacy. This sometimes resulted in some of the most unlikely people being subjected to the blaze of her friendship. The only important attribute that Lady Hester had not learned, and never was to learn, was that of tolerance. It was hardly surprising that she should have had such a lack, for tolerance had been singularly lacking in her childhood, but her energy was such that she saw tolerance of even minor faults or indiscretions as being lazy, bad or sometimes even morally wrong. She saw no reason to be more tolerant with other people than she would be with herself. It was a very high standard, and it sometimes made her very difficult to live with.

When she found what she perceived to be imperfections in those she loved, she found it impossible to bear. She felt compelled to try and right even comparatively minor wrongs. It was not a habit that endeared her to those, like her brothers, who felt the full force of her crusading zeal.

She had always felt maternal towards her half-brothers, a result perhaps of the coldness her stepmother showed to them all. She loved them deeply and was generous in her admiration of their many strengths. What some perceived as her overbearingly bossy behaviour towards them she explained away as a necessary evil. 'If I am severe towards them, it is only from a wish to see them all perfection,' she explained in a letter to a friend, but although Philip knew that he owed his freedom to his sister, he began to baulk at what he saw as her continued interference in his life. The beginning of his resentfulness towards her first began to show when they met on this trip, but the memory of Chevening was still fresh enough in his mind to remind him of how much he owed to Hester. For the time being Philip was content to submit to his sister's criticisms, and peace was maintained.

After spending the winter of 1802 in Italy, the outbreak of war with France meant that Lady Hester had to alter her plans to return home through Paris. She and her party hurried home through Germany only to be met with sad news on their return to England: Lady Hester's grandmother, Lady Chatham, had died whilst she was away and she was now homeless.

Cut off from the only home she had ever known apart from Chevening, Hester was at a loss as to what to do. She turned in despair to the one member of her family who had supported her in the previous months – William Pitt, and he welcomed her into his home without hesitation. His colleagues and friends were frankly astonished by his action: it was not that he was not a generous man, but he was now a man of forty-four, and a bachelor used to living on his own. 'How amiable it is of Pitt to take compassion on poor Lady Hester Stanhope,' an acquaintance of Pitt's observed, 'and that in a way which must break in upon his habits of life. He is as good as he is great.'

One of Pitt's earliest biographers, Earl Stanhope, agreed whole-heartedly. 'He must have felt that he might be sacrificing or greatly hazarding his future comfort,' he wrote. Fortunately, these gloomy prognoses were quite wrong. 'His kind act brought after it its own reward,' Stanhope recorded happily. 'Lady Hester quickly formed for him a strong and devoted attachment which she extended to his memory so long as her own life endured. On his part he came to regard her with almost a father's affection.' And so it was. The three years that Lady Hester spent with her uncle were among the happiest of her life.

CHAPTER THREE

'A light in his dwelling'

William Pitt was forty-four years old when Lady Hester went to live with him. Apart from time spent as Chancellor of the Exchequer he had already served as Prime Minister for seventeen years, but was out of office at the time, having tendered his resignation over the Catholic Question. In appearance he was tall and thin and rather awkward-looking, with a deceptively passive face. The world knew him as a brilliant and independent statesman, dignified, calm, and a man of the highest possible moral standards. Lady Hester also knew him to be infinitely kind and thoughtful, a wonderful uncle who soon began to take the place of the father she wished she'd had. He had been a gifted child and in the days when it was common to go to university at sixteen or seventeen, Pitt was exceptional enough to have been accepted to study at Pembroke Hall, Cambridge, when he was only fourteen. A recurring childhood illness led his doctor to prescribe the drinking of a bottle of port a day in his first year at Cambridge, which makes it surprising that he ever achieved anything at all. Instead, he grew into the youngest and most outstanding Prime Minister England had ever known, but the prescription led him to develop a taste for wines and a capacity for drinking them that was to lead, tragically, to his early death.

Pitt's mother was a Grenville, a cousin of Lady Hester's stepmother, and from her he inherited his patience and tenacity and his great powers of concentration. To those who did not know him personally, he always appeared cold and aloof, but these particular Grenville characteristics were only a façade: he was basically a shy man, only able to relax with his closest friends and family, and the cool exterior he presented to society helped mask his vulnerabilities. People said of him with regard to his father that he was not just a 'chip off the block', but that he *was* the old block. Political skills from both sides of his family combined in him as a superlative talent that won profound admiration and respect from even his most outspoken enemies. Pitt also inherited at least one major propensity from his father that he would have been better without. It was said of Lord Chatham that he had a 'lordly disregard for money', and Pitt was certainly his father's son in this respect: he was spectacularly bad with his personal finances. Although he was a bachelor and whilst in Downing Street paid neither rent nor 'coals and candles', he was never out of debt. Considering he had spent a large portion of his life sorting out the finances of his country, this seems quite extraordinary, but it never seemed to bother him unduly.

His only discernible financial weakness was to spend enormous amounts on the purchase, upkeep and improvement of his houses. He owned two – Holwood and Downe Park in Kent – and was constantly thinking of new things to do to them. Such outgoings were not enough to account for the sorry state of his finances, however, and records show that he was cheated outrageously by servants and tradesmen for most of his life. This was all the more sad because whenever he was in funds he was always generous to those in need. The ability to be generous, he told Lady Hester, was 'the pleasure of being rich'.

Despite his financial problems he resolutely refused to enrich himself from the public purse, and always declined any of the frequent offers of private help that came his way although other politicians made fortunes from patronage. Lady Hester was once approached by a consortium of some friends from the City who wanted to offer him a settlement of £10,000 a year to make him independent of the King. She warned them that he would not accept and she was right. To have done so would have meant he ran the risk of being compromised, for, as Hester observed darkly, 'There are no public philanthropists in the City.'

Pitt never took bribes or accepted presents, even if it meant leaving them to moulder in the Custom House. He was a man of unparalleled integrity and Hester admired him enormously for it.

When Lady Hester first made her home with Pitt he was based at

Walmer Castle, near Dover, which was the official residence of the Warden of the Cinque Ports, a position that he had recently accepted. It was the summer of 1803, invasion from France seemed imminent, and no one was more aware of it than those living on the vulnerable Kentish coast.

'I should not be the least surprised any night to hear of the French attempting to land. Indeed, I expect it,' Lady Hester wrote to a friend. She was quite unafraid at the prospect and deeply cheerful at the prognosis for the French. 'Those who do succeed [in landing],' she foretold, 'will neither proceed nor return.'

Her optimism was based on detailed and first-hand knowledge of the country's defences. Pitt was closely involved in the organization and inspection of the British line of defence along the coastline, and week after week Lady Hester accompanied her uncle on reviews of the troops stationed up and down the coast. She was impressed by how well-drilled they were, even though the powers that were to deploy them seemed to her to be 'wavering fools'.

'Mr. Pitt absolutely goes through the fatigue of a drill-sergeant,' she wrote to Francis Jackson in October. 'It is parade after parade, at fifteen or twenty miles' distance from each other.' Although she was in excellent health, she occasionally found it tiring. 'The hard riding I do not mind,' she continued, 'but to remain almost still so many hours on horseback is an incomparable bore, and requires more patience than you can easily imagine.' The weather was often appalling. 'I have been so drenched that as I stood, my boots made two spouting fountains above my knees.' Her main concern throughout all these rigours was for her uncle. 'If Mr. Pitt does not overdo it and injure his health, every other consideration becomes trifling.'

The amount of wine Pitt drank was beginning to affect his health. He drank alarming quantities of port, madeira, claret and burgundy – all the most toxic of wines – and the gout that had been first diagnosed at an early age was proving more and more serious. He began to have bouts of severe illness, with stomach cramps and painful vomiting. He would recover quite quickly from the attacks, but it was clear that something was seriously wrong. In 1795, he asked for the opinion of a Dr Walter Farquhar who sensibly recommended 'some relaxation from the arduous Duties of Office', but this was impossible for Pitt by virtue of both his workload and his temperament, and he ignored the advice.

Hester was constantly concerned about his health, but was sensitive enough not to nag him about it. 'The extreme care I take,' she wrote to a friend, 'is rewarded by his minding me more than any other person, and allowing me to speak to him upon the subject of his health, which is always an unpleasant one, and one he particularly dislikes.' In 1803 his health seemed much improved, however, and for these first few months at Walmer everything was perfect for Lady Hester. She felt more happy and secure than ever before in her life. She was living with her uncle, whom she adored, and her three brothers were happily settled nearby. She was enjoying the experience of being loved and accepted unconditionally – it was a richness of life that was quite new to her and it brought out the best in her. She was generous and cheerful, enthusiastic and loving.

James, her youngest brother, had left the Navy to join the Guards, and was frequently to be found at nearby Dover Castle. Charles, the middle brother and Hester's favourite, was stationed at Ashford with the 57th Regiment, whilst Philip had settled in Dover having found himself a pretty and amiable wife. As far as Hester was concerned, Philip was still being lazy and arrogant but, unlike him, Charles had turned out to be a very likeable young man. 'Charles is by nature my favourite,' she had confided to a friend a few years earlier, 'he has the least ability of the three, but a degree of openness and good nature which wins every heart, and an air of nobility his quizzical education can never destroy.' Pitt, too, was becoming very fond of Charles, treating him almost as a son, which pleased Hester greatly.

Another source of delight to Lady Hester was the constant flow of men who came to Walmer to see Pitt. She was always happy to be in masculine company, simply because of her low opinion of women, but there were a few women she liked, among them Charles's wife – 'a vastly kind, good little soul; the more I see of her, the more I like her'. On the whole, however, it was usually men who commanded her greatest respect and admiration. She loved to pit her wits against an intelligent and good-looking man and the cut and thrust of informed yet flirtatious banter made her sparkle. In an endearingly straightforward way, she simply loved to be admired, although she would always rather it was her wit and intelligence that impressed rather than merely her smiles and pretty manners. She adored flirting and being the centre of attention, and as she was often the only woman present at

Pitt's social functions, this was a role she was often guaranteed. But she never allowed her enjoyment of a party to let her forget her role as Pitt's hostess; she performed her duties happily and gracefully.

Living with Pitt meant that Lady Hester was suddenly immersed in the political life of the country and, because she was intelligent and logical and had always been interested in people, she quickly found it enthralling. At first she simply listened, but she learned fast and soon began giving her opinions and judgements to the leading figures she met. At first she was listened to as a matter of courtesy, but when it became apparent that she had an unusually quick grasp of new subjects, and could often come up with sensible, sometimes inspired solutions to problems, people began to take her seriously.

There were usually two or three men staying at the castle at any one time, and there were supper parties for eight or nine every other night. The guests were mainly political luminaries, and Hester quickly got to know them all. Castlereagh, Addington, Liverpool and George Canning were frequent visitors, but no one was too grand to escape her advice or her dry humour. The dull, boring men were unscrupulously attacked. Lord Castlereagh was christened 'His Monotonous Lordship', and Lord Liverpool was warned that his trouser pockets were so full of papers they were in danger of falling down. When he searched through his pockets, she told him, he was like a man groping for an eel at the bottom of a pond. Using her gift for mimicry, she sometimes regaled the guests with whole conversations, acting out each part in turn. Earl Stanhope said that whilst Hester lived with Pitt she was 'a light in his dwelling' and that although Pitt was 'on some occasions much discomposed by her sprightly sallies, which did not always spare his own Cabinet colleagues', he was delighted with her lively company. They brought each other much joy.

In the spring of 1804, Pitt was asked by George III to form a government once again, and he moved back to Downing Street, with Hester to act as his hostess, confidante and informal adviser. The politicians and influential people whom she had met at Walmer now became regular visitors, and Lady Hester knew them all well. Her instinctive insight into people's characters was very accurate and Pitt listened to her opinions, and often found them helpful. As time went on her importance in her uncle's household became so widely accepted that people began to approach Lady Hester first when they wanted to consult Pitt: Canning said that Lady Hester 'stood instead of preface and apology' in matters of confidentiality with the Minister. The unwary sometimes tried to extract information from her, but she was neither stupid nor disloyal, and sometimes took enormous and wicked delight in deliberately misleading people who were too persistent.

During this period Hester was one of the brightest stars in London society. Her social standing as Pitt's niece was unquestioned, and she enjoyed an unprecedented degree of political power as well, in much the same way as the wives of American presidents do today. Hester recalled much later in her life that Pitt used to let her write letters and official documents for him, and to sign them in his name as well. It seems unlikely that such a fastidious man as Pitt should have been so relaxed – maybe her memory was at fault – but she also related how Pitt was reproached for allowing her 'such unreserved liberty of action in state matters', so perhaps it was true after all. He was meant to have replied, on being rebuked for his laxity, 'I let her do as she pleases, for if she were resolved to cheat the devil she could do it.' He certainly thought very highly of her talents, thinking her 'fit to sit between Augustus and Maecenas', and when a friend once observed that Hester would never marry until she found someone as clever as herself, Pitt replied, 'why, then, she will never marry,' and he was right.

The King still remembered the young girl he first met in Kent, and he had grown to admire her. One day on Windsor Terrace he informed Pitt with rather heavy humour that he had found a new Minister to replace him. After much polite but alarmed guessing from all those present, the King pointed to Hester. 'There is my new Minister,' he said. 'There is not a man in my Kingdom who is a better politician than Lady Hester and there is not a woman who adorns her sex more than she does.' Hester never forgot it.

Whenever matters of state allowed, Pitt and Lady Hester would retire to Putney, then a village south-west of London, where Pitt had rented Bowling Green House, thinking that the country air would help his precarious health. When they were there life was slightly more relaxed, and although Pitt continued to work too hard, Hester directed all her considerable energies into making his life more enjoyable and relaxed. Her brothers, and some of their friends, would sometimes come to stay, and with their help Hester managed to reanimate Pitt's sense of fun. As a young man he had had a great fondness for schoolboy jokes, as was remarked upon one morning in 1793:

'Some little excess happen'd lately at Wimbledon.... In the Evening some of the Neighbours were alarmed with noises at their doors, but Nobody, I believe, has made reflection upon a mere frolic. It has only been pleasantly remarked that the Rioters were headed by Master P. – late Chancellor of the Ex – , and Master Arden, late Sollicitor Genl.'

One frequent visitor to Bowling Green House was an army friend of Charles's, William Napier, and he tells a delightful story about his usually formal host.

'We were resolved to blacken his face with burnt cork, which he most strenuously resisted, but at the beginning of the fray a servant announced that Lords Castlereagh and Liverpool desired to see him on business. "Let them wait in the other room," was the answer; and the great minister instantly turned to the battle, catching up a cushion and belabouring us with it in glorious fun. We were, however, too many and strong for him, and after at least a ten minutes' fight, got him down and were actually daubing his face, when with a look of pretended confidence in his prowess, he said "Stop, this will not do; I could easily beat you all, but we must not keep those grandees waiting any longer." His defeat was, however, palpable, and we were obliged to get a towel and a basin of water to wash him clean before he could receive the grandees. Being thus put in order, the basin was hid behind the sofa, and the two lords were ushered in. Then a new phase of Mr. Pitt's manner appeared, to my great surprise and admiration. Lord Liverpool's look and manner are well known – melancholy, bending, nervous. Lord Castlereagh I had known from my childhood, had often been engaged with him in athletic sports, pitching the stone or bar, and looked upon him, as what indeed he was, a model of quiet grace and strength combined. What was my surprise to see both him and the Lord Liverpool bending like spaniels on approaching the man we had just been maltreating with such successful insolence of fun! But instantly Mr. Pitt's change of manner and look entirely fixed my attention. His tall, ungainly, bony figure seemed to grow to the ceiling, his head was thrown back, his eyes fixed immovably in one position, as if reading the heavens, and totally regardless of the bending figures near him. For some time they spoke; he made now and then some short observation, and finally, with an abrupt, stiff inclination of the body, but without casting his eyes down, dismissed them. Then, turning to us with a laugh caught up his cushions and renewed our fight.'

Those anxious to speculate about Pitt's never having married would probably have pounced on this story of horseplay with young men as evidence of his homosexuality, yet the episode is recalled with such affectionate yet respectful enthusiasm that it is transparently innocent of any innuendo. Much was written both during Pitt's life and after about his sexuality, for prurient interest in the private lives of famous people was as rife then as it is now. Rude rhymes circulated about his possible homosexuality or impotence or – worst of all to the eighteenth-century mind – masturbation. It was true that he never married, although at one time he was deeply fond of Eleanor Eden, daughter of Lord Auckland, and it was presumed by many people, including herself, that they would eventually marry. It was true that he enjoyed the company of young men, but in the final analysis Pitt's sexual proclivities were simply irrelevant because they were a complete non-event. If he had any homosexual tendencies then he suppressed them ruthlessly, immersing himself in the service of his country. Confirmation of homosexual activity would have meant political death for him, and England would have been the loser. As it was, none of the mud that was slung at him ever managed to stick.

If it was true that Pitt had some traits that were regarded by the eighteenth-century mind as feminine, then it would have to be said that Lady Hester had some 'masculine' tendencies, such as her interest in politics and power. Perhaps this contributed to their keen understanding and appreciation of each other, but it certainly never stopped either of them being assiduously courted by hopeful suitors. Much to Hester's muffled amusement, wherever Pitt happened to be there was a constant stream of hopeful mamas thrusting their daughters forward for his reluctant inspection. The same was true for Lady Hester: many eligible men in London were attracted by her wit and mesmerized by the aura of power that living in the Prime Minister's household conferred on her. She was interested in none of them, until she met a young man called Lord Granville Leveson-Gower, the third son of the Marquis of Stafford. He idolized Pitt, and as one of Canning's closest friends was a frequent visitor to Downing Street. He was charming, attentive, extraordinarily handsome, and quite used to causing palpitations in female hearts. Lady Hester was equally used, by this time, to a slightly smug immunity to masculine charms, but rather to her surprise she fell violently in love with him. It was a disaster, for he was not at all in love with her.

Lady Hester had never learned to hide her emotions, and soon all of London was talking about her passion for Lord Granville. For many years he had been having a comfortable affair with the much older but still lovely Lady Bessborough, and at first he was highly flattered to have his name linked with that of Pitt's niece. Soon it became clear to everyone, however, that Lady Hester was expecting marriage, and he became greatly alarmed. He had absolutely no wish to settle down, and when he finally did decide to marry he was going to choose one of the many, small, coy, rich and biddable young misses who frequented the salons of London. The tall, imperious Hester was not at all his idea of a perfect wife, so he turned to the accommodating Lady Bessborough for advice. 'Is it quite honourable, dear Granville, to encourage a passion you do not mean seriously to return?' she asked him, coolly. 'If Mr Pitt knew even what had passed already do you think he would like it?'

Lord Granville was appalled at the idea of Pitt's possible wrath, and much to Hester's dismay started to make excuses not to call on her. Pitt was quite aware of what had been going on, and in the autumn of 1804 he showed great tact by offering Lord Granville the post of Ambassador to Petersburg. Granville sensibly accepted his temporary banishment, and after having excused himself to Hester with the feeble story that he could never marry her as he loved another, he decamped. Hester was shattered and fled from London to the quiet of Walmer Castle to nurse her heart, her pride and her health, all of which had taken a horrible blow.

'My heart points, like a compass, to the North,' she wrote pathetically to a friend. 'I am not happy; indeed how can I be, when I have shown my taste more than my prudence in admiring an object which fills more hearts than one?'

In an effort to distract herself, she embarked on a project to create a garden for Pitt at Walmer. They both shared an interest in landscape gardening, and had often talked of making the grounds around the castle more attractive, but nothing had ever been done. Her self-imposed exile was an ideal opportunity to turn their ideas into reality. It was a vast undertaking, and it was evident that a huge amount of manpower was going to be needed, but Hester was quite undaunted. She simply seconded several regiments of soldiers stationed at Dover, and set them to level, turf and plant, all under her personal supervision, whilst she charmed Lord Guilford at Waldershare into giving her great masses of shrubs and young trees. The whole project was a resounding success, and formed the basis of the garden which is still there today. Pitt was enchanted and declared it a miracle, which totally satisfied Lady Hester, and by the time it was finished she had, to a great extent, recovered from her disappointment over Lord Granville.

CHAPTER FOUR

'All over with him'

All through the year of 1805 Pitt worked unceasingly, as he had done for most of his life. When he was not in Parliament there was an endless stream of people coming to Downing Street or Bowling Green House to see him. When he was in the House he suffered very much from the cold, and the chilly draughts cut through the thin silk stockings that he wore. He begged Hester, in fun, to start a fashion for muffs and tippets; then, he said, he would put his feet in the muff, wrap the tippets round his legs, and be warm. His days were very long: Hester reckoned he usually slept no more than three or four hours a night. She began to be seriously worried about his health, as were his friends and colleagues. Although his doctors were beginning to realize that his illness was caused by 'the early habit of the too free use of wine', they had no way of knowing that it was beginning to affect his kidneys. His face was becoming swollen and jaundiced, his stomach increasingly sensitive, and his gout worse.

Occasionally Pitt and Lady Hester would manage to get away to Walmer, and she would take heart at the improvement in his health. He had a room at a nearby farm where he could escape from the visitors who followed him down from London. There he would have time to sit and write. 'Oh what slices of bread and butter I have seen him eat there,' Hester rejoiced, 'and hunches of bread and cheese big enough for a ploughman.'

These breaks were not enough to restore his health, and late in 1805 Pitt succumbed to pressure from his friends, and went to Bath to rest and take the waters. Hester persuaded him to take her eiderdown quilt with him for the journey, so he shouldn't be cold. When he returned for Parliament in January 1806, however, she was stunned at the sudden deterioration in his health. He was brought by carriage to Bowling Green House. 'I went out to the top of the stairs to receive him,' recalled Hester. 'The first thing I heard was a voice so changed that I said to myself, "It is all over with him,"' and so it was.

It was so evident to her that he was mortally ill, that instead of rushing to greet him she 'retreated little by little, not to put him to the pain of making a bow to me, or of speaking'. Within a week it was declared that his life was in danger, and four days later, on 23 January 1806, he died.

Towards the end he was delirious, and Hester's brother James sat with him. The doctors had inexplicably refused to let Lady Hester see her uncle, but when they were at dinner, she crept in to see him for the last time, and his delirium lifted briefly. James was witness to their farewell: 'with his usual angelic mildness [Pitt] wished her future happiness and gave her a most solemn blessing and affectionate farewell.' After she had left, Pitt continued to speak of her as he lapsed into fever again: 'Dear soul, I know she loves me,' he said, and 'Where is Hester? Is Hester gone?'

When he died, the whole nation mourned a tragic loss, but for Hester, as for some of his closest friends, the loss was irreparable. Pitt had inspired the very deepest respect, love and affection in those who knew him well. Hester was stunned by his death. Her grief was so deep that it went beyond ordinary distress; for weeks she was unable to function normally, she was unable even to cry. She finally broke down when a visitor came to call. 'Lord Melville came to see me,' she recalled, 'and the sight of his eyebrows, turned grey, and his changed face made me burst into tears.' It was the beginning of a recovery for her, 'I felt much better for it after it was over,' she said, but she never completely recovered from her loss. Although they had lived together for only a few years, Pitt had been, and continued to be, a powerful influence on her life. His impeccably high standards of morality and behaviour had reinforced her own ideals, and together with Lord Chatham, his father and Hester's grandfather, he came to represent to her all that was best in mankind. He was a standard against whom others would always be set, and she talked of him with loving pride and affection for the rest of her life.

With Pitt's death a sad pattern had begun to emerge in Lady Hester's life, a pattern that had started with her mother's death so many years before. It seemed that time and again the people whom she loved and upon whom she depended were to die, often leaving her homeless. Her mother's death when she was four had not been a conscious memory for Lady Hester, but in losing her at such an early age, Hester had been deprived of a warm, loving and secure relationship, a loss that directly affected her attitudes towards women as a whole. Later on, the help she had given to Philip after having left Chevening effectively killed her relationship with her father, and closed the doors of her family home to her. A few years later in 1803, the death of her grandmother, Lady Chatham, deprived her of the only maternal love she had known, and again left her with nowhere to live. Now the loss of Pitt, her beloved uncle, was hardest to bear, for she had loved him most, and with his death she was homeless yet again.

One of Pitt's last requests had been that Parliament should settle an allowance on Lady Hester and her sisters. 'I am far from saying that my public services have earned it,' he had said, with typical modesty, 'but I hope my wish may be complied with.' It was. Parliament settled his debts of around £40,000, and granted Lady Hester £1,200 per year, and her two sisters £600 each. After her dreadful loss, all Hester's instincts told her to gather what remained of her family around her, so with the money granted to her by Parliament, she rented a house in Montagu Square to be a home for herself, Charles and James.

Life in London was very different for Hester now that she was without Pitt. She soon discovered that many of the people who had once sought her company so assiduously now tried to avoid her. A few, including the Duke of York and George Canning, were still happy to see her, but she started going out less and less. Her income did not allow for any extravagances, and she soon realized that she could not even afford to run a carriage and horses. This further inhibited her social life, because if she walked anywhere she ran the risk of being mistaken for a prostitute, even if she had a footman with her. She hated not having enough money. 'A poor gentlewoman,' she later observed, 'is the worst thing in the world.'

Although her political power was now greatly reduced, she still kept in close touch with what went on in Westminster. Canning would often visit her with the latest news, and she had messengers to bring bulletins when he was too busy to come. Another visitor was Sir John Moore, whom Hester had met three years before, when he was stationed at Shorncliffe in Kent. Moore had been a great admirer of Pitt, who in his turn had respected the general as a gentleman and a soldier. Sir John had been greatly saddened to hear of Pitt's death, and when he returned from his campaign in Sicily, where he had been attempting to stop the spread of Napoleon's power in the Mediterranean, he called on Lady Hester to pay his respects. She had always thought very highly of his talents, and when it became apparent that he was being treated rather shabbily by the present government, she decided to take up arms on his account. Letters were sent, and complaints made.

There were three major outcomes of this seemingly minor crusade. The first was that, having had the matter brought to his attention by Lady Hester, George III put Moore in command of the forces in Spain, in so doing acting independently and in direct opposition to government advice. The second result was that Hester quarrelled bitterly with her old friend Canning, who opposed the appointment, and the third outcome was that Sir John and Lady Hester became very close friends. He was a good, honest and straightforward man who had spent many long years in military camps all over Europe, and perhaps it was inevitable that he would be dazzled by someone as sophisticated and intelligent as Lady Hester. She, on the other hand, had learnt a bitter lesson over her infatuation with Leveson-Gower, and she had no intention of exposing herself to ridicule again. They were utterly discreet, yet it seems that by the time Sir John left for Portugal in 1808 there was an understanding between them: when he returned they would become engaged.

When Sir John left he took with him Charles Stanhope, as his youngest major and aide-de-camp, and William Napier. Hester gave him an inscribed seal, which Moore had placed on his fob.

It is hard to know how Lady Hester felt about Sir John and Charles going to war, because little of her correspondence from this time has survived. She certainly felt proud of them both, and had every confidence in Moore's abilities as a general, but she could have had no idea of what was to happen.

Very early in 1809, James Stanhope travelled to Corunna from

England, with despatches from the Duke of York. Within days of his arrival he was standing beside the bed where Moore lay dying, having been mortally wounded in his successful 'masterly retreat' from the French. He had turned down the help of surgeons, telling them to go to the soldiers who needed them more, and the only thing he feared was that he would be a long time dying. He was not, and his final words were to James: 'Stanhope, remember me to your sister.' They were not romantic words, but they were spoken from the heart by a good and brave man dying in a foreign country. Hester was to treasure them for the rest of her life.

James, together with the rest of the men whom Moore had so valiantly commanded, was deeply shocked and saddened by Moore's death, but worse was yet to come. His brother Charles had also been killed. He, too, had been leading his men in battle. At almost the same moment that Moore had received his fatal wound, Charles had been shot through the heart and had died instantly.

Hester was by nature a resilient person, but the crushing blow of this double loss coming so close to Pitt's death utterly overwhelmed her. It was 'a misfortune so cruel', she wrote to a friend, 'that I am convinced I can never recover from it.'

For weeks she would see no one except for Colonel Anderson, an officer and long-time friend of Sir John's, who had been with him when he died. He had been wounded and sent back to England to recover. He brought with him Sir John's personal effects and a blood-stained gauntlet, which he gave to Lady Hester. She insisted that he stay with her at Montagu Square and she took care of him, nursing him back to health. As he recovered they talked endlessly about Moore and Charles. Lady Hester wanted to know every detail of what had happened, and every memory of Anderson's life with Moore; it seemed to help her begin to come to terms with what had happened. The friendship and trust that Anderson and Lady Hester built between them during his convalescence was such that she appointed him to be the alternative executor of her will in case James should predecease her.

During this time many people wrote letters of condolence to Lady Hester, and asked to come to see her, including Canning and Lord Castlereagh, but Moore's campaign had been criticized in Parliament and she would see no one who had been a party to such calumny. 'I am mortified beyond description that you are not the public character I expected,' she wrote in a furious letter to Canning, 'and I am sure this feeling is not softened by your private conduct to those I love.'

Once again Hester's world had collapsed around her. Once again those that she loved most in the world had died and left her. She was broken in her heart, in her spirit and in her health. There was nothing and no one to keep her in London any more, and by April 1809, three months after her awful loss, it seemed that London had become almost repugnant to her, and claustrophobic with unbearable memories. It was as if everything had turned sour, and in desperation she remembered a trip she had once made to Wales where the countryside and the people seemed fresh and pure. Perhaps life could be simple there, she thought, unsullied by the bitter past and unpressurized by a frighteningly bleak future. It was an escape, and she seized it with both hands.

She remembered a little farmhouse in Glen Irfon which she had discovered during one of her rides. She knew it was available to rent, so she wrote to a clergyman who lived nearby with a list of her requirements, which were very exact but far from lavish. By immersing herself in unimportant details she hoped to blot out the awful reality of her bereavement. The technique had proved an effective distraction once before, when she had been upset over Leveson-Gower, and she hoped it would work again for her, now that her need was far greater.

'I want the parlour, the little room above it for my bedroom and the little room next for a dressing-room, a door to be made near the window to communicate with the bedroom. The room over the kitchen for my maids and a bed, in the loft or elsewhere, for a boy. The parlour must have two rush chairs or wooden ones, and be carpeted all over with green baize, or coarse grey cloth, like soldier's greatcoats, a table to dine on, a fly-table and shelves for books. The bedroom must have two chairs, a table – no bed, as I shall bring down a camp bed and furniture complete. Bedside carpets I shall expect to find, a table with a looking-glass, two wash-hand basins, two water jugs, one large stone pitcher for water, two large tumbler glasses, and two large cups for soap, a tin kettle for warm water, and a little strip of carpet before the table. . . . I shall want no attendance from any part of the family. . . . If Mrs Price chooses to put things in this order, I will give her twentyfive pounds for part of the months of May, June, July, August, September, and part of October – in short the season.'

She was so anxious to leave London that she arrived in Wales before the work was finished, but it was soon completed under her own supervision, and her stay in Wales helped greatly towards mending her health and her spirits. For a few months she led a simple, rural existence that provided a total counterpoint to the complex, sophisticated life she had had in London. She kept two horses, and went riding regularly. She bought a cow called Prettyface, and learned to milk it and to make butter from the milk. She visited the neighbours, and made medicines for them when they were ill. She made herself tea from balm leaves. She rested and recovered.

As some kind of order returned to her life she began to contemplate her future, and as she did, she realized that her life was unalterably changed. She could no longer imagine living in London: she had no power or influence there any longer, the activities of her former political friends disgusted her, and many of her other friends had deserted her. On the other hand she could not imagine living permanently anywhere else in England. She had no responsibilities or obligations to tie her down, and when she realized that James was going to have to rejoin his regiment in Spain, she decided to close down the house in Montagu Square and travel with him to Gibraltar.

She had enjoyed her trip through Europe in 1803 six years before, and a journey abroad now would help to cheer her. It would provide her with a distraction from her loss, and she would also be able to postpone having to make any decisions about her future.

CHAPTER FIVE

'Go out of England I am determined'

The journey to Gibraltar meant a long trip by sea around Brittany, across the Bay of Biscay, down the Portuguese coast and in through the Straits of Gibraltar.

Lady Hester estimated that to travel privately would cost her two or three hundred pounds, which she simply could not afford, so she wrote in a typically imperious way to General Richard Grenville, who was not only First Admiral of the Fleet, but also her first cousin:

'My dear General, Go out of England I am determined, & I will go in some vessel I am sure will be taken, for I have not the vast dread of being ill-treated by the French & at all events I wd. rather be at their mercy than at that of any creature called a friend of Mr. Pitt's.

'If after Mr. P [Pitt] has added during his administration, 600 ships (line of B & frigate) to the Naval force of this country, a relation or even friend of his cannot be accommodated with a passage in one of them it is rather hard, & if they do not chuse to do the thing hand-somely they may let it alone. I am much too ill to be worried. I will give you no further trouble on this subject for I will ask for nothing more and refuse every offer I don't like with the contempt it deserves.'

She got her way and was offered a passage on the frigate *Jason,* which was providing protection for a convoy of merchant and trans-port ships bound for Gibraltar. Captain the Hon. James King was commanding officer, and, together with a small group of travelling companions, Lady Hester left England on 10 February 1810. Before she left she redrafted her will and in it made reference to her return to England, but whatever her intentions were, they were not to be. She never set foot in England again.

Her travelling companions included James and his friend Mr Nassau Sutton, her maid Mrs Elizabeth Williams, a manservant, and a young physician named Charles Meryon. Meryon had been recommended to Lady Hester by an eminent surgeon friend, but as Hester was quite certain that she knew how to cure most illnesses better than most doctors, she saw his presence as more of a token gesture than a necessity.

Dr Meryon was, however, to be the most loyal and faithful of all her company: the next thirty years of his life were devoted to her service, and he deserved a better reference than Lady Hester eventually gave him twenty-eight years later. Writing to Lord Hardwicke, she said:

'Should you see the doctor in England, recollect that his only good quality in my sight is, I believe, being very honest in money matters. No others do I give him; without judgement, without heart, he goes through the World like many others, blundering his way, and often, from his want of accuracy, doing mischief everytime he opens his mouth.'

One hopes that Meryon never read these harsh words; they would have grieved him bitterly. Once he had met Lady Hester all he wanted to do was to serve her, and this he did to the best of his ability for the rest of his life. She was a hard person to live with as she got older. Dr Meryon wrote of her: 'Those who have known her can not deny that opposition to her will was altogether out of the question.'

It was spoken from the heart and was indubitably true. Perhaps it was not surprising that after so many years with such a strong-willed woman he was occasionally inaccurate and 'blundering'.

Meryon was a patient, long-suffering man. Not troubled with an over-abundance of intelligence, he was nevertheless quick to see that quality in others. Loyal and brave when necessary, he was also a tremendous snob and totally conversant with all the nuances of the English class system. He took the keenest interest in the social standing of all he met, and was most fully aware of his own lack. At the beginning of the nineteenth century family physicians did not occupy anything like the social position they enjoy today; then they were little more than servants, though perhaps head servants, in a household. Dr Meryon knew his place.

As a newly qualified doctor he considered himself very lucky to have been offered a job with a member of the aristocracy so quickly. He was delighted with his new position, and by the end of their voyage to Gibraltar, he was thrilled with his new employer. He wrote to his sister Sarah in a typically pompous way:

'I find my situation not merely such as satisfies, but one that gratifies me,' he said. 'For instead of encountering all those haughty condescensions, which are always reminding us of our inferiority whilst they profess to overlook it, and which we feel so sensibly when coming from persons to whom we are superior in everything except in wealth, I find civility that sets me at my ease and a treatment that never humiliates me. Yet with Lady Hester and her brother I could brook a conduct almost the reverse of what they show me: for there is in both such an air of nobility, such a highly cultivated mind, which I am convinced nothing but high birth and the first society, and that, too, from one's infancy could give, that on every occasion I am obliged to confess a superiority which they never seem inclined to lay a stress on.'

It is most unlikely that Hester and James set out deliberately to charm and enchant Meryon to this extent, but that was certainly the effect they achieved. These first impressions gained by Meryon were all-important, for they formed the foundation of his whole concept of Lady Hester, of how she thought and why she acted the way she did. At this stage she could do no wrong in his eyes. 'She is the best lady who ever breathed,' he wrote fervently to his sister, and he never really changed his opinion of her, even in later years when, driven to distraction by his manner, which could be pedantic and subservient at the same time, she often treated him quite abominably.

If it is not too unkind a comparison to make, Meryon was not unlike a pet dog in the simplicity of his emotions. Love and devotion, once bestowed, were never to be dented by kicks and curses.

The journey to Gibraltar took almost exactly a month, and during this time the party got to know each other very well. It was a tedious trip, and one that took Hester past the towering cliffs that guard the entrance to Corunna where Charles and Sir John Moore had been killed so recently. Lady Hester thought bitterly of the war that had claimed their lives, and worried for James, now safe with her but shortly to rejoin his regiment in Cadiz.

They may have been beyond the reach of war, but they were completely at the mercy of the elements, and when a violent storm struck them off the Portuguese coast, the convoy was very nearly wrecked on the shoals of Trafalgar. They were forced to stand off the coast, and endured two days of terror and seasickness before it was judged safe to traverse the straits and make for Gibraltar and safety.

It was a horrible experience, and naturally enough the passengers needed time to recuperate. The Governor of Gibraltar, General Campbell, gave them a warm welcome and ensconced Lady Hester and James in his residence, the Convent, whilst Mr Sutton and Dr Meryon had apartments nearby.

Gibraltar was full of English visitors and Spanish aristocracy, and the social life was hectic. As Lady Hester recovered, she was drawn into the social round, taking Dr Meryon with her as companion and escort. Dr Meryon was thrilled with his suddenly elevated social position and Lady Hester was being quite charming to him. On 23 March he wrote exultantly:

'Here, then, we are, receiving all the civilities that the chief people of the place can show us.... [Lady Hester's] disposition is the most obliging you can possibly conceive, and the familiar and kind manner in which she treats me has the best effect on persons around me, from all of whom, through her, I experience the politest civilities. At about six we meet at the Convent to dinner, and the General's table is, of course, made up of the best company in the place.'

Entranced by his new employer, dazzled by her friends and basking in his new-found social acceptability, Meryon was enjoying life as never before. Perhaps his snobbery should be off-putting, but he was so utterly transparent that it is hard to dislike him for it.

The travelling party shrank in Gibraltar: James left for the 1st Foot Guards in Cadiz, and Nassau Sutton, James's friend, left for Minorca. Hester was subdued and saddened by the farewells but, quite unknowingly, she was poised to meet someone who would change her life in the most dramatic way.

Michael Bruce, at twenty-one, was thirteen years younger than Lady Hester. He was travelling abroad at his father's expense, doing the

Grand Tour before taking up a career in politics. He and a friend, the Marquess of Sligo (who was yachting in the Mediterranean), were introduced to Lady Hester in Gibraltar.

Michael was a well-educated young man with a great respect for knowledge. He was also charming, gallant and, as Dr Meryon soon reported, 'handsome enough to move any lady's heart that is not, like my poor patient, too much a valetudinarian to find a moment for love'.

Little did Meryon know. In a very short time Bruce and Lady Hester found that they were most compatible and it was decided that he should join her party. He was in the habit of writing regularly to his father, with whom he enjoyed an unusually liberal and open relationship, and a letter went promptly from Gibraltar.

'Lady Hester Stanhope who is now my compagnon de voyage is a woman of very extraordinary talent,' Bruce told his father. 'She inherits all the great and splendid qualities of her illustrious grandfather [Lord Chatham]. For the last five years she has been in a most unsettled state of health and she is still very unwell. I hope however that change of scene and change of climate will restore health to her body and tranquillity to her mind.'

After a few weeks in Gibraltar, society there began to pall for Lady Hester and she decided to go to Malta. Michael was unable to alter his immediate travel plans, so they decided they would have to travel separately and meet in Valetta.

Lady Hester left Gibraltar on 7 April in a ship called *Cerberus* commanded by a Captain Whitby. Despite the Governor's hospitality she was not sorry to go, for Gibraltar was near to the unrest in Spain, and after the first few parties she had found the diplomats and their friends to be stuffy and pompous.

On the way to Malta, *Cerberus* dropped anchor in Port Mahon bay in Minorca to allow Lady Hester to see the town that her ancestor, the 1st Earl Stanhope, had captured for England in 1708. For this deed he had been awarded the title Viscount Stanhope of Mahon, a title that was now held by Hester's brother Philip. After a brief stay the party carried on to Malta, where they were met and warmly welcomed by General Oakes, the Governor of the island. Graciously refusing his offer of accommodation, she accepted an invitation from the Commissary-General, Mr Fernandez, whose wife was the sister of her maid, Mrs Elizabeth Williams.

Despite the sadness of her recent parting from James, Lady Hester was evidently recovering her form. The party dined nightly at the Governor's palace where, to Dr Meryon's unbridled delight, they mixed again with the top society of the island. 'I found myself directly opposite the Governor,' he recorded ecstatically, 'separated by the breadth (and not the length) of the table, with an Italian Duchess on his right hand, Lady Hester on his left, and a string of Lords and Ladies, and Counts and Countesses, on either hand.'

Unlike Meryon, who was entranced with the Maltese women, Lady Hester did not like any of the ladies that she met, nor did they like her. According to Dr Meryon she contrived to 'affront almost all the women in the place. She has the most thorough contempt for her sex,' Meryon had realized, 'at least, that part of it who converse on nothing but visits, caps and bonnets, and such frivolous subjects. Hence it is that the moment she discovers one to be of that class, and her knowledge of mankind very soon puts her in possession of a person's character, she seldom fails to manifest her disgust and to give rise to as much disgust as she feels.'

This was certainly the Lady Hester that prickled and offended so many of London's top ladies for so many years, and the fact that she was behaving controversially again shows how much she had recovered since leaving England.

She took huge delight in making the acquaintance of General Oakes, however. She would accept invitations only from him, and the pleasure she took in their growing friendship was evidently reciprocated, for despite the fact that she offended nearly all the women of note on his island, Lady Hester and General Oakes became such close friends that they remained confidants for the rest of their lives. This was all the more extraordinary since they were never actually to meet again, and all their communication was accomplished by the very unreliable system of sending letters via friends, acquaintances and passing boats.

Soon, as Michael Bruce established himself in the party, he and Dr Meryon began to quarrel. The compatibility that Lady Hester and Michael had felt from their first meeting was growing into something stronger, and Dr Meryon began to feel left out. He saw Michael as usurping the gilded role of companion to Lady Hester that he had revelled in for so many weeks. Rivalry and jealousy began to make themselves felt.

'I don't like Mr Bruce,' wrote Dr Meryon petulantly. 'He seems desirous of excluding me from the great nobilities with which he is intimate, and of inducing Lady Hester not to bring me forward so much as her accustomed goodness prompts her to do ... he and Lady Hester have dined out twice and I have not been invited.'

He certainly felt most put out, but there was even more at stake for him than met the eye. What rankled equally with him was that if he ceased to be invited to the top-flight social affairs, he would lose his superior ranking in what he called 'the second-rate society ... the colonels, majors, and chief merchants of Valetta'. He could afford to despise them now, but he realized that 'when they find I am accounted unworthy of accompanying Lady Hester out,' they would 'immediately call in question how far I ought to be admitted into their set'.

Dr Meryon's ostracism would have been certain had they heard themselves described as second-rate society. He was so finely tuned in to the nuances of social acceptability that he had not paused to consider that any stratum of Maltese society might have been happily prepared to accept him purely for himself.

Poor Dr Meryon. To have been elevated so suddenly and then to find himself in imminent danger of complete social decline was almost more than he could bear.

In the same letter in which he confided his social worries, Dr Meryon commented about Lady Hester: 'she is mended in health considerably of late, and really begins to look quite winning.'

Having spent many years entrancing most of the men in London, including the King, Lady Hester would have ground her teeth had she heard such faint praise. She had never been a beauty but, when in good health and spirits, had always had a vivacity that made her sparklingly attractive to men. She had been ill, though, and was not one of that minority of fortunate women who can look appealingly fragile when ill; she was one of the majority who succeed only in looking drained and drab.

Dr Meryon had been enchanted by her even when she was at a low ebb. Now her health had returned Meryon saw, forlornly and for the first time, the Lady Hester who had captivated the King of England, the Royal Princes and half of London. She was mended in health; she was also mended in spirit. And she was falling in love.

Michael Bruce was very lucky to have a father who was intelligent, liberal-minded, compassionate and devoted to his children. Born of a solid Scottish family, Patrick Craufurd Bruce – known by his middle name, Craufurd – had dashingly eloped to Gretna Green at the age of thirty-seven with a beautiful eighteen-year-old girl, Jane Smith. It is not known why this romantic act was necessary, but Craufurd and Jane had a long and very happy marriage.

They left England early in their married life to live in Bombay, where Craufurd worked for the East India Company. A canny businessman, he soon started to build up a small fortune. Although romantic enough to elope, he was astute enough to keep his accounts meticulously: every rupee and anna that he spent between the years of 1785 and 1814 was recorded in a vast leatherbound book that still survives today.

Though he was always careful with his money, Craufurd could not be accused of being mean or penny-pinching in any way. Apart from keeping his family in great comfort, many people both known and unknown to him benefited from his kindness. His accounts show that he gave to the poor (1,000 rupees on 10 May 1791); he subscribed to the building of Edinburgh University (500 rupees, 1 March 1792); and on 9 April 1792 he gave 200 rupees to the family of a man careless enough to get himself shot in a duel. Not all of his spending was so altruistic though: he also spent fairly large sums quite often on 'Gold leaf for gilding my chariott'.

Whilst Craufurd and Jane were living in India three of their six children were born. Michael was the first, and was followed by two sisters, Maria and Jane. The family decided in 1791 that they would return to England early the following year. Jane and the children would go first, leaving Craufurd to tidy his business affairs and follow them after a month or two. To mark this important point in their lives, Craufurd commissioned two paintings to be done by a Mr James Wales: a miniature of himself for Jane to take with her, and a large portrait of all the family.

Sadly, the miniature is now lost, but the family portrait remains. It shows a delightfully relaxed and happy scene. His wife Jane is beautiful, and Michael, as the eldest of the family, is casually and confidently holding his father's hand: a handsome barefoot boy.

Craufurd provided a good education for his children. The girls were educated by a host of governesses and tutors, and Michael went to Eton and Cambridge. After the completion of his formal schooling, Craufurd was keen for his son to enter politics immediately, but Michael felt he needed more experience first, so his father readily agreed to send him on a Grand Tour. Suitable companions were decided upon and letters of introduction sought from Lord Grenville and other luminaries to ease the party's progress through Europe. It was during the course of this Grand Tour that Michael Bruce and his party arrived in Gibraltar and first met Lady Hester.

Michael and his father were in constant touch by letter. Michael reported on his progress and activities and gave his impressions and opinions, some of which were extremely outspoken. Craufurd replied with encouragement and advice. When Craufurd first heard from Michael that he had joined Lady Hester's party he was rather alarmed: he knew her to be older than Michael and was aware that she had quite a reputation. After making discreet enquiries, however, he realized that she was of impeccable descent, and that the Grenvilles, who were friends of his, were her relatives, so his initial worry soon abated.

Towards the end of July Craufurd received a letter from Lord Bute who, together with Lady Bute, had been guests of General Oakes in Malta and had often dined with Lady Hester and Michael. Bute remarked about Michael that 'Nothing I could say to you to his advantage would to my mind bear the smallest tendency to flattery. His thirst after acquiring every species of information is quite uncommon and most laudable.' He went on to ask that if Michael's trip was to be extended, perhaps his grandson, the Earl of Dumfries, could be allowed to join the party. Craufurd was very gratified by such praise.

In Malta Lord and Lady Bute had been staying in one of General Oakes's country residences, the pleasantly situated Palace of St Antonio, five miles outside Valetta. When they left General Oakes offered the house to Lady Hester and her party, who moved in immediately, grateful to be in the comparative cool of the countryside now that the weather was getting hotter.

The gardens of the Palace were beautifully planted with oleander and bougainvillea, and the long shady walks and cool terraces were perfumed with the scent of orange trees and climbing jasmine. After the hot, crowded streets of Valetta, St Antonio was an oasis of tranquillity and calm.

Here Lady Hester and Michael strolled in the cool of the evening, when the garden was illumined only by the moon and stars. Here the attraction they had both felt so strongly in Valetta grew rapidly until they realized they were in love, and here, in this idyllically romantic setting, they became lovers.

Of the two, Michael, at twenty-one, was undoubtedly the more experienced in matters of love. Lady Hester had always said and done exactly what she wanted to: she loved to flirt and had constantly scandalized people in London by going without a chaperon, but she had never had an affair. In the prevailing climate of sexual hypocrisy it was assumed that far more went on than actually met the eye, so gossip about her had been rife, as has always been the case with socially prominent people. Whilst living in London Lady Hester had written to a friend who had been unwise enough to believe rumours of an engagement:

'Thank you for your news. I have been going to be married fifty times in my life, said to have been married half as often and run away with once. But, provided I have my own way, the world may have theirs and welcome.'

It was a fact, however, that in an age known for its moral laxity, Lady Hester was still a virgin when she met Michael. Her relationships with Lord Camelford and Leveson-Gower had been platonic, and Sir John Moore had been too gentlemanly to think of anything less than marriage. Her self-esteem and her analytical mind had always prevented her from indulging in any passing dalliances.

Her friend Lady Suffolk understood this well, as Meryon reported much later in his *Memoirs*. 'She never will let anybody do a bit more than she intends,' she wrote, 'what she does is with *connaissance de cause*.' Hester herself agreed with this: 'nobody could ever accuse me of folly. Even those actions which might seem folly to a common observer, were wisdom. Everything with me, through life, has been premeditatedly done.'

Embarking on an affair with Michael was neither wise nor premeditated, but it was perfectly understandable. Michael was still young enough to be impressionable, and he was dazzled by Lady

Hester's wit, knowledge and reputation. She in her turn found an intellectual affinity and unquestioning admiration impossible to resist. They were strangers together in a foreign land. He was also young and extremely handsome.

Affairs were tolerated and indeed accepted as long as they were conducted with discretion. What was not deemed socially acceptable was for lovers to be open or in any way flagrant. This presented a considerable problem for the scrupulously honest Lady Hester. Pride had always been one of her family's weaknesses – or strengths – and in her it was displayed to the full. Now that she had finally embarked on a love affair she was not ashamed of the fact and had no intention of hiding it. The man with whom she had fallen in love was, in her eyes, almost perfect, and someone with whom it was an honour to have her name linked. 'No one was ever so handsome nor so clever,' she declared of Michael, 'and no one was destined to a greater future than he.'

Any attempt at discretion would, for Lady Hester, have been tantamount to deceit. It would have implied that there was something shameful and underhand going on, and that was complete anathema to her.

She had always had very little regard for the opinion of society, and cared not at all for what it would think of her conduct. What Lady Hester did care about, however, was the opinion of people she loved or respected. Craufurd Bruce had already earned her respect by virtue of being Michael's father, so she began to be very concerned about what his reaction to their affair would be.

One major reason for Hester being so appreciative of Craufurd and Michael's relationship was the fact that her own father had been so unsatisfactory. 'Nothing affects me more than parental kindness,' she was to write poignantly to Craufurd, 'because alas I have never experienced it, for like the offspring of a bird of prey I was driven half-fledged from the parent nest.'

Craufurd both liked and respected his son. He listened to his opinions and sought his advice. The 'very early management of himself' that he had given Michael seemed to have been amply rewarded: at this stage of his life Michael was indeed 'kind, correct and honourable', as Craufurd had written to Lord Bute.

This freely given trust was fully appreciated and reciprocated by

Michael, who told his father in a letter, 'I shall ever be thankful for being blessed with the most honourable and most generous of Fathers.'

Lady Hester and Michael were both anxious not to jeopardize this happy state of affairs, but since they were not prepared to hide their relationship it was inevitable that Craufurd was going to find out about it. To Lady Hester there was only one course of action open. It seemed perfectly natural to her, but even she must have realized what an extraordinary step she was about to take. She would preempt the gossip. She would write to Craufurd herself and tell him she was having an affair with his son.

CHAPTER SIX

'While loving him to distraction'

On 27 June 1810 in the Palace of St Antonio in Malta, Hester wrote one of the most unusual letters of her life. She addressed it to Craufurd and marked it private. He could not fail to be astonished by it.

'Sir,' she wrote, 'If your character inspired me with less respect, I should not give you the opportunity of perhaps accusing me of impertinence, in presuming to address you upon a subject which requires all my courage to touch upon, & great liberality on your part, to do justice to those motives which induce me to expaciate [sic] upon it.

'You may have heard that I have become acquainted with your Son, his elevated and statesmanlike mind, his brilliant talents to say nothing of his beautiful person, cannot be contemplated by any feeling mind with indifference; to know him is to love & admire him, & I do both! Should you hear this in any irregular way, it might give you uneasiness, & you might not only mistake the nature of the sentiments I feel towards him, but my views altogether, & imagine that he had fallen into the hands of an artful woman who wd. take him in, as far as it lay in her power.

'Sir, you need not be under any of these apprehensions, the affection I feel for him wd. only prompt me the more to consider his advantage in every point of view, & at this very moment (while loving him to distraction) I look forward to the period when I must resign him to some thrice happy woman really worthy of him. While seeking knowledge & considering plans of future ambition, few persons are perhaps better calculated for his companion than I am, but when he has once taken his line, & become a public character, I shall then like a dethroned Empress, resign to virtue the possession of that perfection which she alone has a right to, & see whether a sacrifice demanded by principle & true feeling, cannot be made with as good a grace as one dictated by policy and interest.

'Sir, if you knew me, I flatter myself that it wd. be unnecessary to give you any further assurance of the sincerity of my intentions, but as you do not, there is no promise however solemn I am not willing to make upon this subject. After what I have said I trust that no feeling of anxiety will remain as far as relates to your Son's welfare. It wd. be a satisfaction to me to learn (tho' I do not wish you to write to me) that this candid confession of my sentiments has not displeased you; do not however mistake the tone of humility I have adopted thro' this letter, which proceeds in fact from my being one of the proudest women in the world, so proud, as to despise the opinion of the world altogether, as far as relates to myself, but when I am addressing the parent of a man I so tenderly love; (& for whom he has so great an affection) a sacred sort of reverence steals upon my mind, which I hope has communicated itself to my expressions, as I have intended they should convey the confidence & respect with which Sir I have the honour to remain.

'Yours &c &c

'Hester Lucy Stanhope'

The letter was a masterpiece which few parents could have resisted. She had managed to convey her admiration and appreciation of Michael, confess her love and promise her protection all in the most compelling way. She was also subtle enough not to draw attention to her own considerable status; she knew it would speak for itself.

Michael sent a letter to his father on the same day. He was ill, but he too pleaded eloquently – in defence of Hester – and demanded, if necessary, to take any blame.

'My dear Father,' he wrote, 'It was my intention to have enlarged upon a subject concerning which you will receive full information in a letter from Lady Hester Stanhope, but as I am very unwell from the effects of a severe blow which I received on the head, and which has been attended with some fever, I can only at present touch upon it very shortly. Indeed the doctors have forbidden me to write at all, but as it is a subject of very great importance and interest to me I cannot refrain from saying a few words upon it.

'Know then that it was very much against my wishes that the letter was written as I was most anxious that the onus of the explanation and the odium of the consequences (if any such should result) should fall upon me.

'Lady Hester with a generosity and elevation of spirit almost unequalled insisted upon sending home what she calls her story. From the decided tone in which she expressed her intentions I was obliged to comply. But in complying, I determined to confess to you that I most strongly sympathized in those feelings of regard and attachment which she entertains for me, feelings which were not called forth by mere personal charms, but by the enlarged powers of her understanding and her most exalted mind.

'Independent of her own intrinsic worth, she has every associated merit which can raise her in my esteem. Highly born, splendidly connected and the granddaughter of the illustrious Chatam [sic] whose noble qualities she inherits. Far from being ashamed I feel most proud in openly confessing to you that I most sincerely love and admire her. Recollect that Lady H. Stanhope in writing to you has performed a work of supererogation, and it is a mark of esteem with which you cannot but be flattered. Her conduct throughout has been most open, most ingenuous and most honourable. As for myself, though it is a duty which every son owes his father but, a more particular one in me, who has always found you a most sincere friend and most indulgent parent. If there is any fault I am the guilty person and upon me you must wreak your vengeance. If the measures we are about to enter into meet with your displeasure it cannot fall upon Lady Hester, as over her you have neither power nor authority, but I must be made (as perhaps I may deserve) the scapegoat of your indignation.

'This letter is not intended as an exculpation or defence of my conduct, but I thought it advisable to communicate to you the simple truth, before your mind [is] prejudiced by a thousand malicious and unfounded reports which will apall [sic] you. I have only one favour to ask, which is that you will well revolve in your own mind the contents of the two letters before you communicate them to any person. In your liberality and generosity I have the greatest confidence and I know that your understanding, when it is not biassed but left to its own free working, will draw the most just and liberal conclusions.

'With every sentiment of regard and esteem I remain
'Your most affectionate Son
'Mic. Bruce'

Whatever Michael had done, a letter of such clarity and confident affection would surely have brought understanding, if not forgiveness. He was right to have gone against his doctor's advice and written a letter to send at the same time as that of Lady Hester. It would not have seemed honourable had her 'story' arrived on its own, and Craufurd's wrath might then have descended on Michael's head with justification.

Although Lady Hester had told Craufurd that she did not wish him to reply to her, it was obvious that he would do so, and Hester and Michael were fairly confident that the combined force of the two letters would elicit a favourable response. They knew, though, that his reply would take many weeks to arrive and the period of waiting was a time of great apprehension and anxiety for them both. In fact the letters took nearly two months just to reach Craufurd, and in the meantime, life had to go on.

During this period in Malta, the tensions that had been apparent between Michael and Dr Meryon suddenly reached a climax, and Meryon's jealousy of the pair erupted. 'Until this unpleasant fellow quits us,' he raged, 'I shall take my meals by myself.' Not being in charge of the party, however, he was forced to conclude rather bleakly, 'When that will be I know not, for he accompanies us on our voyage to Constantinople.'

Perhaps as a result of all these strains, Lady Hester was afflicted most unromantically with a fearful boil on the side of her head. It made her face swell up enormously and confined her to bed for ten days, during which time Dr Meryon grasped the opportunity to tend her most solicitously. He was thrilled to be needed again by Lady Hester and was most impressed by her courage, reporting that 'Her patience and fortitude under illness made it a pleasure to be near her person.' It would have been a pleasure for him even without the patience and fortitude.

Lady Hester's gratitude to Dr Meryon for his careful nursing encouraged her to speak to Michael about the antipathy that existed between the two men. Michael agreed to make an effort, Meryon responded, and soon all was peaceful again within the party.

As July progressed into August, so the heat in Malta grew until it became nearly unbearable. No letters had arrived from Michael's father, and the couple decided to continue with their travels, with General Oakes's assurance that he would forward any mail that arrived for them. The original plan had been to go to Sicily, but the threat of imminent invasion from Murat, recently put on the throne of Naples by Napoleon, made a trip there out of the question. Hester decided she wanted to go to Constantinople via Greece, but there was no vessel bound in that direction. Just as the despairing party were about to charter a boat, the frigate *Belle Poule* arrived in Malta from Corfu, and the captain, according to Dr Meryon, 'very politely offered to convey her ladyship and her party to one of the Ionian Islands'.

The Ionian Islands were then under English rule, having been taken from the French the year before, so Lady Hester accepted the offer gratefully. Her departure from Malta was tinged with sadness, though, for she had become firm friends with General Oakes. She gave him a little box as a keepsake, writing, 'I send you the box I mentioned. If it occasionally puts you in mind of me I shall be much flattered. Were I in France, where they work so admirably, I might be able to offer you one more worthy of your acceptance, for I should order that a little bird should pop up with a spring and sing a little hymn daily, expressive of my gratitude for all the kindness you have shown me.' It was not the only farewell to be said: Hester's maid, Elizabeth Williams, decided that she wanted to stay in Malta with her sister, so arrangements had to be made for another woman, Anne Fry, to take her place.

Dr Meryon was very anxious about the proposed trip. He had no illusions about how uncomfortable it was going to be, and even began to doubt that Lady Hester could survive such hardship. He wrote to his sister on 28 July, 'I can assure you I much fear my patient will not be able to stand it. For when you reflect that we are to travel through a country without beaten roads on mules, and to have nothing better to sleep in than these mules' stables, you will agree with me that it requires the constitution of a mule to stand the fatigue.'

Dr Meryon's professional concern for Lady Hester reflected well on him, but he soon learned that his patient was far more resilient than he could have conceived possible. It was just as well, for although there were many marvellous experiences in store for the party, there were also hardships to come beyond his imagining.

The voyage on the *Belle Poule* was the third leg of the journey for Lady Hester, but it represented far more than it seemed. The great adventure upon which she had embarked when leaving England had begun to seem rather tame in the familiar social scenes of Gibraltar and Malta. There, Hester and her party had been cosseted and entertained together with all the English and European aristocrats who had been unable to travel in France or Spain. So far the party had travelled no further than many others, but with the start of this journey to Constantinople Lady Hester was committing herself and her party to more than just a holiday abroad. Her exhilarating new relationship with Michael Bruce had revived her sense of daring and boldness, by taking her through emotional and physical experiences previously quite unknown to her. With him as her adoring lover and travelling companion her self-confidence was fully restored, and she was ready for a new challenge. Turkey represented a wholly different culture. Although England had a diplomatic presence there, it was not as yet a strong one. Constantinople was not only geographically distant, it was also politically and socially far removed from anything the party had yet encountered. It was exactly what Lady Hester wanted.

The party sailed on *Belle Poule* to Zante (modern Zakinthos) where they stayed for two weeks before travelling to Patras in late August. There they were joined by Michael's friend Lord Sligo, who was a delightful man and a welcome addition to the party. His splendidly flamboyant entourage included a Tartar, a dragoman or interpreter, a Turkish cook, four English servants, an English artist to paint the views, and two Albanians in full national costume which included 'silver-stocked pistols and silver-hilted yatagans' – a kind of short, curved sword. This brought the number of Hester's party to twenty-five, and they were an impressive sight as they crossed the Isthmus of Corinth on horseback and then sailed across to Piraeus and Athens.

Michael and Lord Sligo had known each other for many years, and had studied together under the eminent archaeologist Dr Gell. Sligo had already been involved in several archaeological digs in Greece and had exported many statues and other works of art to his home in

Ireland. To Michael, therefore, he was welcome not only as a congenial male companion but also as someone to share his appreciation of the treasures of ancient Greece, for Lady Hester was totally indifferent to such antediluvian stuff. It was almost incomprehensible to Michael that someone with a mind as brilliant as hers should find archaeology boring, but her academic education had been so desultory that she probably knew little of ancient Greece or its artefacts. By heredity, upbringing and inclination the focus of her most passionate interest had always been politics, people and a combination of the two – politicians. She found it far more invigorating to talk about them than to study long-buried broken statues, and had evidently been indulging in her favourite subject one day when Michael was stirred into what was one of his few recorded criticisms of her. 'Madam,' he said, 'I may say of you what was once said of the GREAT Lord Chatham, as you call him, and whom you have been talking about for these last two hours – I hardly know which most to be astonished at, your extraordinary genius, or your extraordinary ignorance.' Lady Hester's reaction is not recorded, but she made clear her opinion of education: it was 'all paint', she pronounced, 'it does not alter the appearance of the wood that is under it, it only improves its appearance a little.'

In 1810 the harbour of Piraeus was a small fishing port, and as the party sailed through the entrance a man dived from the mole into the sea to meet them. It was one of Lord Sligo's Cambridge friends: Lord Byron. Sligo called to him to get dressed and joined him on shore, and together they rode to Athens to arrange transport for the rest of the party.

Lady Hester and her party stayed in Athens for a month and during that time Lord Byron was a frequent guest. He knew that Michael thought Lady Hester 'the most superior woman of all the world', but he wasn't prepared at their first meeting for her spirited assault on his reputed misogyny. It was reported that Lady Hester 'with that lively eloquence for which she is so remarkable, took the poet briskly to task for the deprecating opinion which, as she understood, he entertained of all female intellect. Being but little inclined, even were he able, to sustain such heresy against one who was in her own person such a refutation of it, Lord Byron had no other refuge from the fair orator's arguments than in assent and silence, and this well-bred deference, being in a sensible woman's eyes, equivalent to concession, they became from henceforward most cordial friends.'

Of course Lady Hester was far too perceptive to think Byron's 'well-bred deference' meant any such thing as concession, but it served as a stable enough foundation for a temporary friendship. In truth, they found each other both irritating and faintly threatening: each was used to being the centre of attention and privately resented any undue attention being paid to the other. They were too alike to be friends, for each would have needed to be the dominant character. Byron left Athens shortly before Lady Hester, and they both reacted in the same coolly disparaging way when asked their opinions of each other.

'In Athens I saw nothing but a well-bred man like many others,' Lady Hester wrote of Byron. 'As for poetry, it is easy enough to write verses; and as for the thoughts, who knows where he got them? Many a one picks up some old book that nobody knows anything about and gets his ideas out of it.' Even his physiognomy was suspect: 'He had a great deal of vice in his looks, his eyes set too close together, and a contracted brow.' The only thing she admired about his famous looks was part of his chin and 'the curl on his forehead'.

So Byron was dismissed as a possibly reprobate but otherwise ordinary plagiarist, and he in his turn described Lady Hester as 'that dangerous thing – a female wit!' He continued: 'I have discovered nothing different from other she-things, except a great disregard of received notions in her conversation as well as conduct. I don't know whether this will recommend her to our sex, but I am sure it won't to her own.'

As usual Meryon missed all the subtleties, and got it quite wrong. 'On the 14th of October we quitted Athens,' he wrote, 'and with regret we left behind us Lord Byron, whom her ladyship was much pleased with. . . . Lord Byron himself, I believe, is a little keen occasionally.'

When the party left for Constantinople they travelled in a more humble style than they had previously enjoyed: frigates were not so freely available this far east and they had to use local transport. The only vessel available was a Greek polacca – a type of three-masted sailing ship used for carrying cargo. It was laden with wheat, part of the tribute then levied on Athens by the Turks, and had only one cabin that was hastily whitewashed to make it habitable for Lady Hester and her maid. The unfortunate servants were forced to sleep actually on the cargo, in the narrow gap between the wheat and the top of the hold. The gentlemen of the party were the most comfortable of all, up on deck, but felt obliged to keep their weapons close at hand, for the crew seemed exceptionally villainous.

The first days of the trip were delightful: 'Dolphins gambolled round our prow,' Dr Meryon reported, 'and light airs filled our cotton sail.' On 25 October in the Sea of Marmara, however, they were first becalmed, then they were hit by a terrible storm as night fell. Much to Meryon's disgust the sailors panicked. The Battle of Trafalgar had taken place only five years before, and there was perhaps an echo of Nelson's famous signal in Meryon's later report. 'Instead of doing their duty,' he snorted, 'they set about collecting money from the passengers, which they tied up in a handkerchief and fastened to the tiller, making a vow to St. George that they would dedicate it to his shrine if we reached some port in safety.'

St George appears to have obliged them, for they finally made a safe landfall at a small port called Erakli in the Gulf of Rodosto. Lady Hester prudently waited there with her maid while Sligo and Bruce went on ahead to arrange accommodation in Constantinople and to hire a more stable vessel, a caïque, in which Lady Hester could complete the journey. It was night when they finally sailed out of the Sea of Marmara and into the mouth of the Bosporus, and as they approached Constantinople the lights and the sounds of the ancient city mingled with the smells of smoke and exotic spices that were drifting on the wind. It was very Eastern and quite different from anything they had experienced before. Approaching a new harbour at night has one major disadvantage, however: without a slow visual introduction one misses all the opening vistas, the contours and perspectives that give each place its unique character, and Constantinople, or Istanbul as it is now called, is particularly spectacular.

'The imperial city commanded, from her seven hills, the opposite shores of Europe and Asia,' Gibbon wrote, 'the climate was healthy and temperate, the soil fertile, the harbour secure and capacious, and the approach on the side of the continent was of small extent and easy defence.' It was no wonder that Constantinople had been a city of huge importance for so many centuries.

Sailing in from the Sea of Marmara, the two opposite shores quickly close in on either side. On the left the land then curves in sharply, studded with towers, and as the city begins, the houses cluster closely together, right down to the water's edge. Domed mosques are everywhere, their pointed minarets punctuating the skyline. In the centre of this part of the city – Stamboul as it was called – lie the old Seraglio, the ancient Acropolis, and the site of the walls of Byzantium, but dominating everything are the domes of S. Sophia, gleaming gold in the sunlight. On the right is Scutari, with its barracks and cemeteries, and once around the corner of Stamboul, the Golden Horn opens up: a magnificent natural harbour shielded by great land masses on either side. On the right is the residential area called Pera, and it was here that Hester and her party had their lodgings.

The history of Constantinople is a rat's nest of politics, corruption, bloodshed, luxury and vice. In 1808, two years before Hester's arrival there, Mahmoud, the last surviving prince of the House of Osman, had taken the throne, and he seemed at first to be as bloodthirsty as his predecessors. It had become the habit when new rulers assumed power for them to kill their brothers to obviate any possibility of any opposition. Mahmoud was no exception. He had also been trained to hate the Janissaries, a formidable body of men formed originally by his ancestor, Orchan, son of Osman, in the early fourteenth century. To ensure the total loyalty of these men to the Sultan, they were indoctrinated from birth: Christian baby boys were captured and brought up by the strictest methods to become fiercely orthodox Muslim soldiers who enforced the absolute will of the Sultan at all times. By the seventeenth century, the Janissaries had grown so powerful, however, that they were, in effect, the rulers of the city and of the Empire. Any Sultan foolish enough to attempt independence from them was simply killed.

When Mahmoud became Sultan he inherited an Empire that was totally corrupt. In an attempt to break the power of the Janissaries he had several of their leaders strangled and thrown into the Bosporus. He then started to introduce new ideas: schools, printing presses and the learning of foreign languages. He soon discovered that he had not dealt strongly enough with the Janissaries: in a blatant attempt to terrify Mahmoud into submission they surrounded and set fire to his palace. It was a drastic move which got terrifyingly out of hand. The fire spread until it seemed as if the whole city was ablaze.

'No one attempted to stay the conflagration,' reported M. de Jucherau, a Frenchman who was staying in Pera, 'which in a short time made terrible progress. Soon the most populous quarter of Constantinople was covered with a sheet of fire. The cries, the groans of women, and old men and children attracted no attention and excited no pity ... the fire was too intense and active to be subdued or arrested, even by throwing to the ground whole stacks of houses: it vaulted over the chasms thus made.'

Although the destruction was far more serious than perhaps even the Janissaries had intended, the point was made, and Mahmoud was forced to abandon his radical ideas for a great many years.

This, then, was the city into which Lady Hester and her party had sailed. They arrived at midnight on 3 November, and Hester was carried in a sedan chair through the steep, narrow streets to a house in Pera, the way before her being lit with a huge lantern. Her passage was marked by 'scores of dogs, like so many Cerberuses', who 'poked their ugly heads out of dark corners and stunned us with their incessant barking'. The streets were filthy and their luggage had been sent to Smyrna. It was not an auspicious start.

The next few months were significant for Hester in a variety of ways. It was in Constantinople that she first got to know the Turks, a people for whom she would have the greatest respect and affection for the rest of her life. She developed a lively friendship with Stratford Canning, first cousin of her old friend Lord Canning, the young Plenipotentiary Extraordinary to the Porte, as Constantinople was also known. Her relationship with Michael Bruce matured and consolidated. After many months of travel the couple had still not heard from Michael's father, and of all the events in Constantinople, perhaps the most immediately important of all was when they finally received letters from Craufurd. Theirs had taken many weeks to reach him, but he had reacted decisively in his reply. After all the months of waiting, Hester and Michael would finally know what his reactions were, and be able to see clearly at last if their life together could continue and, if so, in what form.

CHAPTER SEVEN

'A frankness and a candour which cannot be surpassed'

The long-awaited letters from Craufurd arrived within the first few weeks at Pera, having taken nearly three months to get there. The first was for Lady Hester and was dated 20 August 1810.

'Madam, A few days past I had the honour of receiving your Letter,' Craufurd wrote. 'I will candidly confess the first perusal of it startled me much, my imagination did not then comprehend that decisive peculiarity of thinking and of acting for which I have understood you have been distinguished, and for which I also understood some of your immediate relatives are highly indebted to you.'

Craufurd was referring to Hester's intervention in her sister's and brother's lives, particularly when she enabled Philip to escape from their father and go to university in Germany. Craufurd had evidently made a rapid and thorough investigation into Lady Hester's background, and this had allayed many of his initial fears.

'I have repeatedly read over your Letter,' he went on, 'and I have to thank you for a frankness and a candour which cannot be surpassed, and which gives me confidence you will persevere to act on that firmness of principle which you assure me is your determination.'

He could not resist pointing out in some detail and at considerable length that 'the partiality of Lady Hester Stanhope is not singular, for the most discerning and discriminating judgements have singled him [Michael] out for his promise of Talents and honourable Manly conduct.' He cited three Lords – Hutchinson, Wellesley and Bute – as being amongst those who thought highly of his son, and also, ironically, Sir John Moore.

Having made sure that Lady Hester could be in no doubt about the unique and sterling qualities of his son, Craufurd delivered his verdict on the relationship:

'I have myself long been of the opinion that at the period when a Man is taking his first station in the operations of the World, he may derive the highest benefit and improvement from the advice and friendly communication with a well informed Female Mind, from them we take advice with more complacency and other circumstances and feelings lead us to give it more attention and consequently to make it form more of a principle for our guidance and conduct; – in YOU my Son has placed himself under the direction of a Lady who has from Ancestry a Hereditory claim to the most superlative Talents, and in the very point of character for which I wish him to distinguish himself, as an enlightened Statesman, – permit me therefore Madam, by the Names of your Grandfather the truly Great Lord Chatham, and from the affection and reverence that you must ever bear to the Memory of the ever to be lamented Mr. Pitt your Uncle, by whom I have understood you was [sic] selected and distinguished by his peculiar affection, from respect and veneration to your connection with these distinguished and most honorable [sic] characters, I entreat of you to impress on the mind of my Son all the intentive particles you possess of their genius, in short fullfill [sic] the promise you have spontaneously given in the Letter now before me, and in such case I am sure the Mind of my Son must be inspired with greater genius.'

A triumph for Lady Hester: the appeal and promises she had made to Michael's father in her letter so many months before had been most handsomely accepted. Craufurd continued: 'You have therefore Madam intentionally or not I do not enquire, thereby made yourself responsible for his future character and achievements in life and to you myself and all those friends who are so sincerely and ardently attached to his welfare and reputation, will look for their future examplifiation [sic].'

In handing Lady Hester this almost maternal responsibility for his son, Craufurd Bruce seemed to have made no allowance for Michael's continued responsibility for himself. This is curious, and uncharacteristic of Craufurd, who had always been most careful to allow his son 'management of himself' and had attributed much of his son's success to this independence. Perhaps he was simply carried away by the magnificence of Hester's ancestry.

He ended the letter in a tone so conciliatory as to be almost humble: 'Though I must consider myself as incompetent to maintain [our correspondence] on an equal footing with you, yet I shall be gratified and anxious for a continuance of it, because I have that confidence in your candour, that I shall expect to receive from yourself the truest recital of every communication between you and my Son.'

The trust that Lady Hester and Michael had put in Craufurd's liberality had been fully rewarded; indeed, he and Lady Hester seem to have understood and trusted each other completely. Before finally signing himself as Lady Hester's 'very devoted and most Obedient Humble Servant' however, Craufurd allowed himself one flash of wry humour: 'Our correspondence has certainly commenced' he observed, 'on a very extraordinary footing.' It certainly had.

A letter to Michael from his father arrived in the same packet and it was loving, open and frank. Sensibly, he made no attempt to alter the situation. 'I will not breath an authoritive Command,' he said. 'You have hitherto been left the guide of your own conduct, on the present occasion I am aware it would be folly even in me your Father to dictate a line, when I know you would not because you probably could not submit to any direction.'

Everything seemed satisfactory, and Michael and Hester rejoiced in the paternal blessing, but what then happened was very strange. Having stated his approval of the relationship, Craufurd wrote to Michael again, only days later, expressing the most harrowing doubts about the whole situation, and begging him to reconsider his actions. Instead of sending his appeal direct to Michael, however, he enclosed it with a covering note to Hester, leaving her to decide whether or not to give the letter to Michael. This demonstrated an almost incredible degree of trust and faith in Lady Hester, who after all was personally quite unknown to Craufurd.

'I am doing what few Men would venture,' he wrote candidly, 'and what I certainly should not do to any other Woman but yourself, in committing the enclosed Letter to your charge, to be delivered or returned to me at your option; excuse or palliation I shall not attempt, but I throw myself on your consideration, if I did not judge you capable of heroic conduct I should not have placed myself in the situation I now do,' he continued, 'but I have every confidence you will sympathize with me and that you will do what is proper even should that prove adverse to your inclinations.'

In judging Lady Hester capable of 'heroic conduct' Craufurd showed a remarkable degree of perception considering he had never met her. Honour had always been one of the mainstays of Hester's own personal code of ethics, and to have this discerned, acknowledged and appealed to by a man for whom she held such respect was most compelling. She acted as Craufurd must have known she would, and gave his letter to Michael.

'I call on you, I entreat you to consider,' Craufurd begged Michael, 'that you are not laying up for yourself a store of future remorse and self-condemnation, and whether you are not clogging your future progress. . . . I cannot too strongly or too often say to you that what is not respectable can never meet but with partial success. Reflect Michael on what I have said, you will find that these are not the sentiments of one who is callous to enjoyments or judging from harsh or narrow principles.' And finally 'I would say no more, if your own understanding thus appealed to, if the express avowal of my opinion, if the pain I must feel, shall fail to influence you I have no other means to which I should wish to resort to control your conduct.'

Craufurd did of course have access to another means of control: Michael was totally dependent upon him for financial support, but Craufurd had decided that he would not use this final sanction for fear of losing his son completely.

This letter was so much more censorious than his first one that it puzzled and alarmed Michael and Lady Hester: what could have happened to change Craufurd's mind? One contributory factor was that Craufurd had received a letter from someone who described himself as 'a very old and real friend who loves you and your son'. It was anonymous and vituperative:

'Your son is gone to Constantinople with an artful woman as his mistress, Lady Hester Stanhope. She means to make him marry her, he knew her first criminally at Malta . . . see the danger he runs into from this connexion and move heaven and earth to break it.'

Craufurd was far too sensible to pay too much attention to such a letter, but he was certainly extremely agitated to think that perhaps he had been too indulgent in his first response, and these second thoughts were probably corroborated by his wife and the close friends in whom he had confided after having sent his first letters.

Michael and Lady Hester wrote back immediately, and the letters they sent were as well-constructed as before. Hester's in particular was quite masterly. She contrived to acknowledge the validity of his fears whilst proving them utterly unfounded.

She opened the letter by showing her appreciation of Craufurd's fears, telling him that had there been the slightest danger of estrangement between father and son, she would have returned to England – 'there I should have thrown myself at your feet,' she wrote, 'to implore forgiveness for the unhappiness I had occasioned both you & him, & if I had outlived the misery I had brought upon myself, given you the power to banish me to what part of the globe you thought fit, with a promise never to see him again.' Luckily for Lady Hester she knew there was little or no chance of this melodramatic act being necessary.

She then broached the main point of the letter and told Craufurd that he had no reason to worry about Michael's reputation being damaged. 'A man in no age has ever suffered in the public opinion by his intimacy with a woman who had his real interests at heart,' she wrote convincingly. 'Did Mr. Fox's attachment to Mrs. Armstead, or that of Bonaparte's to the late Empress ... make them LESS great men?'

Lady Hester had hit on the one argument that Craufurd would find irrefutable.

'I believe it has never yet been expected that a man should be a saint, at least till he is married, & if I MOST SOLEMNLY declare that I NEVER HAD OR EVER WILL HAVE FURTHER CLAIMS upon your son, than any woman he might have picked up in the streets, how can he shock the world?' Hester asked. 'At a time when I held my own head very high in society,' she continued, 'I always blamed & lamented that women who had erred from sheer vice, or from some unfortunate attachment, being placed upon the same footing as virtuous women, & thrust into society; if my judgement was a SEVERE one at least it extends to myself, & so far from wishing to be received in society, I shall most scrupulously avoid ever setting eyes upon a modest woman.'

Perhaps this was when Lady Hester began to realize that she might never return to England. Her Stanhope pride asserted itself: 'I am too proud not to dread humiliation & putting the virtuous part of my sex out of the question, I will never give an opportunity to those fair ladies who have married for a title, a house & fine diamonds, having previously made up their minds to be FAITHLESS WIVES, to SNEER at me. Inferior as I may be to one of these class of women,' she continued, 'I consider myself far superior to the other, God & my own conscience are my judges, & you must not imagine Sir because my conduct has been imprudent that my heart is either devoid of sentiments of real delicacy or honour.'

It was a wonderfully effective letter.

Michael's letter to his father was basically a reiteration of his first, except that he spoke of his growing love for Lady Hester, and of how much he had already learnt from her. 'I can only in answer say that I have gained more knowledge within these six months from my conversations with Lady Hester than I have acquired for the last ten years of my life. . . . I wish to God you could see Lady Hester; you would then be convinced that I have not fallen into the hands of an artful or designing woman, but that I have met with one, who is gifted with splendid talents, most elevated sentiments and who is most sincerely attached to me.'

When in due course Craufurd replied it became apparent that the letters had been well received: his misgivings were finally quelled, and Lady Hester and Michael were able to stop worrying about parental censure and start enjoying each other and their travels.

Lady Hester was unhappy with the house at Pera. It was cramped and the streets of the town were dirty and narrow. The fire that the Janissaries had started meant that there were not many alternative houses, so in December Michael and Hester took a villa in nearby Therapia. This was a town about ten miles from Constantinople on the banks of the Bosporus and was a popular resort during the hot summer months. The large, lofty rooms of the villa they chose were not the best accommodation for the long winter months however: when the wind blew from the south it was warm enough, but when it came from the north it was bitterly cold, and Hester quickly became ill with a chest infection. This was the first attack of what was to become a recurring illness for her. She decided it was asthma, but it seems possible that it was the early stages of tuberculosis. Dr Meryon was allowed to look after her, but she insisted on making her own prescriptions; she felt that she knew best, but the habit she had recently adopted of bleeding herself regularly did nothing at all for her health.

Michael and Lord Sligo had planned a trip to Smyrna, on the shores of the Aegean, and Hester urged them to go even though she was unwell. This they did, leaving Dr Meryon once more happily in sole charge of his beloved patient. Hester recovered fairly quickly and whilst waiting for Michael's return began getting to know the inhabitants of Constantinople.

When Lady Hester and Michael had first arrived in Constantinople they had been enthusiastically greeted by Stratford Canning, the twenty-four-year-old man who constituted the entire British diplomatic presence in Constantinople. Canning had been in the Porte since 1809, as First Secretary for Adair, and fifteen months later, when Adair left, as Plenipotentiary Extraordinary, given full, though temporary, responsibility for the Embassy. His brief in this splendidly named post was threefold. He was to defend the interests of the English shipping trade, to try to induce the Turks to prefer the influence of England to France, and to effect a reconciliation between the Czar of Russia and the Sultan so as to free Russia to repel the Napoleonic forces. This was heady stuff for any twenty-four-year-old, however mature, and all the more so because he was entirely without instruction from England: in his own words he was forced to 'steer by the stars'.

Canning was delighted to have Lady Hester and her party in Turkey. As he reported later: 'the diplomatic circle was at zero. The intelligent and educated traveller was a rare bird and at best a bird of passage.' Lady Hester, for her part, was pleased to be there: after the rather stolid ambassadorial circuits of Gibraltar and Malta, she was excited to be in less well-charted political waters: it reminded her of her life with Pitt.

Canning was particularly pleased to have Lady Hester's company in Constantinople not only because she was a lively and interesting person in her own right, but also because she was a fount of interesting anecdotes about Pitt, Moore and Chatham, who were his mentors. 'Lady Hester Stanhope brought with her all the interest which attaches to a person of her sex remarkable for talent and nearly connected with a great public character', he said. 'Not only was she the niece of Mr. Pitt, but she had lived for a time under the roof of that unspotted Minister in the full intimacy of close relationship and daily inter- course. She had known many whose names were familiar to me, and some with whom I was personally acquainted. . . . On these several accounts her conversation had strong attractions for me, notwith- standing its measureless redundancy, and the not infrequent sin- gularities it displayed.'

Lady Hester enjoyed Canning's company too, and reported that he behaved towards her 'in the civilest, kindest manner possible'. He was an extremely earnest young man however, very sedate and sober, and he took his responsibilities seriously. Lady Hester, having had such close friendships with politicians of far greater import than Canning, found it quite irresistible to tease him about what she named his 'primosity', and she was often tempted to say outrageous things to try to make him unbend a little.

'I trust you will not quite crack your brain with politics,' was one such sally, 'particularly SPANISH POLITICS, for you may depend upon it they are not worth thinking about, any further than individuals are concerned. If you had seen all those fools called Generals I saw at Gibraltar, you would think so likewise.'

On another occasion, referring to some gentlemen arrived from England, she admonished Canning: 'Look sharp, or I shall intrude myself under some strange form into the sanctuary you inhabit and burn all the papers, and unprimefy Sir H. Jones, who, if he was not a quiz before, must be turned into one from having been kept under LOCK AND KEY, and bored to death with business ever since his arrival. I am sure I shall more than like Captain Barrie,' she continued, 'if you will not stamp him with mystery and solemnity before I have made his acquaintance. The Doctor tells me that you were so improved with the small portion of country air you allowed yourself to breathe that I cannot but wish you could make it convenient to try a little more of it.'

It was perhaps a measure of her initial liking for Canning that she subjected him to such gentle yet persistent banter, and, for all his 'primosity' and youth, she was impressed with many of his views: 'I am not going to flatter you, but some of your opinions are so like those of my great Oracle [Chatham], that I send you his letters to his nephew, just to compare them.'

In all his dealings with Turkish dignitaries, Canning used the services of the chief interpreter and dragoman Mr Pisani, whom Lady Hester found to be a charming man of 'talent and integrity, and more feared and loved than his Excellency'. Canning found the Turks to be great procrastinators, and rather horridly compared discussions with them to 'cutting into dead flesh'. Lady Hester was amazed when she discovered that Canning had no social contact whatsoever with the people of Constantinople.

She had decided not to socialize with the very few European women who lived in the city not only because they represented the 'modest ladies' whose company she had promised Craufurd she would avoid, but also because she thought they were extremely dull. She determined instead that she would get to know the proud and handsome Turkish men and their graceful wives, although initially it seemed impossible to make the significant first contact. Eventually, with the unlikely help of Dr Meryon, she managed to breach the apparently insuperable social barrier.

Word had quickly got around that a great English Lady had come to live in Constantinople, a Lady who, moreover, had an English physician in her employ. Representatives of the great Turkish families began to pay their respects, at first to request Meryon's professional services, but increasingly, as time went by, to meet Lady Hester socially.

She was enchanted by the Turks. 'The manner of the Turks I like extremely, they have fine understanding which is expressed in their countenances, & a natural politeness which the best bred English man of the present day cd. not imitate with success . . . the Turkish women I have seen I think very agreeable, every gesture is so remarkably just that you can almost understand them without comprehending their language.'

Being Muslims, the Turks adhered to all the principles of that religion, including social segregation of the sexes, polygamy and the occasional keeping of harems, all of which was diametrically opposed to the respect and personal freedom which Lady Hester had always assumed as her right. Having seen for herself though, that the Turkish ladies were not only perfectly charming, but also perfectly happy, she was forced to concede that the Muslim way, though different, was quite acceptable.

Since Lady Hester was a European and a putative Christian she was not expected to live as a Muslim woman. Unlike most European women in a Muslim country, however, she saw no particular reason even to modify her dress or her general conduct whilst appearing in public. She had always enjoyed riding, for example, and when no escort was available to accompany her, she would go on her own. On one such trip she came across the magnificent sight of the Sultan Mahmoud and his gorgeous and prolific retinue on their way to the mosque to pray. Preceded by slaves sprinkling water to lay the dust, accompanied by his Ministers of the Porte and surrounded by burly bodyguards, the Sultan was an awe-inspiring sight, splendidly dressed and glittering with jewels. As the crowd around her bowed low to show their respect, Lady Hester sat upright on her horse, watching with interest, alone and unveiled.

Dr Meryon wrote: 'There is probably no other example of a European female having ridden through the streets of Constantinople in this manner on that day; and it may be reckoned as a proof of her courage that she did so, and of her conduct that she did so without insult.'

She certainly meant no disrespect by acting in this way, and it was a measure of the deference she innately commanded that not once was her conduct ever construed by any Turk as being insulting or unacceptable. Her height, commanding demeanour and the fact that she rode astride her horse occasionally led to her being mistaken at a distance for, as Meryon said, 'some young Bey with his mustachios not yet grown'. This may have afforded her some kind of protection. It certainly nearly got her into trouble once when, on entering a bathing house and being taken for a man, dozens of naked women scattered, screaming, in all directions.

Lady Hester very quickly carved herself a unique niche in the society of the Porte: she was accepted by the Turkish ladies by virtue of being female, and was accepted by the Turkish men by virtue of being foreign, high-born and intelligent. Both sexes responded to her charm and good nature. Lady Hester noted rather ruefully that the men were fairly versatile in their sexuality: 'The women are so beautiful,' she wrote, 'more so even than the men, yet sad to tell, they are rivalled by dancing boys.' The Turkish men found Lady Hester particularly intriguing: she was a woman, with all the usual feminine instincts, and yet her whole attitude to life seemed to them to be masculine. She was quite a challenge.

Before, in European society, Lady Hester had often been infuriated by the meaningless small talk that the women engaged in, mainly because there were usually men present who talked of far more interesting things. In mixed company, therefore, she was never fully relaxed: if she talked with the women she felt that she was missing the more interesting conversations that the men were having, and if she conversed with the men she was thought by their wives to be showing off and flirting. Because of this recurring problem, Lady Hester found it suited her very well to have her new friends segregated into groups of male and female. When she was feeling vigorous and energetic she would go riding with the men, and afterwards drink coffee and talk politics with them. When she felt more languid she would retire with the women, to bathe and relax and admire the intricate jewellery that the Turkish women wore. She thoroughly enjoyed being able to indulge the two different sides of her personality in two entirely separate social systems.

The initial liking that the Turks had for Lady Hester soon increased to admiration and respect, and she began to be included in their circles to a degree totally unprecedented for a European woman. She wrote jubilantly to Mr Canning: 'When did four Turks, and one the brother of a Captain Pacha, visit and dine with a Christian woman? I wore my sword with such an air that it has made a conquest of them all, and they begin to find their own women rather stupid (at least they say so, but men fib sadly).'

Another triumph was a conducted tour of a vessel of the Turkish Fleet, the *Sultan Selim*. The invitation was issued by the same Captain Pasha on the condition that she did not wear women's clothes whilst on board. The delighted Lady Hester didn't hesitate. She donned 'a pair of overalls, and military greatcoat and cocked hat', and inspected the ship from top to bottom. She was most impressed by the ship, pronouncing it magnificent, and the Captain Pasha ranked equally highly. 'The decorations in his cabin are superb,' she reported, 'he is a very handsome agreeable man, but a great tyrant. He had been cutting off heads one day when I came in but was just as composed as at another time.' Canning was much shocked by Hester's tour, and she started to despair of ever being able to make him less pompous and dull. He had never approved of Hester's relationship with Michael, but had been obliged to turn a blind eye. As Lady Hester socialized more and more with the Turks, though, he started to be critical of her conduct and seemed almost to cast himself in the role of older, and disapproving brother.

It is not hard to imagine what Lady Hester thought of such an attitude coming as it did from someone ten years her junior, a man she knew to be occasionally bigoted and extremely prudish. Their friendship began to deteriorate, and Lady Hester's opinion of Canning fell until on 11 September 1811 she wrote to a friend: 'for the good of the country I trust he will not remain long in this part of the world or we shall lose the little influence we have at the Porte . . . Canning has no influence with the Turks, all the merchants complain bitterly of him and strangers dislike him, laugh at his mysteries.' They were always to remain on perfectly civil terms with each other, but there was to be one major disagreement between them before Lady Hester left Turkey that went so far as to involve letters home to the Government.

In the meantime, Lady Hester was revelling in her acceptance by the Turks. She had rapidly and accurately assessed the way to 'gain the good will of any Turk', and it was how Lady Hester was naturally: 'Unaffected easy manners, accompanied with great civility, totally devoid of obsequiousness.' As a naturally proud and dignified race of people the Turks admired these qualities above all others, and they were greatly impressed by Lady Hester's unpretentiously aristocratic bearing. It was an admiration that was fully reciprocated.

'I must confess I think them a very superior people,' Lady Hester wrote to a friend, 'they have no advantages, no education, yet they never say a silly thing. They have all high spirits, great composure of manner and a degree of good breeding which would make our courtiers blush. . . . You have no idea how eagerly they learn, one day they had got some maps and I was describing the places I had seen and pointed out where battles had been fought and they were so delighted.'

She began to realize that she could be of use to England either in a diplomatic or an advisory role, but recognized that for the British

Government to place such a trust in a woman was out of the question. She was not rich enough to perform such a role unpaid, and it irked her: 'I wish I had a large fortune,' she commented to a friend at this time, 'I think I should contrive to pick up more information and do more good than one of your Cabinet ministers. Lord Camden, for example, would be just as useful to the world in a smock frock, and his money in my pocket would turn to some advantage.' It was not, in fact, until over one hundred years later that Britain finally realized just how valuable a contribution might be made by a similar woman in a similar situation: in 1919 Gertrude Bell was appointed to an advisory role in Iraq. Even then such an appointment was an innovation, so any formal political career for Lady Hester had always been an impossibility.

It was here in Constantinople that Lady Hester first came to admire, respect and understand the Near-Eastern people. It was here also, in her first winter in a Muslim country, that the roots of Lady Hester's legendary fame and her unique and unquestioned power were first established.

CHAPTER EIGHT

Constantinople

During the months that Michael was away the weather in Constantinople was appalling. On 28 February there was a fall of snow a foot deep, followed by a few mild days which preceded, as Meryon rather ungrammatically recounted, 'a series of snowstorms and tempests exceeding almost what I had ever witnessed elsewhere. Such weather,' he continued, 'in a country where there are no fireplaces and the houses are hardly weather-proof made Lady Hester feel much regret at having quitted Athens, there we might have sat, as we were told, with our windows open all through the year.'

One consolation during the bitterly cold weeks was a contraption called the tandour. In a letter to Michael's father, Lady Hester explained how it was used: it was, she said, 'a table brought up close to the sopha, under which wood ashes are set, it is covered with a thick wadded, coloured tablecloth which [the Turkish ladies] spread over their knees. Tho' I have abused the poor tandour,' she admitted ruefully, 'I have found great comfort from it this winter.' No doubt most of Lady Hester's considerable correspondence home that winter was written whilst she was tucked cosily into this splendid invention.

Whilst Hester was busy with her letters and her growing social life, Dr Meryon was free to make professional calls on the various local dignitaries who had heard of his presence in Constantinople. One such visit was to Hafiz Aly, the Captain Pasha who had conducted Lady Hester around his ship. He was an intelligent and charming man who appeared to have been suffering from haemorroids: 'a plethoric habit arising from a sedentary way of living.' Meryon's treatment must have been acceptable to him, for he presented Meryon with a crimson cashmere shawl, then asked him to attend his wife. Meryon was used to the peremptory manner in which most Turks seemed to treat their women, and was delightfully surprised by the Captain Pasha's conduct towards his wife. 'There was,' he said, 'nothing in the behaviour of the Pasha that marked any undue assumption of superiority over the female sex; on the contrary,' he marvelled, 'it was all kindness. She was addressed in the tenderest manner by the Pasha, who desired me to bestow all my attentions on her case.' When Meryon examined her, however, he soon realized that the unfortunate lady, who had originally been part of the Sultan's harem, was consumptive, and despite his attention she died shortly afterwards.

Hafiz Aly was profoundly impressed by Lady Hester; in fact, he was so taken with her that he decided he wanted to marry her, and asked Meryon for his advice. Unfortunately, Meryon was far too discreet to make reference to this in his memoirs, so we shall never know what he said to the Pasha, but Lady Hester was never asked. Michael, in an annoyingly patronizing way, was most entertained by the idea. 'You will not be a little amused,' he wrote to his father, 'when I tell you that the Pasha had serious thoughts of making proposals of marriage to Lady Hester. . . . He expressed a great admiration for her talents and said that she would produce a noble race of Dgired players.' Perhaps Lady Hester could have done worse than consider his proposal.

A final episode in the Captain Pasha's dealings with Meryon was not so happy. The Pasha acquired a concubine of quite exceptional beauty, and when she became pregnant he asked Meryon to give her an abortion. 'Childbearing,' he was reported to have said, 'would destroy the symmetry of her person.' Meryon had already discovered that this was a common practice amongst the Muslims and responded quickly. 'Without listening to what the Pasha had further to say, I told him plainly that, by the laws of my country, I should be considered a criminal if I were, in any shape whatever, consenting to such a deed.' By couching his refusal in such terms, he avoided a loss of face on either side: 'He said no more about it,' Meryon recalled with relief, 'and the subject was never introduced before me again.'

The only other patients on whom Meryon felt it worth reporting were, 'those whose rank may entitle them to notice'. One of these was the splendidly titled 'Princess Marouzi, wife of the ex-Hospodar of

Wallachia'. 'When I paid her a visit,' Meryon recalled, 'everything was done with a view to inspire me with a notion of her greatness. . . . It was usual for me to be conducted up a flight of steps to the first or second floor, between two ranks of servants, then led through a suite of apartments, and, when arrived at the door of the room where she was sitting, a page would draw aside a crimson curtain, and there I found the Princess, seated on a crimson sofa edged with gold.'

Though snobbish, Dr Meryon was always gallant, and therefore did not record the Princess's various ailments. After each attendance, however, he was presented with 'an embroidered scarf, an antique ring, or some such present, with a little speech of her own in French, calculated, by its amiability, to render the present more acceptable'.

The winter of 1811 was enjoyable and gratifying in every way for the doctor. With Michael and Lord Sligo still away, Lady Hester was more than usually appreciative of his company, and he was in constant demand professionally. It was all very good for what he perceptively called his 'self-love', – his ego. 'Eastern countries,' he pronounced, 'became every day more agreeable to me.'

Lady Hester, on the other hand, was feeling more fragile and less settled than was usual for her. She and Michael had received his father's blessing on their relationship, but Hester was not entirely comfortable about the affair. There were two other people whose opinions mattered very much to her. One was her brother James, who was still with his regiment in Spain, and the other, perhaps surprisingly, was General Oakes, the Governor of Malta, with whom she had struck up such an immediate friendship. In the spring of 1811 she wrote to them both, telling them in veiled terms of her affair with Michael.

It is interesting that Hester, usually so positive about her actions, should suddenly have felt the need of approval from even her closest family and friends. Perhaps, however, it is too easy for us, from a distance of nearly two hundred years, to underestimate the audacity of what she was doing. By openly living with a man who was not her husband she was risking total social ostracism. Since she was no longer living in England, or indeed in European society of any kind, this threat was not immediate, and most probably she would have scorned it anyway, but it still made her feel uncomfortable. She suspected also that there would be a scandal about her in England, and she was right. Apart from the shocked gossip that was whispered round the salons, snide remarks appeared in the papers and Lady Charlotte Bury received a letter from 'Monk' Lewis in November of that year, full of malicious enjoyment:

'I hear that Lady Hester is living at Constantinople with young Bruce, avowedly as his *chere amie*,' the letter read, 'and that she says nobody was ever so handsome, nor so clever, and that he is in short, and *is to be* , one of the finest characters in these Kingdoms. I wish him joy of his conquest, and had rather he than I.'

Fortunately Lady Hester had never cared about gossip. What did matter to her however, as always, was the good opinion of those few about whom she really cared. With each day that passed she was drawing further away from everything she had ever known: her country, family, friends and even familiar social customs, and perhaps she felt unaccustomedly vulnerable.

While she was waiting for replies from Captain Oakes and James, Michael and Lord Sligo returned from their travels. On the way to Smyrna they had visited many places – Scutari, Brusa, Magnesia and the Plains of Troy, and arrived back in Therapia laden with exotic presents for Lady Hester including a particularly fine horse, with which she was delighted.

Michael had come to a fairly momentous decision whilst he was away: he had decided to ask Lady Hester to marry him. They had just spent several months apart and yet he had found himself to be still very much in love with her. He was very aware that to live together openly as they were was an extremely irregular situation even though they were so far away from England, but he intended to return to England and take up politics. What was an irregularity in the East was a total impossibility in England. It was a problem that Michael undoubtedly discussed with Lord Sligo many times whilst away. They were both romantic and basically conventional young men: marriage to Lady Hester must have seemed a natural and happy solution to the problem.

What neither of them had anticipated was that Lady Hester would refuse Michael's proposal, but she did, despite the fact that it caused her considerable distress to do so. She had already promised Craufurd Bruce, Michael's father, that she would lay no claim on him, and that she would freely give him up to the 'thrice happy woman' he would eventually marry. Although it is hard to understand why she had ever made such a promise – there was no legal or moral reason why they should not have married – she had always been a woman of her word and it says much for her that she was able to resist the reality of marriage to the man she loved.

During the months that followed, Lady Hester's spirits were at a very low ebb. Having endured illness and weeks of bitterly cold weather in a house ill-equipped to deal with such extremes of temperature, she was now having to live with her decision not to marry Michael. Records do not show how he reacted to her decision, but it seems likely that he would have been peeved and rather humiliated, which would not have made things any easier for Lady Hester. Ironically, at the same time she suddenly seemed to be facing criticism over her affair from every quarter. Stratford Canning was silently critical, and letters arriving from Malta and Spain showed that whilst General Oakes was mildly unenthusiastic in his response, James appeared apoplectic. His response to the news that his sister was living with a man was 'not exactly satisfactory', according to Bruce's great-grandson, Ian. In fact he wanted to shoot Michael and he wrote Hester a thunderous letter telling her so. It was a harsh reaction from someone on whom Hester had lavished so much love and attention for so long.

Lord Sligo was soon to go to Malta in order to be invested with the Order of St Patrick, which had been sent down from England by the King, and he promised Lady Hester that he would talk to both Oakes and James on her behalf. Unfortunately Sligo was not very skilled at diplomacy. No details can be found as to exactly what he said and did in his role as intermediary, but General Oakes wrote Lady Hester a revealing note. 'He has, I am sure, a good heart, with the best intentions,' he said, 'and the natural effusion of his genuine feelings may probably prevail, but I wish on this occasion he was a little older, and had a greater knowledge of mankind and of the world.'

General Oakes was obviously a kind and wise man, and Hester need not have feared she would lose his friendship. James, younger and more volatile, calmed down in the end, but Hester could certainly have done without his anger and accusations.

What Lady Hester needed at this stage was a change and a rest, and this is what she got – the party decided to go to Brusa, also called

Bursa, a town beautifully situated at the foot of the Turkish Mount Olympus, and famous for its health-giving sulphur baths. Since there was some doubt as to the standard of accommodation available, it was decided that Dr Meryon should precede Lady Hester by a day or two to get things sorted out.

'To avoid the heat,' he wrote to his sister, 'I set off at midnight, on the first of May, in an open four-oared barge with an awning, accompanied by Aly, a janissary, and my servant.' The boat made remarkably good time and arrived at Mudania, the nearest landing-place to Brusa, within twelve hours including a stop for breakfast – a distance, according to Meryon, of sixty or eighty miles. The oarsmen were not only able-bodied but also very fetchingly attired: 'Their shirts, of a texture like Chinese crape, are open at the bosom,' Meryon observed, 'so that their muscular forms and brawny arms are seen to great advantage. They wear a red cloth skull-cap and white balloon trousers; the feet and legs are naked.' A splendid crew indeed.

Lady Hester was enchanted by Brusa. 'The finest country I ever beheld!' she exclaimed in a letter to a friend. 'Italy is nothing to it in point of magnificence!' Dr Meryon had found three cottages just outside the town 'on the sloping foot of Mount Olympus'. From there the party had a commanding view of Brusa and the whole of the encompassing valley. There were reputed to be one hundred mosques in the town. Scores of slender minarets soared above the low, whitewashed houses, and great numbers of stately plane trees and gracefully curving palms gave welcome pools of shade to the houses and people below. The vale of Brusa is unusually fertile, as it has a constant supply of water from the snows on Olympus even through the hottest summer, and Hester described the sight of the valley spread below them: 'an immense plain more rich and beautiful than anything I ever saw, covered with trees, shrubs, and flowers of all description; the rides are charming and the horses better than any of those I have met with out of England.'

Meryon was equally impressed: 'One may ride for miles in a con-tinued shade of walnut, chestnut, fig, cherry and mulberry trees. These are the trees by the roadside, but within the hedges as being less handy to be gathered, grow peach, apricot, pear and apple trees ... and surrounding the vale on every side, sloping hills, covered with villages and diversified by cornfields and vineyards bound the horizon. Its fertility,' he concluded rather enigmatically, 'is past conception.'

Whilst in Brusa Dr Meryon was called upon once again for his professional services, and this in turn led to copious invitations for the party from 'some of the persons of distinction of whom Brusa is so full'. Visits were made to the famous baths of which there were many. 'The principal of them is a large building,' the doctor recalled, 'consisting of three spacious rooms with vaulted roofs, in which are bell-glasses to admit a dim light, and to confine the heat.' The first room, where the scaldingly hot water rose from the spring 'a foot in diameter', was the steam room. The others were full of huge 'cisterns', also fed from the same water, where 'the bather may immerse himself.'

Meryon was impressed by the baths, but not by the standards of hygiene: 'I occasionally resorted to them, and should have done so oftener,' he recalled with regret, 'but for the vermin with which the Turks filled the carpets and cloths.' He was also unimpressed by the inhospitable reaction he drew from the local Turks. 'A Turk would as soon receive a viper as an infidel into his house,' he sniffed. 'The women, as they pass, cover themselves to the very tips of their fingers, lest the poisonous eyes of a Christian should bring evil upon them. The shopkeepers and artificers will, it is true, supply you with their commodities,' he admitted, 'but with so ungracious an air, that one's self-love is sorely wounded.' Even allowing for Meryon's undoubted insularity, his description of the problem certainly highlights the extraordinary degree of acceptance that Lady Hester was managing to achieve among these same Muslims.

After two restful but invigorating months in Brusa Lady Hester decided it was time to return to Constantinople. Dr Meryon had proved so efficient in his role as house-hunter that he was despatched back to Pera to find new accommodation for the party, their lease on the house in Therapia having expired whilst they were away.

There had been another fire in their absence and there were even fewer houses than before from which to choose. He decided on a house owned by Baron Sturmer, the Austrian 'Internuncio' or Under-Minister, and arranged to rent it for six months. Since Napoleon had taken power, any communication between the English abroad and the French or their allies was very much discouraged, even in a neutral country like Turkey. This led to the slightly ridiculous situation of Meryon having to negotiate rent with the Baron in his garden, where it was felt less likely that 'ill construction' would be put on their meeting.

This same unofficial ban led, however, to a rather serious argument between Lady Hester and Stratford Canning. Hester had loved the French ever since she was a child, when the French Ambassador had visited Chevening, and had always scorned what she termed 'war with individuals'. After her return to Constantinople in July, she decided that she would like to spend the following winter in France, Napoleon or no Napoleon. She arranged to meet Monsieur de Maubourg, the French Chargé d'Affaires, in order to get a passport, but the meeting had to be cloaked in secrecy. A rendezvous between the two was organized. They met on the Asiatic side of the Bosporus where they could walk together in private and discuss the possibilities of a visit, but unfortunately they were followed by 'one of Canning's spies', according to Lady Hester, who wasted no time in informing his master of what he had seen. Canning was furious. As far as he was concerned, communicating with the enemy meant one thing and one thing only: treason.

He went straight to Lady Hester's house and confronted her. They argued bitterly for half an hour, then Canning stalked out, threatening to write to Lord Wellesley, who was then Secretary for Foreign Affairs. Once back in his own house he ordered that 'the English Palace was to be shut against Lady Hester's suite', and all the secretaries and dragomen of the Embassy were commanded to 'hold no intercourse' with them.

Hester was simultaneously amused and infuriated. The sight of the pompous young Canning in a rage with her was enough to make her smile, but she was incensed that this as yet undistinguished youth should dare to question her motives, or presume to criticize her behaviour. She was utterly outraged that her patriotism could even be questioned – she, William Pitt's niece, granddaughter of the great Chatham.

When her fury had subsided, Lady Hester decided on a plan of action that was entirely typical of her. If Canning was going to write to Lord Wellesley and make the whole affair a matter of public knowledge in England, why then, she would preempt the situation by writing to him first. This was exactly what she had done with Michael's father, and as on that other, similar occasion, the letter she wrote to Lord Wellesley was a masterpiece. She sent a copy of the letter to Canning with a little note of explanation.

'That your Excellency may be aware that deceit forms no part of my character I enclose a copy of a letter to Lord Wellesley,' she wrote. 'I wish people in England neither to blame nor pity the situation in which you have placed me, and if I defend myself not exactly in the way most pleasing to you, recollect it is your conduct which has made it necessary.'

Her defence, not unnaturally, took the form of criticism of Canning. It was, however, a very mild attack, and liberally spiced with a dry humour guaranteed to infuriate the young, pompous Plenipotentiary.

'He [Mr Canning] has thought it his duty to take leave of me,' she wrote to Lord Wellesley, 'and also to forbid any of those persons belonging to him to visit me, which, as far as it affects my comfort is of no consequence, as they were all horribly dull (except M. Pisani).' She explained why she had hidden her meetings with the French Ambassador from Mr Canning. 'Mr Canning is young and inexperienced, full of zeal, but full of prejudice. I guessed, therefore, what might be the line of conduct he would pursue on such an occasion. Respecting as I do his many virtues, I did not wish to quarrel with him, or appear openly to disregard his authority, or publicly to ridicule the very idea of any person presuming to doubt my patriotism.'

She concluded the letter with a touch of malice, thinly veiled in a tone of kindly patronage: 'if I have acted with more moderation than is usual to me, it proceeds from what may (though true) sound like conceit to confess – the persuasion that Mr C. & I do not stand upon equal grounds, and that he is by no means a match for me, were I determined to revenge what, to others, carries the appearance of insult.' And, finally: 'The best recompense for his services would be to appoint him Commander in Chief at home & Ambassador Extraordinary abroad to the various Societies for the Suppression of Vice and Cultivation of Patriotism. The latter consists in putting one's self into greater convulsions than the Dervishes at the mention of Buonaparte's name.'

Poor, overzealous Canning. He was indeed no match for Hester. He must have had awful visions of the whole Cabinet having a good laugh at his expense. In the event, however, neither the argument nor the letter appeared to have made much impact at all in England. There were far more important things happening there than a minor quarrel taking place two thousand miles away. The Luddite riots against the mechanization of the textile industry were starting, the war with Napoleon was still dragging on, and George III had finally succumbed to porphyria, the illness that had dogged the Royal Family for so many years. He had been declared insane and the Prince of Wales was Regent.

One can only guess at Lady Hester's reaction to these events in England: no letters giving any opinion have survived. She had never liked the Prince of Wales, or the Princess Caroline, although they had both sought her friendship when she lived in London. Her favourite had been the Duke of York, to whom she was still sending letters and presents.

A letter that Michael sent to his father, however, shows a rare flash of compassion for the King: 'Poor Man!', he wrote. 'He has lived too long for his happiness and certainly for his glory. Kings ought to pray for short reigns; their subjects unfortunately like novelty, and are as fond of new kings as they are of new shoes, or new anything else.'

The time had come for the party to leave Constantinople. The idea of spending another chilly winter there was not enticing, and although Lady Hester and Canning had managed to patch up their quarrel, their former easiness with each other had gone. Michael had also realized that he had been spending far too much of his father's money. On 19 October Michael wrote to Craufurd. 'I am afraid that you will think I have abused your generosity in having drawn for so much money,' he apologized. 'The only excuse I have to offer is the extravagant price of every article of life, and the number of presents I have sent home. The money likewise which has been given to servants has very much tended to swell the account.' He went on to explain how necessary it was to 'distribute' money among people like the Pasha's attendants: 'If you omit it you are despised by the Masters and insulted by his servants. I hope for the future that our expenses will be a great deal more moderate.'

Michael and Hester had planned to spend the coming winter in Athens awaiting their passports for France. Fortunately, perhaps, M.

de Maubourg was unable to produce any documents for them, so Lady Hester's plans for France were thwarted. They decided instead to winter in Egypt. A Greek boat was found and hired to take them to Alexandria for £65. Lady Hester, Michael and Dr Meryon were to be accompanied by Mrs Fry, Hester's maid, and a friend of Michael's called Henry Pearce. The party began to look forward to the trip and the prospect of a new and exciting country.

If they had known what was in store for them they would never have left Constantinople. It was what every sailor has always dreaded above anything else. Shipwreck.

CHAPTER NINE

Shipwreck

The boat in which Lady Hester and her party were to sail to Alexandria was a large, wooden, lateen-rigged caïque very similar in appearance to modern Greek caïques and Arab dhows. The main feature of these boats was and still is the extremely wide deck and shallow draught which, together with the unusually prominent prow and stern, give these Near-Eastern boats a very distinctive shape. The beaminess of a caïque means that there is plenty of room on deck but together with the lack of depth it also means the boats have a horrible tendency to wallow sickeningly as soon as the sea gets up. Luckily most of the party were good sailors. The caïque Lady Hester had hired for the journey appeared quite sound but was very dirty, so she employed some men to make it habitable for the journey. The interior of the boat was whitewashed and the hold partitioned to provide separate sleeping accommodation for each person. Live poultry and sheep were taken on board, and the galley stocked with plenty of wine and other essentials. Letters were written and farewells made. Nothing was overlooked.

On 23 October the party boarded the boat, and, leaving the town where they had lived for almost exactly a year, set sail for Alexandria.

They drifted down the Bosporus with a following wind, the sounds and the scents of the city carrying with them for a long way. When they reached the mouth of the river the wind backed completely, and they decided to drop anchor at Prince's Island and wait until it turned again. After five days a more favourable north wind sprang up and they set sail once again, across the Sea of Marmara, through the

Dardanelles and out into the Aegean Sea. The Turkish coastline and Greek islands were beautiful, even in late autumn. The fierce summer sun had lost its burning heat and was once again pleasantly warm. The sea was still azure and turquoise and the periwinkle blue of the sky was smudged by a few wispy clouds that heralded the more changeable, temperate winter weather to come.

The party made good progress as far as the island of Chios where a gale sprang up and they took shelter for ten days. They were happy to break the journey there, for, as Dr Meryon wrote, 'the vivacity of the inhabitants and the novelty and beauty of the country afforded us much diversion.' The captain of the boat was keen to complete the journey in reasonable time, however, so as soon as the wind moderated they set out again.

'We unmoored from Chios and were carried without any accident as far as the Island of Rhodes, where we stopped but a few hours to take in water and fresh bread,' Meryon reported to his sister. 'We then sailed, little imagining how soon we should return thither, and quitted Rhodes on Saturday night, the 23rd November.'

The island of Rhodes is the southernmost piece of land when you leave the Aegean Sea for the passage to Alexandria on the North African coast. After Rhodes there is no possibility of landfall until you reach Egypt – in a straight line it is a journey of roughly three hundred miles, but of course few passages are quite that simple. This one was no exception.

In late November of the year 1811, the weather was very changeable, with frequent, radical shifts in wind direction and strength, as often happens in the Mediterranean. As Lady Hester's boat left Rhodes they had a strong northerly wind behind them, and they made cracking progress, running before the wind for two days under 'a press of sail'. Meryon estimated that they had made half the distance to Egypt when everything started to go wrong.

The weather began to change ominously. Heavy lowering clouds built up and the wind altered direction yet again, this time coming at them head on, from the south and with increasing ferocity.

Caïques are not designed to go into the wind; they are too broad and too shallow. If they try to do so the effect is such that for every degree they make to windward, they are pushed sideways the same amount or more. Since they were already halfway to their destination however, the Greek captain decided to give it a try. For twenty-four hours they plunged to and fro into the wind and sea; huge grey-green waves crashed over the bows to slop and gurgle out of the gunwales. With every change of direction the timbers of the boat creaked and groaned, and the passengers in their bunks below wedged themselves against the sickening corkscrew motion and prayed for delivery. It was not to be. The gale increased.

Finally the captain decided to give up the attempt to reach Alexandria and turned around to run before the wind, back towards Rhodes and safety. Once on the new course the terrifying slamming of the boat into the waves ceased completely, and Lady Hester and her party were able to compose themselves and breathe a little more easily. Their relief was shortlived. Perhaps the pounding the boat had taken had loosened the hemp caulking in the joints, or maybe the continual strain had caused a timber to spring. Whatever the cause, the horrifying result was the same: the boat sprang a huge leak and they were possibly two hundred miles from land.

The cry went up 'all hands to the pump', but it was a useless exercise for, as Dr Meryon recalled, 'It is seldom that the Levantine ships have pumps, or, when they have, they are so little used as generally to be found unserviceable when wanted: and such was the case with ours.' Instead the sailors and all the other men on board including the servants, the doctor, Mr Pearce and Michael all started bailing with buckets at every hatch and stairwell. Lady Hester, who had been down below, realized the immediate danger of the situation and behaved with exemplary courage.

'She dressed herself and quietly directed her maid to furnish a small box with a few articles of the first necessity, to be prepared against the worst,' Meryon later wrote. 'There was a cask of wine in the cabin, which had been brought to drink on the voyage. This her Ladyship, with her own hands, drew and distributed among the sailors to cheer them under the labour, which became very severe.'

The men struggled on with the hopeless task until about midnight but they were fighting a losing battle. 'The boat heeled gunwale down, and was so waterlogged that she never recovered an upright position afterwards.' Servants began to panic, 'throwing themselves flat on the deck, [they] vented the most womanish lamentations, nor could they be induced by either threats or promises to work any more.' All seemed lost when miraculously, the south-west point of Rhodes was sighted off their lee bow. The men set to again with renewed energy, but the ship was so full of water that she would not respond to the helm, and as they watched in desperation, they could see that they were in danger of being swept past Rhodes completely. They dropped an anchor, hoping in that way to stop the boat, but the waters were too deep and it was of no use. There was only one thing left to do – abandon ship.

The longboat was hoisted out and lowered into the sea with great difficulty and everybody clambered in. There were twenty-five people in all – almost too many for safety – so orders were given that no luggage be taken by anybody. Lady Hester had only a small box with her, and Dr Meryon salvaged a bag of dollars, his sabre and a pistol. Everything else was abandoned, including, much to Lady Hester's distress, a little dog who could not be persuaded to jump.

As the longboat emerged from the lee of the sinking caïque the waves started to break over them, but they managed to drift and row to a large rock, which was about half a mile away. A little creek on the leeward side was just big enough to shelter the boat, and they managed to scramble ashore. There Lady Hester and Mrs Fry squeezed into the shelter of a tiny cave and the men collapsed exhausted on the spray-swept rocks. They were hungry and thirsty and in their hurry to leave the caïque had forgotten to take any food or water with them, but, as Dr Meryon primly observed: 'Fatigue ... was at present the most urgent sensation, and we all composed ourselves in our wet clothes to sleep.'

They woke at midnight and had an urgent discussion as to what to do. The wind had dropped a little by then and the captain proposed to row ashore with his crew to get help; if everyone went, he said, the boat would probably sink and all would be drowned. Lady Hester and her party thought this seemed reasonable, so the captain set off once more in the longboat, promising to light a fire to signal his safe arrival on the island. After two hours the fire was sighted and the group on the rock settled down to wait for their deliverance.

'Daylight came,' Meryon wrote, 'and we remained without food or drink, anxiously looking out for the return of the crew. Our reflections were by no means comfortable: for, knowing the character of the Greeks we could not be sure that, once safe themselves, they would not abandon us to our fate.' They realized they had been far too trusting and began to wish they had sent at least one of their party with the dubious captain and his crew.

'We watched all day, and it was not until about a quarter of an hour before sunset that a black speck was seen on the sea, which we at length distinguished to be a boat.' It was the crew of the caïque, but without the captain, who had 'declined the danger of coming off again'. They brought with them bread, water, cheese and arak so the party were able to break their involuntary thirty-hour fast, but the ordeal was not yet over. The sailors had been so relieved to reach safety that morning that they had immediately celebrated with a great deal of arak. They drank more on reaching the rock and in Meryon's words 'grew riotous and insolent'. It must have seemed the last straw for Lady Hester. In the middle of the night, the sailors, drunk, unruly and mutinous on the wet rock, decided not to wait for morning but to row back to Rhodes immediately. Lady Hester and Michael pleaded with them to wait until daylight and until the wind and rain abated, but, as drunks often are, they were implacable: they would go, and Hester and her party had no choice but to go with them.

'The sea was high,' Meryon wrote, 'and as they were pulling almost in the face of it, the labour of the sailors was very severe. But, for the same reason, the nearer we approached the shore the smoother the water became. At last the stern touched and a wave that filled her from head to stern almost at once overwhelmed us. Lady Hester was hoisted out of the boat and each made his way on shore as he could. The boat, soon after, was swamped and staved.' They had survived.

The stretch of coastline on which they had landed was quite desolate, with no sign of human habitation except for a small windmill where they decided to spend the rest of the night. There was room enough inside for the two women and Lady Hester was soon fast asleep, but Mrs Fry was so terrified by the scampering of the rats up and down the mill ropes that she refused to stay in the mill and instead joined the men of the party outside where they had managed to make a fire although the rain was still teeming down. The miller was sent off to his village to arrange for transport for the party and returned at daybreak with men, asses and mules, which carried them all to a nearby village.

It was not a well-appointed place, but rather 'the most miserable that can be conceived as the habitation of human beings'. The cottages all let in the rain, and 'the filth within and about them was to the last degree disgusting: add to which they all swarmed with fleas'. All had been lost in the shipwreck: the doctor's medicine chest, Lady Hester's jewellery, books and correspondence, there was not even a change of clothes for anyone, so the hardy Dr Meryon was despatched to the town of Rhodes to get money and basic necessities. Whilst he was there Lady Hester wrote to Michael's father from her 'bed of straw in the corner of a hut' where she was recovering from the recent ordeal. She headed her letter with rather wan precision, 'From a miserable village near the extremity of the Island of Rhodes. Early in December', and her first concern was to assure Craufurd of Michael's safety. 'The idea of his being lost to you and his friends was my only affliction', she wrote, informing him that Michael was 'if possible . . . more worthy of yr. affection than before this incident for his conduct was admirable and in the midst of all our dangers he did not for a moment lose his presence of mind'.

Michael also wrote to his father praising, in his turn, Lady Hester's conduct: 'It is impossible for me to do justice to Lady Hester for the coolness and intrepidity displayed by her during the whole of this trying incident. She has lost property to the amount of two and three thousand pounds and only saved two pelisses, a dressing box with her combs and tooth brush, a snuff box which Lord Sligo gave her and her Brother's hair. Everything else went to the bottom.'

The village in which they were staying was so uncomfortable that they decided, whilst waiting to hear from Dr Meryon, to start the journey towards Rhodes. After eight hours journeying by mule over a stony mountain track they arrived in the town of Lindo, where they were offered hospitality by an exiled Greek named Philipaki. (The doughty Mrs Fry insisted on calling him Phillip Parker.) Despite his kindness, the journey proved too much for Lady Hester who collapsed with a fever. Michael was extremely concerned. 'The real hardships which she underwent,' he wrote to his father, 'affected her frame so strongly that at Lindo I was under serious apprehension of losing her.' Dr Meryon was summoned back from Rhodes immediately, but Lady Hester seemed only to have been suffering from exhaustion. After a few days of rest she had recovered sufficiently for the party to complete the journey to Rhodes. 'Do not fancy us dull,' she later wrote to

General Oakes, 'for we (myself included) danced the Pyrrhic dance with the peasants in the villages in our way hither.'

For three and a half centuries Greece and her islands had been part of the Ottoman Empire and under Turkish control. Greece was a wild and rugged place and travel there was nearly as dangerous as it was in Syria and the rest of the Near East. The people who lived there were not united as people in any way – not all were even Greek. There were Albanians who had settled many generations before, and thousands of Turks, who were to some extent the ruling class. The Greeks themselves were divided by religion: some were Christian, some Muslim. Loyalties were further divided according to tribe and locality. The island of Rhodes was no different in this respect from mainland Greece, and as the party travelled through the rough, mountainous countryside, they saw many different types of people all with varying customs and clothes. This helped Lady Hester to solve the unique and pressing problem of what to do about her clothes. The only ones she possessed were those she stood up in: all the rest had been lost in the shipwreck. European clothes were, quite simply, not available in Rhodes. What was she to do? There was no question of her adopting Greek clothes, since she despised the Greeks. If she dressed as a Turkish woman she could not be seen to talk to a man and would have to wear a veil when in public so that, too, was out of the question. It was a difficult situation, but one that she solved with her usual panache. She decided to dress as a Turkish man.

Having made the decision, she sent out to all the local outfitters and set to with glee. In a letter to her London solicitor she described her new appearance: 'a silk and cotton shirt, next to that a striped silk and cotton waistcoat; over that another waistcoat with sleeves; and then a short cloth jacket without sleeves beautifully worked in a coloured twist'. After that it became even more dashing: 'a large pair of breeches, Turkish boots, and a sash into which goes a brace of pistols, a knife and a sort of short sword; a belt for powder and shot made of variegated leather, which goes over the shoulder and pouches of the same'. The crowning touch to this splendid new costume was 'a turban, put on in a particular way, with a large bunch of natural flowers at one side'.

'I can assure you,' Hester wrote in a later letter, 'that if I ever looked well in anything it is in the Asiatic dress.' People in England who heard of her new wardrobe were scandalized, but it was simply the idea of her dressing as a man that appalled them. In reality the breeches were so full-cut and voluminous that decorum was thoroughly preserved. Everyone who saw her admired her new appearance: she must have looked marvellous. She dressed this way for the rest of her life.

During the last few weeks in Rhodes, Dr Meryon went to Smyrna on the Turkish coast to get provisions for the party, and whilst he was gone the servants rebelled. Lady Hester had promised them new clothes, but told them they would have to wait until they got to Alexandria. Fearing that she was trying to cheat them, the servants demanded new outfits immediately, thinking that Hester would comply for fear of losing them. They underestimated her. She dismissed them all on the spot, and proceeded to Alexandria with the faithful Mrs Fry and a young Greek of seventeen as her only servants.

This time, instead of sailing in a dirty, leaking caïque, Lady Hester travelled in style. Captain Henry Hope had heard of the shipwreck and came from Smyrna to offer Hester passage to Alexandria on his frigate *Salsette*. She was extremely touched and grateful, and dubbed him 'Chivalry Hope', declaring that not even the Knights Templar had been as courteous and kind as he. He was unable to guarantee the weather, however, and once again the voyage was beset by storms. They arrived safely, if belatedly, on 11 February 1812, and although Hester was glad to be on dry land again, she hated the town. She pronounced it 'quite hideous', and said that if the rest of Egypt was the same she would leave as soon as possible. Dr Meryon agreed with her when he arrived: 'Alexandria was more dusty than Blackfriars Bridge on a windy day, and more crowded with blind than a hospital for the opthalmania [sic].' They were obliged to stay at least long enough to find new servants, though, before leaving for a leisurely trip down the Nile, with Cairo as their destination.

They spent a few days at Rosetta whilst the boats were being prepared. It was a busy trading town with constant activity in the port, as barges plied to and from the river mouth, loading and unloading at the crowded warehouses. There were 'fine, lofty houses' in the town which was also celebrated for its beautiful orchards, but they also found the place to be 'more full of fleas than a beggar's tent'. When they set off for Cairo, the Nile was at its lowest ebb, so even the shallow-bottomed barges they hired for the journey were constantly running aground. There was no hurry, however, and the barges were so large and comfortable that the whole journey was very restful, and made a pleasant change from being shipwrecked.

They arrived at Bulak, the quay area of Cairo, on the fifth day, and from there travelled into Cairo on asses. On the way they passed the Palace of the Ruler of Egypt, and by chance he happened to be returning from an early morning ride. 'The Pasha cast his eyes upon us and naturally concluded we were strangers.' They had not known that they should have dismounted as a sign of respect. No sooner had they unpacked, however, than an invitation to go to the Palace was received from the Pasha, and so it was that Lady Hester first met one of the main characters in the history of the Near East: Mehemet Ali, Ruler of Egypt.

Mehemet Ali was not Egyptian, neither was he an Arab. He was an Albanian born in the town of Kavala, where he lived as a shopkeeper until he was thirty. He then entered the Turkish Army where, although he had had very little formal education, he was quickly promoted to the rank of officer. In 1801 he was sent to Egypt to help drive out the French contingents left there by Napoleon after his defeat by Nelson at the Battle of the Nile three years earlier. By a series of events Mehemet Ali was rapidly promoted to become the military master of Egypt and then was appointed as the Sultan Mahmoud's Viceroy and Pasha of Egypt. Having fought against European troops he saw that their methods were infinitely more successful than the Muslim ways, so he decided to employ European instructors and drilled his army to a degree of skill and efficiency unprecedented in the East.

Although Egypt had been part of the Ottoman Empire for centuries, for most of that time the actual rulers of Egypt had been a group called the Mamelukes. This race of people were descended from the slaves of the Arab rulers of Egypt who had overthrown their masters in 1250, and who had remained in power more or less ever since. They had quickly established themselves as a land-owning, ruling caste who had no relationship with the Egyptians themselves except to exploit them mercilessly. By the time Mehemet Ali came to power in 1805, Egypt was nearly ruined, and it was clear to Ali that if he wanted to rebuild his country, he would have to break the power of the Mamelukes.

He decided that ruthless measures were called for, and dealt with the Mamelukes in much the same way as Sultan Mahmoud had attempted to deal with the Janissaries in Constantinople, only his method was even more bloodthirsty and dramatic. Secretly massing his Albanian troops around the city walls, Ali invited all the leading Mamelukes to a banquet, and as soon as they had entered the city gates, the troops opened fire and massacred them all. By this slaughter Mehemet Ali achieved his aim of reestablishing Egypt as a prosperous nation, but the massacre remains one of the most infamous events in the blood-stained history of the Ottoman Empire.

Britain's reaction to the assassination was one of approval, and although it had taken place only the year before, Lady Hester had no qualms at all about being summoned to the Palace. She had no time to be worried about things that were past history, for she had more immediate problems on her mind. She didn't know what to wear.

It was a ticklish decision for her, and she gave it much thought, but finally she decided on a Tunisian costume, and bought a sumptuous outfit of purple velvet beautifully embroidered in gold. There were pantaloons, a waistcoat and pelisse – a kind of long mantle – and as a turban and girdle, she wore two rich cashmere shawls each costing fifty pounds. She also decided to buy a new sabre and saddle for her horse, and the thrifty Meryon calculated that the outfit had cost her more than three hundred pounds: extravagance indeed. Michael's outfit was judged to have cost at least as much, whilst Meryon, mindful of his position, contented himself with 'the common costume of a gentleman or an effendi'.

What Lady Hester had not realized was that Mehemet Ali had never met an English woman before. As a token of great honour, he sent an escort and five richly caparisoned horses to carry Lady Hester and her party to the Palace. A great number of silver sticks were carried in front of the entourage to signify its importance, and when they reached the Palace, they were allowed to dismount at the inner gate, another privilege.

Once inside, they were ushered into a painted and gilded pavilion in the gardens of the harem, where the Pasha, in a sign of great respect, rose to greet Lady Hester. The room was magnificently decorated.

The floor was covered with a scarlet carpet, and they were invited to sit on sofas of scarlet velvet lavishly embroidered with gold. Gorgeously dressed servants stood to attention all around and a fountain played quietly in the middle of the room.

Mehemet Ali was a small, middle-aged man dressed plainly but richly, and he and Lady Hester were delighted with each other. He plied her with green sherbet served in cut crystal glasses, then coffee in china cups supported by 'gold zerfs, ornamented with precious stones'. Lady Hester was also offered the traditional pipe, but declined, as she had not yet learned to smoke one. Sources do not relate what they talked about, but by the end of her hour-long stay, the Pasha was so enchanted with Lady Hester that he promised he would review his troops in her honour – something never before done for a woman. This was just the sort of thing that Hester adored, and at the review she could not resist showing off her horsemanship, and was rewarded with congratulations and two magnificent Arab horses. Michael had to content himself with an ornate sabre and a cashmere shawl.

Lady Hester was delighted with her conquest and wrote to Stratford Canning that 'Mehemet Ali was civiler to me than he ever was to anybody in his life.' For the rest of their stay in Cairo, she spent much of her time meeting the cream of society. It seemed that everyone had heard of the strange English lady who wore men's clothes and who had so charmed the Pasha, and they all wanted to meet her. She visited Mehemet Ali many more times : 'I rode with him, paid him visits when I chose, where I chose and at my own time ;' she wrote to Canning, 'I talked to him for hours together and everything I asked was done.' At the same time she visited the widows of the some of the slaughtered Mamelukes, and had no compunction in telling the Pasha all about it.

It seemed that the further she travelled from England the more conventions Lady Hester managed to cast off. Perhaps the loss of all her possessions in the shipwreck had been symbolic for her, but her decision to dress in Arab clothes almost certainly made her feel quite a different person. It was in Cairo that she first felt confident enough to share a house openly with Michael, relegating Pearce and Meryon to other quarters, and significantly it was at this time that she began to realize that Michael was not as perfect as she had once thought.

Answerable to no one but herself, she felt in control of her life for the first time, and she was revelling in it. On 3 May the party left Cairo for the Holy Lands, where, after an unusually uneventful passage, they arrived in Jaffa.

CHAPTER TEN

Arrival in Syria

Tel Aviv-Jaffa is a major city on the coast of Israel, but when Lady Hester landed there it was simply the pretty, stone town of Jaffa. Easter was just over, and the narrow sloping streets were bustling with people from every Eastern country and religion, many of them pilgrims returning home from Jerusalem. Traders throughout the Lebanon took advantage of this yearly passage of pilgrims to bring their goods to trade and barter. Silks from Damascus, Barbary shawls and the softest cloth from Angora were exchanged for pearls, precious stones, gums, herbs and medicines.

The teeming market town was a microcosm of what has long been known as the Holy Lands. Situated as it is, a long rectangle of land bounded by the Mediterranean on the West and mountains and desert to the East, the history of the area reads like one long list of foreign invasions. It has always been of vital geographical importance: the isthmus that joins eastern Europe to Africa, and the Mediterranean countries to those of the Middle East. Armies have invaded, conquered, been defeated and left, boundaries have moved and place names changed. As part of the vast Ottoman Empire that stretched all around the Eastern Mediterranean from Romania to Morocco, it had no specific internal boundaries in the early nineteenth century, and encompassed the present-day states of Syria, Lebanon, Jordan and Israel. As well as being known as the Holy Lands it was also called the Levant, or greater Syria, but whatever its name it was part of a continent almost wholly unexplored by Europeans. Lady Hester was going into what was largely unknown territory.

Of all the thousands of people packed into Jaffa that May, none was more polygenous than the British Agent, Signor Damiani, who came rushing down to the port to greet Lady Hester. Born in Syria of Italian parents, his father had served in the English Navy, and he now bade Lady Hester welcome to the Levant on behalf of her country. He presented an extraordinary figure as he stood on the quay. He wore a long Turkish djellaba, a garment rather like an ordinary shirt extended to the ground, but instead of the usual turban, his long grey hair was tied back in a thick pigtail, on top of which was perched an ancient cocked hat. He was intent on providing hospitality for Lady Hester and her party, impressing upon her rather too many times for subtlety that she should not give him too large a present. She had decided to visit Jerusalem however, and despite Damiani's blandishments stayed in Jaffa only long enough to assemble enough servants and transport to make the journey.

The party was completely reprovisioned by now, after the shipwreck, and so there was a lot of luggage. Traditionally, asses were used as beasts of burden for short trips, and camels for longer journeys; Hester had no less than ten camels laden with tents, marquees, clothes, provisions and gifts, and numerous donkeys and horses to carry herself and her party. Two Mameluke servants given to Lady Hester as a departing gift from Mehemet Ali were joined by eight Syrians, and the Governor of Jaffa had provided two bodyguards for the party, for travel of any kind in Syria was dangerous.

It is hard for us to realize fully quite how daring it was for Lady Hester to be travelling into Syria. Europeans had journeyed there before, but comparatively few of them, and all of them men. Gertrude Bell, who was so admired for her travels through Syria and Arabia, did not set out until nearly one hundred years later: Lady Hester had died, an old woman, thirty years before Bell was born. Apart from the inherent dangers for a woman travelling in an unknown country, there were differences and difficulties almost impossible to imagine. One fact that perhaps brings this into focus was that when Lady Hester travelled in Syria there were no roads and no wheeled vehicles: all travel was done by foot or on horses, donkeys or camels. The roads that had been established in Biblical times had fallen into complete disrepair over the centuries, owing to lack of coherent policy from Constantinople; therefore all carts and wagons had become useless and were no longer even made. It was a different world.

Travel was difficult and dangerous for other reasons as well. The Ottoman Empire was so vast that direct government from Constantinople was impossible, so some kind of local rule was necessary. Each area had its own Governor who was allowed complete autonomy unless, as frequently happened, they became too corrupt or too ambitious. Constantinople would then step in, often appointing the brother or son of the existing Governor in his place, and leaving the protagonists literally to fight it out between them. One set of travel documents was not enough when travelling between these different regions: new negotiations had to be made every time. The many mountainous areas throughout the length and breadth of the country were impossible for any Governor to control, however efficient or fierce he was, and so they provided refuge for all those who either could not, or would not submit to the local rule. Recalcitrant ex-rulers, persecuted tribes and assorted brigands and villains, all managed a healthy existence in the mountains, swooping down on unsuspecting travellers to augment their meagre income. Bodyguards were not a luxury but a necessity for any party of substance that intended to travel through these desolate areas.

It was a splendid cavalcade that set out for Jerusalem. Lady Hester rode at the head of the column with two saises, or grooms walking at her horse's head. She was magnificently clothed in a Mameluke travelling costume bought in Cairo. A satin vest and red cloth jacket were matched by 'trowsers of the same cloth, gorgeously embroidered with gold at the pockets, as well before as behind'. Dr Meryon was entranced with her appearance and, as always, managed to describe it in great detail: the 'trowsers' were 'large and loose as is the fashion in Turkey, and when worn, formed, by their numerous folds, a very beautiful drapery. Over the whole, when on horseback, she wore the burnooz or white-hooded cloak, the pendent [sic] tassels and silky look of which gave great elegance to her figure.' Another beautiful cashmere shawl was worn as a turban, and as a final elegant touch, her saddle and bridle were matching too – crimson velvet embroidered with gold.

As they rode through the countryside, they passed large fields of watermelons and great flights of storks rose flapping into the sky, startled by the sight and sound of the caravan. There were orchards of every description: lemon, orange, peach, almond and pomegranate, but most were young trees. Fifteen years before, when the French Army had invaded, all the mature trees had been hacked down to use as firewood. It was a wonderfully fertile place and the recently planted trees were approaching maturity, but even as they approached the end of their first day's ride they came across a plague of locusts. At one place the insects had covered a house and tree so completely that both seemed to be bright green. Great swarms were seen 'marching in a strait [sic] line, not to be stopped by any impediment . . . and dreadful was the havoc they had made'.

Making sure they were well out of the path of the marauding locusts, they made camp for the night in an orchard of olive trees. It was now over two years since Lady Hester and Charles Meryon had left England. They had come a long way together, not only geographically, but also in understanding of the Muslim people. At first the linguistic and cultural differences had been so enormous that they had made the inevitable British mistake of assuming foreign ways to be inferior. They had learned by now, as they travelled further eastwards, to respect and often admire the customs that had at first been so puzzling to them. They had also begun to appreciate the Turkish language and were able to understand most of what was said to them. It was a short step to being able to speak Turkish themselves. Lady Hester loved the personal freedom she had and the respect she was paid by all she met; Meryon was enjoying his new prosperity, security and social status. The Near East was beginning to feel most comfortable to them both.

Michael Bruce was not so appreciative. He had always been an impatient man – an unrewarding thing to be with Arabs or Turks – and he seemed to find them increasingly difficult to deal with. He was no less in love with Hester than he had been from the start of their affair, but he found it hard always to be in second place to her during their visits with local dignitaries. Now that time had passed and Hester was not quite so dazzled by love, she was beginning to suspect that the ambitious predictions she had so confidently made for Michael were unlikely to come true. He still seemed keen enough to learn from her, but he remained strangely immature in many ways. Henry Pearce had left the party at Jaffa, and perhaps Michael missed a male companion – certainly life was not quite so blissful now. He was prone to bad moods and sulky behaviour, he constantly found fault with the servants, who began to depart with alarming regularity, and the old animosity he had felt for Meryon began to emerge once more.

It was therefore with very differing feelings that the three main members of the party prepared for their first night under the stars of the Syrian sky. Lady Hester and Michael had a magnificent marquee that was romantically painted with flowers, Meryon had a smaller tent and there was a large one set apart for the servants, two of whom were employed solely for the pitching and striking of camp. The countryside was utterly beautiful, and Meryon waxed eloquent again. 'In a climate where the sky is more serene than a mirror, where the most delicious fruits are more than abundant, where the bosom expands with hilarity from the very air one breathes, you cannot forgive the man who is not happy! Everything was enchanting!'.

Michael, sitting glumly in his beautiful marquee, would have been driven to new levels of exasperation by such fervour.

In the morning the party pressed on. The path they took wound through the mountains and the territory of a marauding sheik called Abu Ghosh, who levied a tax on everyone passing through his domain. This tax was usually taken by force, but when he saw the richness of Lady Hester's caravan and realized that she was an important foreigner, he decided the polite approach might be better advised.

'Abu Ghosh received us very courteously,' Meryon wrote in his journal, '[he] killed a sheep for us, gave us corn for our animals, and supplied all our wants.' This infamous brigand was fascinated to meet Lady Hester and most impressed to see that she was not at all frightened of him. He ordered his four wives to cook a meal, and they all vied with each other to produce the most delicious combination of meat and rice, which was the extent of their larder. Dinner consisted of lamb stuffed with rice, lamb coated with rice, lamb chopped up in rice and lamb and rice wrapped in vine leaves, but the conversation was sparkling and made up for the somewhat monotonous food, so all was not lost.

When it was time for her to retire, one of Lady Hester's Mamelukes sensibly suggested putting guards around their camp to protect them from possible treachery on the part of their host or his men. There was a very real danger that they might be robbed, or worse, and Hester was wondering what best to do when she had a flash of inspiration: she decided to ask Abu Ghosh if he himself would provide guards for them. By doing this, Lady Hester was placing the lives of herself and her party in Abu Ghosh's hands, but she knew it was the right thing to do. Ever since she was a child Lady Hester had relied on her intuition about people, their intentions and motivations, and although it was a long way from the drawing rooms of London to the draughty tent of a dubious Arab in the mountains of Palestine, her intuitions were just as finely tuned, and just as trustworthy as they had always been. Meryon was often astonished at how quickly and acutely she could make an assessment of someone, but he too learned to trust what he could not understand, even when on this occasion, as on many others to come, the gamble they were taking was with their lives.

As nearly always in matters of this kind, Lady Hester was right. Abu Ghosh was so gratified at being trusted by this great English Lady that he promptly abandoned any thoughts of pillage he might have had and insisted on keeping watch himself. He sat up all night by a large fire, and in the morning he and Hester parted, the best of friends. She gave him a handsome present, and ever after he spoke of her with great admiration and respect.

As the party travelled towards Jerusalem, the Holy City became visible to them from a great distance across a deserted plain, and this helped to create a mood of solemnity in them. Jerusalem has always been a place of great significance to all Christians everywhere, and Lady Hester and her party were no exception. They crossed the great expanse in silence, entered the city gates with a feeling of reverent awe, and made their way to some lodgings, but as they settled in, their contemplative mood was rudely shattered. They were beset by the equivalent of modern-day touts all offering to sell them things and wanting to be their guides. It was 'the dragomans of the monastery, the greatest harpies that Jerusalem can boast of, and equally devoid of principle and of morality'. They followed Lady Hester into her rooms and pestered her until she threw them all out, and even then they hung around outside and made great nuisances of themselves.

The next day the party made a visit to the Holy Sepulchre but word had spread through the city that a great and wealthy visitor had arrived. Huge crowds of people gathered to see the English Lady and her friends, and the Turks at the Sepulchre were forced to beat them back with whips and sticks. This was the first time that a crowd had gathered specifically to see Lady Hester, and even for her it must have been disconcerting. It was the pattern of things to come though, and the first sign of the legendary fame she came to enjoy, and which was to last so far beyond her death.

Once inside the building Hester and her party were further startled by the chattering of the monks and the 'tumultuous behaviour' of the local Christians. Inside the chamber of the Sepulchre there seemed at first to be a different and more appropriate atmosphere: 'the solemnity of the place,' the doctor reported, 'coupled with the reflections to which it gave rise, was inconceivably imposing, far exceeding anything I had ever felt before.' Even there, though, the profundity of their reflections was marred. The priest who escorted them was bored; he had done it all before, and he too was 'indecorously deficient in gravity'.

This, sadly, seemed to be the pattern of their stay in Jerusalem. Everywhere they went they were besieged by souvenir sellers, sightseers and would-be guides. They were glad to leave the city, but before they left they met a man whose existence in later years was frequently denied: the only Mameluke ruler to have escaped the massacre at Cairo. His name was Emin or Ishmael Bey and he told his story to Lady Hester and Michael. He said that when he and his companions had ridden into Mehemet Ali's ambush only his swift reaction had saved his life. Realizing that he was in mortal danger he had put his horse to a low part of the wall and with a prodigious leap escaped into the town. He had made his way into the desert with the help of some guides who then set upon him in the night, robbing him and leaving him for dead. A passing Bedouin rescued him and took him through the desert until he finally arrived in Jerusalem where he had placed himself under the protection of the Pasha of Acre. There was a price on his head, and he was only safe as long as the Pasha of Acre and Mehemet Ali remained enemies.

Lady Hester could never refuse anyone in distress. She gave him money and wrote to Stratford Canning to try and get some protection for him, but sources do not relate whether or not she managed to get anything done.

After their rather disappointing visit to Jerusalem, Lady Hester and Michael made their way back to Jaffa to collect some firmans – travel documents – before setting off northwards towards Lebanon. On the way back they stayed with Abu Ghosh again, and, as Dr Meryon reported, 'passed the night very securely'. When they left the following morning, Abu Ghosh accompanied them for part of the way, and the doctor rather unadvisedly beat him in a horse race, never a wise thing to do to a volatile Arab bandit. It was a measure of his regard for Lady Hester that Ghosh accepted defeat manfully, and slunk back to his four wives, leaving a victorious Meryon to observe haughtily that Ghosh had, after all, been mounted on a grey, flea-bitten mare, not worth more than fifteen or twenty pounds.

After collecting the firmans, the party made its way up the coast towards the ancient town of Acre. Lady Hester wanted to go to Damascus, and there was a half-formulated plan in the back of her mind to visit the legendary Palmyra, but she needed to get closer before she could find out whether or not it would be possible. Only three Europeans had ever been there before, all men of course, and they had been lucky to escape with their lives. It sounded just the kind of place she wanted to see.

Their progress up the coast of Palestine was quiet. There was time to observe in detail their surroundings, and the few people they came across. There were no bandits such as Abu Ghosh, since the strip of flat land between the coast and the mountains did not afford sufficient protection. Most of the people they saw were simple villagers, dressed in exactly the same clothes that are described in the Bible. 'The dress of the men was a cotton shirt,' Meryon reported, 'buckled round the waist with a leathern belt; over which they threw a long woollen cloak called an abah or meshlah, without sleeves.' The women dressed in the same way, with the addition of a veil of coarse white cotton.

Meryon loved to see the women carry water from the wells, and greatly admired their posture. Although he realized the work was 'very toilsome', his doctor's eye noted rather pedantically that 'far from giving a curve to the spine, depressing the neck, or in any wise shortening the growth of the body, the resistance of the muscles seems to increase in proportion to the pressure, and much elasticity of action is the result'. When dressed in their best clothes the women wore yellow slippers, silver bracelets around their wrists and ankles, silver relic cases on a chain round their necks and, most becomingly, 'silver rims of mail or coins which take in the oval of the face from the temples to the chin and have a very pretty effect'. The doctor was becoming quite a connoisseur of women.

As they approached Acre, the slip of land between sea and mountain narrowed until they felt as if they were travelling along a garden path. They pitched their tents within the ruined walls of the Venetian Castle Pellegrino, and the next day saw the great bay of Acre open in front of them.

Acre was a fortified ancient town and one of the major trading ports of the East. Silks, perfumes, and porcelain from China had all been part of the regular trade until the discovery of the new sea routes made the old overland trading roads redundant.

The Austrian Consul in Acre was a man called Mr Catafago, and he had invited Lady Hester to stay in his house, an offer she gladly accepted. He sent his son and nephew to meet her on the road, and they escorted the party through the single city gate and narrow cobbled streets to his home. Mr Catafago and his family made Lady Hester and her party extremely welcome – Meryon actually called his hospitality 'unremitting' – but Acre was not a happy town. The previous Pasha was called El Djezzar, and he had been a man of ferocious cruelty. His nickname was 'The Butcher', and his favourite form of control and punishment was mutilation. On every street men and women with no eyes, ears or noses could be seen. Amputation of sexual organs was also popular with him and once, in a fit of jealous rage, he had all the ladies of his harem sewn into sacks and thrown into the sea.

Lady Hester was sickened by what she heard and saw, but allowed herself to be shown around the town. She inspected the battlements that had held so successfully against Bonaparte and saw the famous mosque that had been constructed from granite, porphyry and marble ransacked from the ruins of Caesaria and Ascalon. She was not, however, tempted to stay for too long in the town.

Mr Catafago had a summer house at Nazareth, and the party decided to make a short trip there out of curiosity. Whilst they were there they were amazed to be addressed in English by what had seemed to be a perfectly ordinary Bedouin. Although the man was dressed poorly in a coarse cotton shirt, he had blue eyes and a broad Germanic face. It was the famous traveller Burckhardt, who was travelling incognito as a poor peasant. He was delighted to meet some fellow Europeans, and stayed for two or three days before continuing his travels. Strangely enough Lady Hester took a dislike to him, though she never said why. Maybe the fact that the two of them had chosen such diametrically opposite ways of travelling indicated something very different in their personalities. In a letter to Craufurd Bruce in September of that year she wrote: 'To go to Palmyra or anywhere else like a thief I do not like, to scalk [sic] about fearing to meet this and that tribe of Bedouins, I go as a friend of them all.'

Burckhardt later wrote warmly to Michael offering his services to Lady Hester if required, and furnishing her with some amazingly detailed information about breeds of Arab horses that she had evidently requested. There were undoubtedly benefits to be gained from both ways of travel.

It was now July, and the weather was becoming unbearably hot. On 24 May Michael had received a letter from his father complaining about how much money he was drawing. This had been a great worry to both Michael and Hester, and they had both written to Craufurd trying to explain why so much expense was necessary. After having lost everything in the shipwreck at Rhodes, they had been obliged to reprovision, and that had cost a lot. They had spent over £3,000 since December and Michael's allowance for the year was only £2,500. Michael felt humiliated: 'If you are not satisfied,' he wrote to his father, 'and should imagine that I had been guilty of any wanton extravagance, I shall feel most deeply mortified as I would rather remain on the bleakest mountain of Scotland and feed upon bread and water than that it should for a moment be supposed that I was capable of abusing your generosity.'

Hester adopted a more pragmatic approach. When she had first met Michael he had been extremely careless with his money, 'leaving his money in the hand of his servant & never inquiring the price of anything & paying a bill without looking at it'. She had changed all that and had insisted that meticulous records be kept. The ledgers from Constantinople had all been lost in the shipwreck, but all their expenses from Alexandria and on were available. She pointed out to

Craufurd that although Michael had many natural attributes, 'information must be acquired' and it was no good hiring cheap guides or dragomen since they knew nothing and could therefore impart no worthwhile local knowledge.

The giving of lavish presents to all they met was another part of the drain on Craufurd's pocket, but this has always been the custom in Eastern countries, and is even mentioned in the Bible. In the first book of Samuel X. 27 it says: 'and they despised him and brought him no presents.' It was taken as an insult to make a visit without bringing a gift, and of course the greater the personage, the more magnificent the present had to be. Lesser people such as court officials and superior servants also expected their baksheesh, and would often make life very awkward if it was not forthcoming.

Lady Hester evidently felt that nothing should be spared in the advance of Michael's education, but told Craufurd: 'If I have mistaken your views I am sorry for it, and expense shall cease.' She had, of course, her own allowance of £1,200 a year, and had been living quite happily within her means before she met Michael, so perhaps the accusations that were later levelled at her of being profligate with Craufurd's money were unfair.

The party moved on from Nazareth to Sidon, which was rather dull, but no sooner had they arrived than Lady Hester received a most exciting invitation from the Emir Beshyr, Prince of the Druses, to visit him in his mountain eyrie. The Druses were a strange Islamic sect who lived in the chain of mountains between Sidon and Tripoli, and who were considered heretical by orthodox Muslims. It was said by their detractors that the principal tenets of their faith were transmigration of souls, belief in there being no future, and approval of incest. Hester was understandably transfixed with curiosity about this tribe of people and confided in Meryon that she had intended to visit them even if she hadn't been invited. The Prince, or Emir, sent down a cavalcade for her use: twelve camels, twenty-five mules, four horses and seven foot soldiers, and they set off for the Druse capital of Dayr-el-Kamar.

The mountains were all but impassable. 'I have travelled for nine hours together and never found a place large enough to pitch a tent,' Hester wrote to Craufurd. 'The vineyards are like staircases, and every little flat place stuffed with mulberry trees for the silkworms, the roads are horrible, and the people savage and extraordinary, the women wearing a great tin trumpet on their heads and a veil suspended upon it, and seeming very proud of these frightful horns.' Hardly an auspicious start.

The 'frightful horns', or tonturas, were an important part of the women's costume, and served to indicate a woman's rank. The horn of a poor woman was made of pasteboard, whilst those of ladies of higher rank were fashioned out of silver, and 'incrustated with diamonds and precious stones'. The horns were generally held onto the head with long scarves although the very rich used wide bandeaux of pearls instead. In public the horn was always shielded by a veil, it being a grave breach of decorum to expose it to public gaze, far worse than exposing the face or breast. It was not removed even for sleeping, which must have posed considerable problems, for the horns were about two foot high. The angle of wear indicated which village the women came from: they could be vertical, horizontal, or at a rakish tilt in between the two.

Lady Hester was received in the Prince's Palace with great ceremony and stayed there for a month. 'They say he is a very good man,' Meryon wrote with restraint. 'It is true he blinded his three nephews and had his prime minister strangled ... but these things go for nothing in Turkey.' The Palace was not particularly beautiful, but the suffocating heat of the lowlands was swept away by the mountain breezes, and the building had been constructed so that a stream of water ran through every room, providing a delightful coolness.

The Emir himself was a tall, handsome man with a big bushy beard, strangely pale eyes and great charisma. Although he was the religious as well as temporal leader of his people this had not stopped him from recently becoming a convert to Christianity. Quite how he coped with this spiritual anomaly is not related, but Lady Hester was fascinated by him. According to one of her letters, anyone prying into the religious affairs of the Druses was liable to be murdered, but it goes without saying that she totally ignored this risk. 'I can ask questions no other person dares to put to them,' she wrote, 'but it would not be proper to repeat here those I asked even the sages, and still less their answers.' Maybe it was all bravado, but she certainly managed to prove one rumour to be true – the Druses ate raw meat.

'I purchased of a Druse an immense sheep, the tail weighing eleven pounds, and desired it to be taken to a village.' The villagers assembled and had a gruesome feast. 'The moment it was killed, it was skinned and brought in raw upon a sort of dish made of matting, and in less than half an hour it was all devoured,' she recalled with a shudder. 'The women eat of it as well as the men. The pieces of raw fat they swallowed were really frightful.'

Whilst in the mountains she also visited the Druse Governor, Sheik Beshyr, who was 'a Lucifer' compared to the Emir. All kinds of mass-acres had been perpetrated at his command, and for fear of poison, he had an official taster for Lady Hester's food as well as his own. Lady Hester pretended to be used to it, but noted nervously that 'this man upon his knees before me looked more solemn than usual.' She sur-vived unscathed and stayed with the Druses for several more weeks before deciding to journey on. As soon as they descended from the mountains, they were hit by the appalling summer heat and Michael started arguing bitterly with Meryon once again. It was accepted that Michael had a short temper, but tension between the two men rapidly reached such a point that Meryon wrote secretly to his sister in England, saying that he had decided it best to leave. His indignation at how Michael was treating him led him to make some scathing remarks that probably had a lot of truth in them. 'Indulged from his infancy by the fondness of a weak father, who at an early age let him loose on the world with the command of a large fortune,' he fumed, 'he has been flattered and caressed until the slightest opposition to his will makes him sulky and churlish.'

Meryon was not an unkind man, indeed he was always ready to believe the best of anyone. He must have received enormous and sustained provocation to criticize Michael so strongly.

His decision to leave was a desperate move, for he still idolized Lady Hester, and loved his life with her. He told Hester of his plan and at first she reluctantly agreed it might be best if he left, but then she changed her mind. Meryon was an ideal travelling companion, depen-dable, brave and loyal and she had no wish to lose him. She still loved Michael dearly, but was no longer blind to his many faults, and could see that he was making Meryon's life a misery. Michael had been wanting to go to Aleppo for some time, whilst Hester herself favoured going to Damascus, so she suggested that the party split for a few weeks: Michael would go to Aleppo, accompanied by M. Bertrand, his dragoman, whilst she and Meryon would travel to Damascus. There she would have the opportunity to investigate the possibilities of a journey to the deserted city of Palmyra, and whilst Meryon and Michael were apart, the tensions between the two men would have time to ease and perhaps all would be well.

Another reason for them to split up for a while was that Michael was often over-solicitous with her, and if he were away for a while it would enable her to make a dramatic entrance into the city of Damascus. She had been in touch with the newly appointed Pasha there, who had courteously invited her to his city, but he had made the mistake of telling her that she must wear a veil when in public: not only was Damascus one of the most rigorously Muslim of cities, but there had been some recent unrest. Christians were despised throughout the Levant, but perhaps nowhere as much as in Damascus. There they were required to live in a particularly unsalubrious part of town and were scarcely allowed to enter the Muslim areas. If they made themselves conspicuous in any way, even by wearing a jaunty turban or yellow slippers, for example, they ran the risk of being physically attacked. Riding a horse was also forbidden. To most European women it might have seemed a prudent step at least to wear a veil.

Of course she refused. Having seen Michael and M. Bertrand off to Aleppo, she set off for Damascus. With a terrified Meryon riding behind her she approached the city at mid-afternoon. Inside, the streets were packed with people. With either great courage or great foolhardiness, she rode in through the gates in her most splendid clothes, unveiled and with her head high. It worked. The crowds fell silent and let her pass unscathed. Lady Hester had become a law unto herself.

CHAPTER ELEVEN

A Queen in Damascus

The city of Damascus is the oldest continuously inhabited city in the world, and was known to both Franks and Muslims alike as the 'Pearl of the Desert'. It has always been a place of immense religious and strategic importance. As a direct result, it has been one of the most beleaguered cities in a country that has suffered invasion and conquest since it was first inhabited.

Unlike some of the more mundane cities of Syria, Damascus has a rich history of beliefs and legends that have woven their way into the very fabric of the city. One of these strands relates how God created Adam from the clay of the River Barada, on which Damascus stands. Another belief that has survived the centuries is that the painted Virgin of Seidnaya weeps real tears. The tomb which purports to be that of John the Baptist is in Damascus, though various other places also claim that honour, and, even more equivocally, there is the tomb of Abel, twenty feet long, and so narrow as to be quite out of human proportion. Almost hidden amongst these uncertainties are a few marvellous nuggets. There is a road running through the town which is called Straight, and on its dusty, undeviating length is, indubitably, the site of St Paul's baptism.

Many historical facts and legends about the city have survived the centuries; much of the physical fabric of the ancient city has also withstood the passage of time. Now, though, the old narrow lanes are overshadowed by ugly concrete tenement blocks that make it hard to remember that Damascus is meant to have been built on the site of the Garden of Eden. The ancient and famous Great Ommayed Mosque still stands however, and, walking within the profound tranquillity of its cloistered walls, it is possible to imagine a time when all around there was an oasis of peace and beauty. There is a mosaic on the walls of the mosque that seems to echo the legend of the Garden of Eden, because unlike most mosaicwork, this one is representational, and depicts exquisite pastoral scenes from some unknown, halcyon time. The site of the mosque has been sacred for three thousand years, and if its story were ever to be told it would reflect the whole history of Damascus: not only Muslims, but Aramaeans, Greeks, Romans and Christians have worshipped their gods there. It is a peaceful place. In August 1812, when Lady Hester rode unveiled and daring through the city gates, Damascus was a busy, bustling town of about 200,000 – 300,000 people. Lady Hester had been given lodgings in the Christian sector, as was usual for any visiting Europeans, but as Christians and Greeks were so despised, this area of the town was almost like a ghetto, and Lady Hester decided it simply would not do. Hardly had poor Meryon recovered from the ordeal of their entrance into the city than he reeled again as Hester sent a quaking dragoman to the Pasha of Damascus with a firm request for relocation to a better part of town. Not knowing who he was taking on, the Pasha turned down the request, but Lady Hester was so persistent that, by the end of the same day, the Pasha was forced to relent. The unfortunate dragoman was then conducted from house to house until one was found that suited Her Ladyship. It was in the best quarter of Damascus, close to both the Palace and the bazaars, and it was beautiful.

Damascus was architecturally very similar to many other towns in the Levant. Minarets and palm trees towered over the narrow, winding streets and jumbled whitewashed houses. Five times a day the call to prayer echoed out over the city, and the loudest noise the muezzin had to contend with was the coughs and grunts of the camels, and the bustle and chat of everyday life. But there was an additional and lovely sound in Damascus – that of playing water. Scores of small streams from the River Barada had been diverted to criss-cross under and through the town, and these fed the countless gardens that graced the city and the fountains that played in every courtyard and square. In every public place and nearly every private house, the air was cooled and the senses refreshed by running water. Lady Hester's new house was no exception.

'It opened through a narrow passage into an oblong marble paved court. In the middle of the court was a large basin shaded by two very lofty lemon trees, into which two brazen serpents poured a constant supply of fresh water.' Two large recesses in the courtyard walls allowed for outside seating areas, and twin staircases wound up the outside of the walls to lead to Lady Hester's rooms on one side, and, on the other, a 'saloon' in which to receive visitors.

It seemed that everyone in Damascus wanted to meet Hester. She made one decision almost immediately that gained her favour with the Turks. The superiors of two local monasteries were in the habit of making calls on visiting Europeans, but since she had been granted the concession of living in the Turkish quarter, she requested them not to visit her for fear of offending her Muslim neighbours. Her thoughtfulness was appreciated.

She rested for two days before venturing out. Word had spread like wildfire through the town that a hugely important and rich foreign lady had arrived. Rumours had sprung up that Lady Hester was English royalty, that she was, indeed, the daughter of the King. When she finally emerged through the narrow doorway from her house it was to see a crowd of hundreds who had been patiently waiting for a sight of the great Elendi, or Queen.

She had decided to make her first excursion around Damascus as she had entered the city – unveiled – and accompanied only by her young interpreter, Giorgio, and her janissary, Mohammed. Although Meryon was getting resigned to her daring escapades by now, he was almost beside himself with worry. He knew that one critical or ribald comment from the crowd might precipitate a riot. He need not have worried. The crowd adored her. They were won over by 'a grave yet pleasing look, an unembarrassed yet commanding demeanour'. Her conduct was so unlike what Muslims had come to expect from a Christian, and so similar to the qualities most admired in Turkish aristocracy that a new rumour started. It was murmured round the crowd that here was an English Queen of Ottoman descent. Was not the instep of her foot as high as an Arab's? Did she not dress as a Turkish ruler? The inconvenient fact that she had a very fair complexion was also explained away: it was paint, they decided, but so skilfully applied as to be undetectable.

One important event of these early days in Damascus was, of

course, Lady Hester's visit to the Pasha. Not only was it a courtesy on both sides for them to meet, but if Lady Hester were to make an expedition to Palmyra, she would need to enlist the Pasha's help. Sayd Suleiman Pasha had spent his life at the court of Sultan Selim in Constantinople and was a proud, dignified and very formal Turkish gentleman. When Lady Hester arrived at the Palace to meet him, it almost seemed as if he was trying to intimidate her. First she was escorted through several echoing antechambers lit only by guttering candles whose uncertain light reflected off the arms of countless soldiers and attendants, who stood lining the route in utter silence. She was then ushered past row upon row of the Pasha's court who watched her avidly, eager to see the strange English woman who dressed as a man and who had presumed to dictate to their Pasha where she should live. For almost anyone except Lady Hester it would have been an unnerving experience. The dragoman who accompanied Lady Hester followed her with all the enthusiasm of an aristocrat approaching the guillotine.

The Pasha was at the very end of the final room, a small man sitting very straight on a crimson sofa. Unlike many other governors whom Lady Hester had visited, he did not accord her the intimacy of rising when she approached, but merely indicated with a regal wave of his hand where she was to sit. Hester's dragoman was trembling so much by this time that he was quite unable to act as interpreter, and could only stand there, stuttering and shaking. Lady Hester was unperturbed by this show of nerves, and waited quietly until the poor man was able to stammer out the mutual salutations. The interview passed off successfully, and although one gathers that Sayd Suleiman was not quite so entranced with Lady Hester as most other Pashas had been, gifts were exchanged and everyone was satisfied.

After her visit to the Pasha everyone was keen to meet the great English Queen. All the dignitaries vied with each other to provide the best hospitality – the most delicious sherbet, the finest ground coffee. It was not long before Lady Hester was fêted wherever she went. Women came out of their houses to strew coffee in her path, as they would for an important leader, and when she entered the bazaars, people rose as if she herself were a great Pasha.

Lady Hester's main reason for coming to Damascus was to see if a trip to Palmyra was possible, and if so, to organize it. Although the two cities were over a hundred miles apart, it seemed to her that Damascus was a good base from which to organize the expedition. She soon decided that she could, and would, go to the desert city, and she launched into her arrangements with enthusiasm. As soon as her plans became known, everyone wanted to give her advice, but it seemed to her that very little of it was either impartial or even helpful. People were offering help and counsel for all kinds of political, religious and financial motives, so, sensibly, she decided to listen to everyone, then ignore most of what she heard. She found a good friend in the leader of the Delibaches – the cavalry based in Damascus – a simple, honest soldier who had no liking for intrigue. A rich Jewish serraf, or banker, was another ally, and of course she had the protection of the Pasha at all times. It says much for Hester's adaptability and receptiveness that she should be able to strike up genuine friendships with such very different people. The network of contacts she was building began to spread and multiply. Everyone wanted to be the friend and adviser of the great English Queen.

Like Damascus, Palmyra was a town shrouded in legend and mystery, but unlike Damascus, it was derelict and only sparsely populated by a few hundred desert people who camped in shacks amid the ruins. Palmyra, also known as Tadmor, was an ancient city known to have been in existence from the beginning of the second millennium BC. It was reputedly built by Solomon, but since there are records of its existence long before Solomon's time, he was probably responsible for enlarging and improving it, for it was a massive place of stunning classical beauty. As a town frequented by Cappadocian merchants since the closing years of the Third Dynasty of Ur, it had been a vital link in the trade routes linking Mesopotamia with Egypt. Only three Europeans had ever managed to visit it, and they had had to travel in disguise and secretly, because the desert that surrounded it positively bristled with ferocious Bedouin tribes. In 1750 two men called Wood and Dawkins had been the first to succeed in getting there, and the series of engravings that they subsequently produced fired the imagination of generations of travellers. Many people knew of its existence, but only one other person had definitely succeeded in making the trip, and that was Burckhardt, whom Lady Hester had met. He had been discovered by the Bedu, stripped naked and thrown out of the territory.

The very fact that Palmyra was so inaccessible and had never been seen by a European woman was enough to make it irresistible to Lady Hester, but there was another, more personal attraction for her as well. The last ruler of Palmyra had been a woman with whom Lady Hester found it rather tempting to identify. Queen Zenobia was a powerful political leader. She was also famed for her attractiveness, her limitless energy and her unusual mental powers. She was, in short, a woman very like Lady Hester and her story was dramatic. She had taken command of Palmyra and its territories when her consort, the previous ruler Odainatti, died in AD 266. Under her rule Palmyra's power spread all over the Middle East, culminating in the occupation of Egypt in AD 270. It was not long before Aurelian, the Roman Emperor, realizing that the Palmyrenes were getting too powerful, began a series of campaigns against Palmyra's garrisons. At a crucial confrontation at Emesa, Zenobia herself went to battle, but lost, and retreated to Palmyra for safety. Aurelian followed her and laid siege to the city, finally forcing Zenobia and her son to flee for their lives. They were captured on the banks of the Euphrates in AD 272 and imprisoned in Tibur, where Zenobia spent the rest of her life. Although deprived of their leader, the Palmyrenes revolted against Roman rule, but with devastating results. Aurelian returned to Palmyra, massacred the population and destroyed the city.

When Lady Hester was living in London, well before she set out on her travels, she had been greatly intrigued by a prophecy that had been made for her by a man called Richard Brothers, who was an inmate of Bedlam. He had predicted that she would go to Jerusalem, spend seven years in the desert, and be crowned Queen of the East. It was tempting for Lady Hester to see a special significance in the quite separate and spontaneous rumours now circulating around Damascus that she was, in fact, a Queen, and she was also privately intrigued by the similarities between herself and Zenobia. She was far too intelligent to take the comparison too seriously, and there were times when she laughed at herself for even thinking about it, but the genuine affinity she was beginning to feel for the Muslim people, combined with the very real power she was beginning to exert amongst them, was an intoxicating mixture. Could it possibly be, she asked herself, that she was to become another Queen of the Desert? For now, however, it was simply romantic speculation, but one in which even Michael was

3rd Earl Stanhope, Lady Hester's father.

Chevening House, Kent.

Philip Stanhope, Lady Hester's half-brother; 'charming, incomparable Mahon'.

Lady Hester Stanhope, a portrait from memory.

William Pitt, the younger, Lady Hester's uncle.

Sir John Moore.

Walmer Castle, Kent.

Michael Bruce, on the left, at the time of his trial for
helping Count Lavalette escape from a French prison.

Prince Pückler Muskau, one of Lady Hester's admirers.

Türkisches Militär.

The Janissaries of Constantinople.

caught up. He wrote of Lady Hester to General Oakes in March, just before they were finally to leave for Palmyra – 'Who knows but she may prove another Zenobia, and be destined to restore it to its ancient splendour?'

The preparations for the journey to Palmyra continued. There were two main difficulties to be overcome. Palmyra was surrounded by twenty miles of desert which had to be traversed. This problem of transport and provisioning was calculable: thorough planning of the expedition would ensure they ran no risk of being stranded or of running out of food. The second problem was not so easily solved. The desert was full of unpredictable and hostile Bedouin tribes. Living as nomads, they were completely unanswerable to rule from Constantinople – they were, literally, outside the law. As direct descendants of the Bedu who had lived in the area since pre-Biblical times, they quite understandably regarded the desert as their own property, and reserved the right to deal with 'trespassers' as they saw fit. The only people they killed, on the whole, were those rash enough to come into the desert armed and aggressive, but the Bedu were not averse to a spot of robbing, and sometimes liked to take people hostage in return for large sums of money. The desert was therefore not a safe place for a rich foreign lady to be.

The first plan Lady Hester hatched with the help – and hindrance – of her new friends was to go to Palmyra under the protection of the Bedouin Arabs, but the Pasha and his Ministers objected to this. It was far too dangerous, they said; the Bedu were an untrustworthy lot and besides, they were the Pasha's enemies, and Suleiman could not let it be thought that they were offering her more hospitality than he himself. She should, he decided, be accompanied by a small body of his own men who would be heavily armed. Lady Hester was happy to accept the idea, but when the number of her escort was inexplicably raised to 1,000 men, she had to decline his offer for the expense would have been ruinous. Lady Hester later discovered that he had been threatened by Mahannah, the chief of the Anizi tribes of Bedu Arabs, who owned the land on which Palmyra was built. Although the balance of power in the desert was always in a state of flux, Mahannah was the most powerful leader in the whole area, and a considerable force to be reckoned with. The Bedu chief had threatened to cut off the Pasha's beard and strip all his men naked if he took Hester into the desert. He said that the desert was his, so the honour of escorting Lady Hester should be his also. Rather than risk his beard and total humiliation, the unheroic Pasha speedily withdrew his offer to accompany Hester to Palmyra, leaving her once more undecided about her plans.

The Pasha had other things on his mind, more pressing, perhaps, than Lady Hester's schemes. Whilst he had been negotiating with her, an alarming rumour had been heard that 40,000 Wahabees, led by the famous Ibn Saud, were on the march from the Arabian peninsula. They were said to be ransacking and burning every village on the way, and their destination was Damascus. The Wahabees had tried to take Damascus once before and had only been repulsed after a furious battle. The Pasha was extremely worried, especially because he had dissension in his own ranks. He had somehow managed to offend his Delibaches, who were under the command of the son of the previous, deposed Pasha. The infantry, who were composed of Albanians, were on the present Pasha's side, and relations between the two vast units of men were tense. 'Every day a battle is expected,' Lady Hester wrote in October.

The situation was made even more volatile by the fact that the Anizis, the strongest group of Bedouin Arabs, disliked the current Pasha, and automatically joined any faction who opposed him. The threat of the Wahabees may have helped to prevent the internal squabble from erupting, however, for if they attacked they would be indiscriminate in whom they killed – Delibache or infantryman. The outcome was rather an anti-climax. Lady Hester told the Pasha she was sure that no Wahabees would materialize and, as usual, she was right. The argument between the Pasha and his Delibaches was resolved and order was restored.

Michael had not been having a very enjoyable time in Aleppo. He had missed having a male companion when Lord Sligo left and the only good thing that had happened whilst he was away was that he had become good friends with Mr Barker, the British Consul-General in the Levant.

When he and Mr Barker heard that Hester was poised to leave for Palmyra, they decided that she couldn't possibly make the journey on her own, and set out for Damascus immediately. They were both horrified to discover that she had been planning to go with only a small escort, and Michael sent a barrage of messages saying she must wait for them and that they must all travel with a large caravan, which would be much safer. Hester replied promptly and firmly, telling him that even if there were a caravan going in the right direction she had absolutely no intention of joining one. This alarmed Michael so much that he replied with instructions that she must travel in a contraption called a tartaravan, which he and Mr Barker would bring with them from Aleppo. A tartaravan was a kind of sedan chair drawn by mules, and nothing could have been calculated to appeal to Hester less. She was a superlative rider, and, knowing her as he did, it is quite staggering that Michael should have even given the idea a second thought: perhaps Mr Barker's influence was at work.

Hester's reaction was predictable: 'What an absurd idea,' she scoffed. She could see exactly what would happen in the event of attack: 'to be stuck upon a machine, the tartaravangees running away and leaving you to the mercy of two obstinate mules.' She was completely vindicated in refusing both propositions when, only a few days later, a large caravan passing between Homs and Damascus was attacked even though it had fifty armed guards. Sixteen people were killed. 'Who is right?' she demanded. 'I, or the Consul-General?' She knew where she would rather be in an emergency, and it was astride 'the swiftest horse one can find'.

Hester was furious at this high-handed interference in her plans. 'It seems very cross to be angry at people being anxious about you,' she wrote in November, 'but had Bruce and Mr. Barker made less fuss about my safety, and let me had perfectly my own way, I should have been returned by this time from Palmyra.'

All these delays meant that it was now too close to the unpredictable winter months for safety, so the expedition was postponed. Just as she was wondering what her next step should be, Lady Hester received a visit from a young Bedouin called Nasar, who was Mahannah's eldest son. He had come to invite Lady Hester to stay for a few days in the desert with his father and his tribes. He was eloquent, polite and charming. 'Instead of the ferocious animals she had been taught to expect,' Meryon later wrote, 'Her Ladyship saw in the Bedouins a well-bred people, apparently dignified in their sentiments, and who, in bidding her repose confidence in them, knew how to inspire it.'

Nasar indicated that he and his father would also like to provide

Lady Hester's escort to Palmyra. 'To a personage like you,' he said, 'the road is open wherever you choose to go. We know what is due to an illustrious princess.' He admitted that they often robbed travellers in the desert, 'but only those who come armed against us'. Others they treated differently: 'Towards those who claim the rights of hospitality from us we know how to exercise them.'

Hester was very impressed by the young man, and decided that she would accept his father's invitation. If her stay with Mahannah was a success then she would also accept his offer to escort her.

Now that she was no longer relying on the Pasha for help in crossing the desert, Hester decided it would be better to spend the winter at a town called Hamah, situated on the River Orontes, halfway between Damascus and Aleppo, and on the fringes of the Palmyran desert itself. It was much closer to Palmyra, and the Bedu occasionally came into the town to buy cloth and other essentials, so it would also be a good base from which to meet Mahannah. Michael and Mr Barker had left Aleppo by this time. Hester still felt extremely disgruntled with them, and was not inclined to be sympathetic when Mr Barker fell ill on the way back to Damascus. Sending Dr Meryon to help Michael nurse the Consul-General back to health, she made what she called an 'experiment on the good faith of the Arabs'. She went to Hamah and then into the desert, alone save for an interpreter and a few servants, and met the Arab chief Mahannah el Fadel, whose reputation was one of power and unyielding ferocity. Mahannah was a man of about fifty-five; with a large shaggy beard and bushy eyebrows. He was rather deaf, and made up for his lack of hearing with piercing eyes that missed nothing. With the exception of a fine vest of red and yellow striped 'Damasc satin', he was roughly dressed, like any of his men; the only tangible sign of his rank was that his tent was bigger than any of the others.

As a delicate compliment to her host Lady Hester dressed as the son of a Bedu chief and looked superb. She wore 'a Bedouin handkerchief' on her head 'bound on with a sort of rope made of camel's hair, a curly sheepskin pelisse, a white abba, with a little gold on the right shoulder, crimson loop and button, and two crimson strings to fasten it'. Mahannah was charmed. Meryon reported that when this fearsome chief saw 'a fair and elegant woman who had ventured upon those wastes where many a man has trembled to go, . . . and where he knew she had been taught to expect nothing but brutality, [he] looked on her with admiration'. More than that, he developed a respect and almost paternal affection for her, which guaranteed their subsequent safety in the desert, and always afterwards referred to her as one of his family.

Lady Hester was utterly entranced with Mahannah and his Bedu. She stayed with them for a week and marched for three days with his encampment. She was treated with the greatest respect and hospitality and the visit was completely unlike any experience she had ever had before.

'Horses and mares fed upon camel's milk,' she wrote afterwards. 'Arabs living upon little else except a little rice, and sometimes a sort of bread; the space around me covered with living things, 12,000 camels coming to water from one tribe only. The old poets from the banks of the Euphrates singing the praises and the feats of ancient heroes, children quite naked, women with lips dyed light blue and their nails red and hands all over flowers and designs of different kinds.'

Lady Hester felt an immediate and powerful affinity for the desert people which was entirely reciprocated: she felt that their pride, self-respect and independence in the face of utter poverty was the antithesis of the rich and corrupt Europeans who so lazily condemned her way of life, and who dismissed these same Arabs as savages. Her friend Mahannah was obeyed like a great King, although his appearance was as rough and unkempt as those of his people. Hester herself was treated as a Queen, which suited her perfectly. She was electrified by the feeling of power evoked in her by their unanticipated deference, rather as one might feel if a dangerous wild animal came to lie at one's feet. An emotional surge of something akin to love and gratitude reinforced the feelings of respect and admiration she felt for these untamed Bedouin people. She examined her feelings and used an example in an attempt to understand her unexpected exhilaration: 'to look around one, free as the air of the desert – to observe something like a flight of crows at a distance – to look proudly that way, move your hand, and in one instant see fifty lances spring in your defence; to see them return, exclaiming "schab –friends".' Multiply the number to 40,000, the size of Mahannah's tribe, and it was intoxicating stuff indeed.

And so began the last great love of her life. It started with the Bedu people, and although it was not confined to them, they were the embodiment of all that she sought to embrace for the rest of her days. What she fell in love with was a strange mixture. It was honour and chivalry; it was freedom tempered with integrity. But since she was as used to life with leaders in Downing Street as she now was with Pashas in Syria, these high ideals were inevitably mixed with something perhaps more human: the spice and intrigue of power.

CHAPTER TWELVE

'A most disagreeable winter'

Winter in Hamah was dismal. After a fine start the weather degenerated into the worst that had ever been known there. First it snowed heavily, and then it began to rain. It rained continuously for weeks, and so hard that the whole town was swamped. Houses fell down under the weight of water, killing their occupants, whilst others were drowned. It was impossible to travel from one area to another. The River Barada broke its banks, and water rose up out of the wells. Conditions were appalling.

Hester and Michael were cooped up with the rest of the party in a house that belonged to a powerful Delibache called Mulla Ismael. Hester liked him very much. 'He is a very jolly Turk,' she wrote, 'and has four wives here and, I believe, fifty women – so many that I cannot count them; they are all very good to me and less shut up than any women I ever saw in this country.' Many Pashas, jealous of Ismael's power, had tried to cut off his head, but none had succeeded, because apart from his influence he was very popular with the desert Arabs and had been able to take refuge with them twice. For this kindness he fed every Arab who came into Hamah. Unfortunately for Hester, Ismael's house, though grand, was no better equipped than the rest to keep out the rain. 'Every room is a pool,' she said. It was very trying.

The party had changed since Damascus. The dragoman who had been so frightened by Lady Hester's behaviour had been replaced by a man from Aleppo, M. Beaudin. He proved so invaluable that when he fell badly from his horse one day and had to take to his bed, the whole household became completely disorganized. Mr Barker was still with them, although at this stage Lady Hester did not like him. Later they were to become friends, but he had blotted his copybook with her before they had even met, when he tried to interfere with her plans for Palmyra, and she had not yet forgiven him. He had still not quite recovered from the recurring fever he had contracted on the way from Aleppo, but Lady Hester had no time for what she saw as hypochondria. He was a 'very troublesome patient', she declared, saying that his fever was still there only because 'he had fixed a certain term for its duration.' He recovered as fast as he was probably able, and departed for Aleppo, no doubt thankful to leave behind both the appalling weather and Hester's disapproval.

Mr Barker was not the only one to fall ill. The dreadful conditions led to general illness throughout the retinue of servants, and poor Mrs Fry developed pleurisy. She was very ill for a while, and the one person who could have speeded her recovery was not there. Dr Meryon was in the desert, tending Sheik Mahannah who was suffering from a chronic illness. Meryon had been thrilled to be sent for by the great Arab chief, and had made his preparations quickly, having been assured by Hester that it would be safe to go. She advised him to dress as poorly as he could, so as not to 'excite the cupidity of the Bedouin'. Not relishing the prospect of being set upon and robbed in the desert, the doctor agreed heartily and went to buy some rough clothes: 'two very coarse cotton shirts with long sleeves tapering to a point, a pair of cotton drawers which were to serve as breeches', and 'two tanned sheepskin pelisses, one long and one short'. This modest wardrobe was colourfully completed with a red skull cap, a green and orange *keffiyeh* or scarf, and, rather jollily, a pair of 'uncouth red boots'.

On 2 January 1813, Meryon set off through the floods in excellent spirits with Hassan, an Arab guide, and an interpreter called M. Lascaris. They were well mounted on stallions and each carried a bag of provisions. After travelling for two hours they entered the edge of the desert.

'That name does not imply always a sandy barrenness,' Meryon wrote, 'but rather the absence of towns and villages and the want of water and cultivation.' This first part of desert was a country of hills and plains, covered with flowers in the spring, but burnt up with heat by the autumn. Now, in mid-winter it was a bleak and barren-looking place. They passed the ruins of castles and empty villages, saw immense flights of birds and the occasional small herd of antelope. As they zigzagged deeper into the desert, looking for Mahannah and his tribe, the smooth plains became gravelled and rocky, and the hills gave way to craggy mountains. It took them several days to find Mahannah, and they came across various small Bedouin tribes on the way, with whom they spent the nights. On each occasion they were treated with civility and respect, especially when they let it be known that they were Lady Hester's friends. There was plenty of opportunity for Meryon to observe the customs of these nomadic people. He enjoyed the ceremonious making and drinking of coffee and marvelled at the sight and sounds of the returning herds of camels, goats and sheep at sunset.

'The musical call of the herdsmen, joined with the bleating and lowing of such vast numbers of animals, covering . . . a circle of a league, formed a pastoral scene that can nowhere be witnessed but with the Arabs.'

He watched the women cooking the evening meal of mutton, rice and flat, round cakes of bread, and was appalled, in his English way, by the lack of hygiene and manners. 'It cannot be denied that they approach nearer to beasts in their manner of eating than any other people,' he observed primly.

They continued the search for Mahannah, and finally, on about the fourth day, found him on a high plain in a small range of mountains. Meryon was greeted by Nasar, Mahannah's son, with kisses on each cheek, and taken in to the old chief's tent.

Meryon travelled with Mahannah and his tribes for eleven days, but despite the chief's unshakeable belief in the powers of Western medicines, he was unable to cure his illness. Realizing that a full cure was impossible, Meryon prepared to take his leave of the old man, but whenever he mentioned his plans, Mahannah 'grew out of humour' and demanded that first he be cured. When Nasar and his brothers then began, half-jokingly, to demand gifts from Meryon, he started to feel quite alarmed. He was only finally allowed to leave after he invoked Lady Hester's name, saying she would be most displeased if she heard that he had been detained against his will.

On the morning of 14 January, Meryon and his guide Hassan left Mahannah's encampment with relief. Since they were fairly near to Palmyra they decided to try and get there. Not only did Hassan's family live there, but Meryon wanted to make sure there was suitable housing for Lady Hester. They struck out in a north-easterly direction, and after a successful escape from a small band of rather incompetent would-be robbers, were soon within sight of Gebel el Abyad, the White Mountain that guards Palmyra. They crossed the vast salt-encrusted plain of El Mezah, which is bounded by Gebel el Abyad on the left and Mount Ayan on the right, and entered a narrow valley enclosed by small hills. Here they found the ancient reservoir that trapped the fountainhead of water that used to supply Palmyra. They then followed the route of the league-long aqueduct to the Valley of the Tombs, just outside the city.

By this time it was night, and the doctor found it an awesome experience to thread his way by moonlight past the ancient monuments to long-dead Palmyrans. The valley was a mile long, and as he and Hassan approached the angle in the hills from which the panorama of Palmyra would unfold before them, Meryon was taut with excitement. He could scarcely believe that he was finally going to see Palmyra, and it seemed almost perfect that his first sight of the fabled city was to be by moonlight. Poor Meryon. It was a huge anti-climax. The moonlight was not strong enough and he could see nothing. His feelings of disappointment were almost overwhelming, but he sensibly reminded himself that he was tired, hungry and thirsty, and that things would seem better in the morning. He and Hassan made their disconsolate way down to the longed-for but still unseen ruins, and finding Hassan's relatives, settled down in a mean mud hut for the night.

It is impossible to tell from the records whether or not Hester had asked Meryon to go to Palmyra on this trip. She had often sent Meryon ahead of her to arrange accommodation in new places, but her impending visit to Palmyra was so important to her that it seems strange that she would run the risk of tarnishing the glamour of her trip by sending Meryon there first. By now the journey to Palmyra had assumed giant proportions. She had written letters to Craufurd Bruce, General Oakes and many others about her intentions. Hundreds of people had become involved in her plans and preparations, and she was sufficiently determined to go to wait for months in Hamah under conditions of extreme discomfort. Unlikely as it seems, however, I think that Hester had indeed requested Meryon to go to Palmyra to arrange suitable housing for her. She probably rationalized it on two counts. The salient differences between her proposed trip and any that had gone before were that firstly, she was a European woman going where none had gone before, and secondly, that she intended to go not as 'a thief in the night', as all the others had gone, but with the highest possible profile. Another indisputable point was that Meryon was only able to go safely into the desert by using Hester's name. Using these criteria it seems likely that she did not perceive Meryon's trip as undermining the importance of her own. She would still be the first European woman to go to Palmyra: the triumph would still be hers. Meryon stayed in Palmyra for six days, and, surprisingly perhaps, was disappointed in what he saw. There, certainly, were the massive columns and stately temples he had expected, but to him they didn't look as impressive as those in the plates that Wood and Dawkins had produced. Situated as it is, at the foot of huge craggy mountains, he felt the city correspondingly diminished. He could see that the vast pillars carved from a single block of Egyptian granite were impressive, but to him they 'dwindled to the size of tapers' when seen from the distance of a few hundred yards. The glorious golden ochre of the stone was another dissatisfaction. 'The face of the soil is precisely the same hue,' he complained. 'Tints must be opposed to set each other off.' Perhaps he had been expecting too much; there was nothing to please him. He organized some houses to be prepared for Lady Hester, made one or two excursions, and returned to Hamah.

Lady Hester had been worried about Meryon, for he had been gone longer than she expected, so she was glad to see his safe return. When he had recovered from his journey he told her all about his experiences with Mahannah and of his stay in Palmyra. She made no comment; perhaps after all she was a little jealous. She had been having a very dull time. The weather was still appalling, and there had been only one European visitor to Hamah all winter. The only other company she and Michael had had was that of some dreary, deposed governors who had been exiled to Hamah. Michael had got hold of a copy of Adam Smith's *Wealth of Nations* which he had been trying to read, whilst Hester divided her time between letter-writing and keeping everybody's spirits up. She had become keenly interested in desert politics, and had several orderly Arabs who kept her well informed. 'I receive despatches every two or three days,' she wrote to Henry Williams Wynn in a marvellous rambling letter dated 15 January, 'giving me an account of what is going forward in the desert, of what battles have been fought, and with what tribes war has been declared etc. etc.' Good news for the Syrians was that Mecca had been recaptured from Ibn Saud's followers, the Wahabees, who had been forced to retreat to their own capital of Dariya. More sombre tidings had come from the coast, however – plague had come to Sidon, Acre and Tyre, and judging from past experience, would spread inexorably inland along the caravan routes.

Hester was unconcerned by threats of plague, she wanted news of her friends in England: 'Do tell me how you find [Ebrington], what is the matter with him and why so out of spirits? Dear creature that he is, when everybody loves him, how can he be unhappy? When you write to me fill a whole page about him for he writes me little squeezy letters, and says very little always about himself.' 'Tell me how dear old Sligo is,' she continued, and 'What is Taylor doing?' She also wrote revealingly of Syria: 'There are some men of great talents in this country, but, generally speaking, the greatest rascals upon the face of the earth. But you know I like rascals better than fools, the latter do about the same portion of mischief in the world and bore one to death besides.'

In a letter to Mrs Fernandez, the woman with whom she had stayed in Malta, she wrote amusingly of how Meryon had become almost more Arabic than the Arabs. 'Oh, I forgot to tell you that the gentlemen have all long beards, and the doctor is such a quiz you can have no idea of, his head shaved and a pigtail coming out of the crown a yard long, a copper-coloured sheepskin and a pipe, six feet long, never out of his mouth. He never stands two minutes and squats about all over the house,' she continued with glee, 'when in the air, pulls a mat after him to sit down upon, washes his hands every five minutes and always eats with his fingers.' Even allowing for the undoubted exaggeration, it seemed that Meryon had adopted Arabic ways with enthusiasm.

The long weeks dragged by and the weather showed no signs of abating. It had been a long time since they had received any mail, for there was plague in Constantinople, and no ships would call there for fear of catching and carrying the disease. A packet of mail finally arrived for them though, and there was much excitement. Their exhilaration at getting the letters was shortlived, however. The most important letter in the packet had taken eleven months to arrive, and was not a cheerful one.

Craufurd Bruce was having financial problems. He had spent a colossal amount of money in 1811 on buying estates all over England and Scotland, and somehow things had gone wrong. The money that Michael and Hester were spending was an additional drain on his pocket, and although he didn't mention his financial worries, he wrote to ask them to curtail their spending. He was also looking ahead to the time when Michael and, as he thought, Lady Hester would return to England. He foresaw massive problems. As he had done once before, Craufurd enclosed his letter to Michael with one to Hester, asking her to pass it on to him, or not, as she saw fit. Once again the compliment, and his trust in her, was enormous.

The letter was vastly long and very serious. He had received a visit from Lord Sligo, who had told him that Hester had refused to marry Michael. Craufurd was full of praise for Hester's motives: 'they were exalted and beyond what any other woman similarly situated and with the enthusiasm of affection she so unreservedly professes for you, would have been equal to,' he told Michael. The problem that he foresaw was that it was now too late for them to become a respectable married couple, even had Lady Hester wanted it. 'The world is in possession of your misconduct,' Craufurd wrote. Their social reception in England was going to be difficult or impossible: 'You must expect to have mortifying remarks made against you ... your line of conduct will often be most difficult ... what caution and reserve will it not often be required on your part, to avoid discussion, to abait the spirit of resentment and keep in bounds of moderation, when the babbling Blockheads of the World will tell their story.'

Despite the problems it had created, Craufurd admired Hester's strength in refusing to marry his son, and the next part of his letter showed what an utterly honourable man he was. 'Your honour is pledged,' he told his eldest son. 'You have entered into an engagement more binding, more sacred to a feeling mind than all that the ritual of the Church can give to the ceremony of marriage. In short, my friend, I speak it with a deep anguish of heart ... you cannot now ever marry another woman. Lady Hester has a sole and entire claim on you, and if you was to forsake or desert her I should depreciate you as an ungrateful and unfeeling, I can almost add, bad character.'

What agonizing and heartache must have gone into this letter to his beloved son. Craufurd could see no way out of the dilemma. His feelings of honour and respect for Hester were so strong that he would deprive Michael of any legitimate heirs rather than do wrong by her. The only possible solution could be if Hester were to voluntarily and willingly revoke all claims on Michael which she had said she would do in her original letter to Craufurd in 1810. She had promised to give Michael up to 'some thrice-happy woman', but Craufurd genuinely could not believe that she would be able to do this, nor did he expect her to.

His sense of loyalty towards his wife and her position in society was also strong. He had decided that when Michael and Hester came back to England, however high his respect and admiration for Hester was, he could not invite her to live under his roof: it would be asking too great a sacrifice of his wife, because she too then would be involved in the scandal.

Michael and Hester replied separately to this gloomy letter. They both knew that Craufurd was a very wealthy man, but since he hadn't confided in them about his financial losses they were at a loss to understand his worry about their overspending. All the money that Michael drew was his father's, however, and they respected that, and had no wish to abuse his generosity. They promised that, although too much time, effort and money had been invested already in the expedition to Palmyra to cancel it now, as soon as they returned from the desert all excessive expenditure would cease.

Their responses to the more complex emotional content of the letter reflected well on them both. Michael showed a new, calm maturity as he gently rebuked his father. Referring to his father's decision not to let Hester live in his house, Michael reproved, 'This was not very kind, nor was it called for. It is not doing justice to that conduct which has every claim upon your admiration and gratitude.' He went on, 'It ought to be remembered that this is no common case. There has been no seduction, no binding promises, none of the artifices usually practised by the sex, but it is that of a woman who has refused marriage, the only compensation in my power to offer, and an honour to which I had no right to aspire.' He accepted Craufurd's decision, but regretted it. 'The world may condemn, because the world are ignorant of all the circumstances, but its opinion ought never to influence your actions.' He had been away from society, and under Hester's slightly anarchic influence for so long that perhaps he had forgotten what social pressures could be like.

Hester replied to Craufurd with calmness and dignity. Nothing had changed for her. 'The promise I made you in my first letter I shall religiously keep. I should not have made it had I known myself incapable of performing it, & this appears to me to be all you need be anxious about. . . . The line of conduct I have laid down for myself I shall follow,' she continued, 'and it does not even depend upon B [Michael] to make me deviate from it.'

Lady Hester was utterly confident about reiterating her promise to Craufurd because she had come to a private decision, one that she had shared with no one, least of all Michael. She had decided quite unequivocally that when he returned to England he would go alone: she would stay in Syria, and it would be the end of their relationship.

There was a host of reasons behind this decision. On the positive side, she had discovered a new independence for herself; up until now she had always relied on other people for her emotional security. First it had been her father, then her grandmother, then William Pitt and afterwards Sir John Moore. At the beginning of her relationship with Michael he too had provided her with an emotional stability, but as time went by, her need for that particular support had grown less. The period of her affair with Michael had seen a major change in her image of herself. She was no longer a person to whom things happened, she had become a person who controlled her own life, who made things happen, and naturally she liked it. Michael had been a very large part of that change, but, as sometimes happens in relationships, she had changed faster than he had, and they had, to a certain extent, grown apart. She was grateful to him for the happiness they had shared, and she would always love him, but she was no longer blindly in love with him. She could see his faults now, and they had begun to irritate her occasionally.

Michael was not such an analytical person as Hester, and he still seemed to be besotted with her. 'My dearest love,' he had written to her only months before, 'if anything were to happen to you I would take a vow to spend the rest of my days in the desert.' A declaration of love indeed, for Michael could see no attractions at all in the barren wastes of the desert, and this illustrated another chasm that was widening between them. Michael still liked comfort and good living, whereas Hester, whilst perfectly at home in the most luxurious surroundings, was finding herself increasingly attracted to a more ascetic way of life. 'I respect poverty and independence,' she had declared, and the desert Arabs personified that particular dignity to her.

Hester knew that if she were to state her case to Michael now, it would have disastrous effects. Firstly, he would be very distressed: he seemed still to love her very much, and he was also a romantic who believed in the importance of love. Secondly, as an honourable young man he would be caught in a dreadful dilemma. He would feel compelled to make promises and vows that Hester would not want to hear. She was wise. She said nothing, deciding to wait at least until after the trip to Palmyra. Perhaps something would happen to make any dramatic announcements unnecessary.

CHAPTER THIRTEEN

Palmyra

The trip to Palmyra was imminent. All the arrangements had been made and Mahannah had promised his protection to Lady Hester and her party. Although he commanded many thousands of Bedu, there was still a considerable element of danger, because he was constantly at war with another vast and fragmented tribe called the Faydans, and it was these Arabs that might cause trouble, for they were known to be in the area. The danger was all the greater because of the rumours that had spread concerning Lady Hester's wealth. It was said that she rode a fabulously valuable horse using stirrups of solid gold and that she received a thousand sequins, or gold coins, daily from the English Sultan's treasurer. It was also rumoured that she had a book with her that showed where treasure might be found at Palmyra, and that she possessed a herb that transmuted stones into gold.

A few days before they were to leave, Mahannah visited Lady Hester in Hamah to finalize the arrangements. She had agreed to pay him the sum of 3,000 piastres, the equivalent then of £300, to ensure their protection from the Faydans, and to help guard against the annoying habit all Bedouin had of appropriating other people's belongings. One third was to be paid in advance, and the other two thirds on their safe return from Palmyra.

Mahannah's tribe, the Anizis, consisted of many smaller groups of Arabs who were ruled by lesser chiefs, from whom they got their individual names. Thus peoples like the Beni Hez, the Beni Kaleds, and the Sebah tribes were independent, but also part of the Anizis. As part of Hester's protection Mahannah decided to range a selection of these tribes along the route to Palmyra, each to be within a few hours ride of the next. In case of attack, Hester and her friends, who were all mounted on strong, fast horses, should be able to escape to the comparative safety of a nearby Anizi encampment.

On 20 March 1813, Lady Hester set off for Palmyra at the head of a huge entourage. Months of planning and six weeks of intensive provisioning meant that nothing had been overlooked. The road out of Hamah was packed with people who had come to see the great English Lady ride into the desert. Many cheered as she rode past, whilst others moaned and wailed, convinced that she was riding to her death. Others still had come out of sheer curiosity; the crowds were so dense that dragomen had to clear the road to let the procession through. It was a tremendous affair.

All the party, even the long-suffering Mrs Fry, were dressed as Bedouin Arabs. Hester rode at the front with Nasar and one of his brothers, who had provided a dozen of their bravest men as her personal bodyguard. They were an exotic-looking band as Meryon showed in his description: 'their long lances plumed with ostrich feathers, their curling hair hanging in ringlets over their cheeks and neck, their gay-coloured keffiyahs drawn over their mouths like vizors . . . everything about them was novel and calculated to set the fancy of all of us to work, as to where we were going and what would be the issue of our journey.'

Behind this elite group came the rest of Lady Hester's personal caravan. Forty camels carried every conceivable type of provision including, most importantly, water. There were twenty horsemen – dragomen and Mamelukes, valets, cooks and tent-pitchers, grooms and slaves. An armed escort of Arabs rode at either side of the column, and Dr Meryon and Michael brought up the rear. Hester had tried to convince Michael that it was essential to security that he ride at the back but he was not over-excited at his relegation, and was in a cross, sarcastic mood. The simple truth was that Michael and Nasar were profoundly incompatible: Hester was forced to keep them apart, and Nasar, as their guide and host in the desert, would have to be in front. Michael had never liked the Bedu. He thought they were an unreliable, dirty bunch of thieves, to whom he was infinitely superior. Not surprisingly the Bedu didn't like him either, and Mahannah had underlined this by warning that if Michael were to go into the desert without

Lady Hester he would cut off his head. Having had the two parties
declare themselves in this way, it was sensible of Lady Hester to
separate the two arrogant young men. Had they ridden together a
quarrel or fight would have been inevitable, and Hester would have
been forced into the role of mediator, which she did not want. She was
embarking on the grandest adventure of her life, and she wanted to
enjoy it. It was a beautiful spring day as the caravan wound its way out
of Hamah. The camels padded ponderously along watching the horses
who, infected by the mood of excitement, were inclined to prance and
frolic. Hamah was soon left behind, and the procession headed for the
desert, following the curved banks of the Orontes where the almond
trees that had survived the winter weather were in full and glorious
blossom. Hester was in scintillating form, Nasar was entranced by her
and the first day seemed to pass very quickly.

It was impossible to reach the desert in one day, so they spent the
first night in a tiny village called Genan. Almost as soon as they
arrived, Dr Meryon was called to the bedside of a dying man. Even as
he was trying to explain to the onlookers that it was too late, the man
died, and their first night was interrupted by the immediate funeral. It
was not too onerous an affair, as Meryon described it. Four or five
professional mourners with whitened faces and dishevelled hair performed a funeral dance 'with sabres in their hands . . . accompanied by
occasional howls'. Mrs Fry was far more distressed by the number of
rats in the cottage she was sharing with Lady Hester. As once before in
Rhodes after the shipwreck, Hester slept happily in amongst the
rodents, whilst poor Mrs Fry sat outside for most of the night, wide
awake and shivering.

The next day they entered the desert. The copious rains of winter
that had wreaked such damage in Hamah had brought about the
yearly miracle in the stony, scrubby desert lands. Millions upon millions of seeds that had lain dormant since last summer's scorching heat
had burst into life. The rolling hills were smothered with a luxurious,
rippling carpet of grass and flowers that stretched as far as the eye
could see. Picking their way through this living tapestry of colour,
Hester and her retinue made for their second stopping place: an
encampment of the small tribe of Beni Hez, a ride of seven hours. They
spent this second night under canvas, and everyone felt that the
expedition had truly begun.

The Bedu of Lady Hester's day lived exactly as they had in Biblical times, and as they have continued to do right up until the discovery of oil around the Arabian Gulf. The pivot around which their lives revolved was their animals, of which the camel was perhaps the most useful. Camels were their beasts of burden, carrying the women and children and every other good and chattel an Arab might possess. They provided milk to drink, meat to eat; tents and rugs were made of their hair, and it was said that a drop of camel urine would purify even the most dubious water. Goats and sheep were also an important part of the Bedu's life, but the most important animal of all to a Bedouin was his horse.

Every Arab boy was brought up to appreciate the finer points of a horse, and to be a daring and skilful rider – a necessity when most tribes were constantly involved in petty warfare with their neighbours. Many desert Arabs owed their lives to a quick getaway. They were amazed and impressed to see a grand English Lady who was as skilled and as knowledgeable as they, and this mutual love and appreciation of horses provided an instant bond between the Bedu and Lady Hester that was far more genuine than the spurious affection engendered by expensive gifts.

On the third day of travelling Lady Hester and her caravan reached the ancient wells of Keffiyah where Mahannah's tents were pitched. A great feast had been prepared for them of roast camel, rice, huge bowls of yoghourt and flat, unleavened bread. Many Bedu leaders had come in from outlying areas to meet the English Queen who came bearing gifts. As men whose chief recreation was making war, they were hugely interested in a Frankish leader they had heard about – Napoleon. They had been taught by the Turks to fear invasion from Russia, and had decided that the French Army under the command of such a great leader would be their best defence. They were probably the strangest group of politicians that Lady Hester had ever met, but she sat with them for many hours and told them all the news she had; they sat discussing European and Arabian politics until late into the night.

The fact that so many Bedu chiefs had come to see Lady Hester showed that it was common knowledge that she was in the desert, so the risk of attack from the Faydan was very great. On the next leg of the journey therefore, Nasar sent out his best scouts both in front of and to either wing of the caravan, and Hester was provided with an enormous black slave armed with a huge battle-axe and a ferocious scowl to stand guard over her tent at night. He was so menacing that he frightened everybody – even those he was supposed to be protecting. The journey was not dull. Nasar's men entertained the caravan by performing mock fights with each other, and sometimes in the evenings two of them would recite poetry and tell epic stories of brave deeds.

Each night, after the bustle of encamping was over, Lady Hester would hold an audience, calling into her tent those to whom she wished to speak. Nasar had been called every evening and had always responded with alacrity. On the fifth day, however, perhaps succumbing to taunts from his men about taking orders from a woman, the young Arab decided to test Lady Hester to see whether or not she was really worthy of his respect. When he was summoned to her tent he sent a message back to her saying that he was the son of a Prince and that if she wished to speak with him she could come to his tent, not he to hers. The servants were most alarmed, and when Nasar's men started hinting that if their chief was displeased perhaps they would all have to turn back, the whole camp was buzzing. Lady Hester reacted in the best possible way by doing absolutely nothing. She adopted an air of sublime indifference to the whole matter, and although she quietly warned her servants to be on their guard that night, the whole rebellion fizzled out. Nasar was thwarted.

He tried again the following evening. Crying out that the Faydan were near and had stolen some of their mares, Nasar and all his men leapt on their horses and vanished into the night, leaving Hester and her party suddenly and completely alone. It was a critical situation: Hester had no idea whether or not Nasar was bluffing or even if he and his men would come back. They were totally vulnerable. Without a guide they didn't know where they were or where the next waterhole was, and if the Faydan were really there, they could have attacked at any moment. It would have been easy to panic, but according to Michael, Hester 'remained as calm as if in a ballroom'. She ordered everyone to take up their muskets and stationed them all around the little encampment. In less than twenty minutes, however, Nasar reappeared rather sheepishly with an unlikely story of having seen off their enemies. Hester maintained a dignified silence about the whole affair; her bravery had been tested and not found wanting. Nasar gave her no more trouble.

By now they were nearing Palmyra. The smooth rolling hills of the outer desert had given way to the rocky wastes and towering mountains of the more desolate interior. As they entered the range of mountains that lay between them and their goal, they came across a huge tribe of Sabah Bedouin moving in search of pasture. Thousands of the nomadic people mounted on camels and horses spilled down from a high mountain pass and flooded onto the plain, followed by scores of young unladen camels and colts that scampered after their mothers like puppy dogs. The tribe had come from an area so remote that they had no conception of there being people who did not understand Arabic, and they were astounded to see a white woman. Hester and her friends were equally amazed at the Sabahs' appearance. The women had heavily tattooed faces and rode in massive saddles shaped like the skull and horns of a ram, and the tribe as a whole were so pared down by poverty, wind and weather, that they seemed almost a race apart from humans.

Shortly after this encounter Meryon left the party to ride ahead to Palmyra with two guides to make sure all was ready for his employer. It was a hard, fast ride of many hours for the three horsemen. They dared not stop for fear of being set upon by unfriendly Arabs, and Meryon was almost left behind by his guides. 'My horse grew sluggish,' he wrote. 'I hallooed to them but they would not pull up and I found that I had no resource but in the use of my stirrups, whose sharp corners I drove repeatedly into my horse's sides.' The exhausted travellers finally arrived safely at Palmyra and the next morning, having supervised the cleaning of some housing for Lady Hester, Meryon set out once again to meet her in her approach to the ancient, ruined city.

He rode out once more through the Valley of the Tombs and found a vantage point on top of a 'small mountain' overlooking the plain across which Lady Hester's caravan was to approach. He saw a great cloud of dust in the distance which seemed to be moving slowly towards him, but was greatly puzzled as to what it might be, for the slow-moving caravan did not create anything like such a disturbance. After an hour's anxious wait he was able to see the cause of it: it was indeed the caravan, but surrounded by frenzied horsemen charging to and fro, shooting wildly in all directions. 'My mind misgave me,' he wrote tremblingly, 'I thought that Lady Hester and her party were attacked by the enemy.' As he watched fearfully, straining his eyes across the vast distance, he could see increasingly clearly that a major skirmish was indeed going on, but that the caravan was advancing steadily, and, pathetically, 'no dead or dying were left by the way.'

Quite unable to understand what was happening, he bravely went down onto the plain to meet the caravan. 'My apprehension did not subside until I joined them,' he said, and he was finally able to see what was happening. A great group of Palmyrans had gone out to greet Lady Hester, and were performing a mock attack to impress and welcome the great English Lady. Fifty horsemen 'galloping in all directions, with rude kettledrums beating and colours flying' were accompanied by fifty men on foot 'who, naked down to the waist, without shoes, stockings or breeches and covered only with a sort of antique petticoat, ran by their side and kept pace with them'. Meryon noted with slight alarm that they 'fought with a pretended fury that once or twice might almost have been thought real'.

Meryon was hugely relieved that Lady Hester was in no danger, and, with his usual attention to detail, observed the Arabs closely. 'The tanned skins of the men on foot formed a curious contrast with the cowry shells, or blackamoor's teeth, studded on the two belts which crossed their shoulders, and to which were suspended their powder-flasks and cartouche-boxes.' The Palmyrans were fierce fighters and constantly at war with the Bedu who plundered the great salt caravans that went from Palmyra to Hamah and Baghdad. An unspoken truce had been called between them on this occasion, but neither side could quite resist the odd bit of foul play. 'Many were the severe pokes the poor footmen got from the lances of the Arabs,' the doctor observed rather anxiously, 'and in return, many a bruise did they receive from the stones that were hurled at them by the Palmyrans.'

This exciting and rather alarming entertainment continued until they entered the Valley of the Tombs, when Hester decided that she wanted to see rather more than the swirling clouds of dust would allow. They passed quietly through the sombre valley, threading their way past the vast mausoleums and more humble graves. Approaching the vantage point from which Palmyra would first be seen, and which the unfortunate Meryon had reached in darkness, Lady Hester was gripped with excitement. At last she was going to see Zenobia's ancient city that had obsessed her for so long.

Finally rounding the last corner, there it was, and unlike Meryon, she was not disappointed. The great golden city lay sprawled in magnificent disarray below her, seeming to stretch to the horizon. The vast classical columns with which Solomon had embellished the city lay where they had fallen more than seventeen centuries before, when the Roman Emperor Aurelian had destroyed the city to break the spirit of the Palmyran people. Very few structures of value had escaped his ravages. One of these, the Temple of the Sun, rose massively from the ruins on the far side of the city, and closer at hand there was the gracious sweep of colonnade terminating in Zenobia's triumphal arch, built to commemorate her taking of Egypt. All else was devastation, but the breadth of vision that had inspired the building of the city and the knowledge of the sheer length of its recorded history gilded the ruined city with a dignity that was felt by everyone present.

The people of Palmyra had prepared a magnificent welcome for Lady Hester, one which perhaps echoed the reception they would once have given their Queen Zenobia. They poured out to greet her and guided her along the vast crumbling colonnade towards the triumphal arch, the first European woman ever to set foot in the city. On each huge column the marks of cramp irons on small projecting consoles showed that marble statues had once stood there. In the place of each of these long-gone statues stood a young, beautiful Palmyran girl, draped in robes and posed in a classical stance. Each of the living statues carried a garland in her hand and remained motionless as Lady Hester rode by. 'When she had passed,' Meryon later wrote, 'they leaped on the ground, and joined in a dance by her side.' Surrounded by a growing throng of rejoicing people, Hester finally reached the triumphal arch where she was greeted by yet more girls bearing palms, and one, suspended over the arch, held a crowning wreath over Lady Hester's head. The Palmyrans formed a circle around her, 'the men and the maids intermixed, they danced around her singing by turn in her praise, whilst all the spectators joined in chorus.' Poets 'from the banks of the Euphrates' sang odes and played upon their instruments. 'I have seldom seen a sight which moved my feelings more,' Meryon wrote, and Hester herself was deeply touched. It was a tumultuous, joyous mêlée of welcome, and Lady Hester truly felt she had been given a royal greeting. The prophecy that said she would be crowned Queen of the Desert had been fulfilled.

Although she had little interest in archaeology, Lady Hester was fascinated by the ancient city. Armed with the plates of Wood and Dawkins, she set off on horseback around the ruined acres. To allay the Palmyran's fears that she was looking for treasure she invited their leader to accompany her, and rode off at a tremendous pace, but he was on foot and he soon begged to be excused saying he could go no further. She continued to explore every day, scrambling over huge broken blocks to reach hidden places. 'Her Ladyship visited everything,' the admiring Meryon wrote in a long letter to Lord Sligo, 'climbing up into places almost inaccessible to a woman.' She went with Michael and the doctor to examine the sanctuary in the centre of the Temple of the Sun. There were no windows or doors and they had to crawl in through a tiny hole, but once inside were able to admire, by the light of torches, several bas-reliefs and two wonderful ceilings covered with signs of the zodiac.

There was a wedding whilst they were in Palmyra and Lady Hester was invited to watch the bathing ceremony that was customary for all Muslim brides. This took place at the Fountain of Ephca, a hot sulphurous spring that arose in a 'vaulted grotto' and spilled out in a quick, deep stream through an archway to a pool below. The bride and her attendants undressed in the cave, which, as Meryon surmised, 'cost them but little trouble, for they wore only one covering . . . a shift of coquelicot-coloured [poppy-red] silk, with white diamond spots like India handkerchiefs'. Having bathed, the laughing women all came shooting out under the arch, and splashed down the stream of water like a playful string of shiny brown seals. It sounded so delightful that Hester might have been tempted to join in. Perhaps she did. At any rate she naughtily described the morning's activities to the men that evening in such a way that made them 'laugh exceedingly'.

They spent several more days exploring the vast stretches of ruins before a rather worrying incident made them decide to return to Hamah immediately. Four Faydan Bedouin had been caught skulking outside the city and although they had been stripped naked and locked up, two of them had managed to escape and make their way back to their tribe. Nasar was furious, and, convinced a Faydani attack was imminent, decided they must leave the next day. Before they went, Hester sent her interpreter to talk to the two remaining prisoners who sent a message saying she need have no fear of the Faydans. They said that whilst it was true that they would attack the Anizis wherever and whenever possible, they 'set [Lady Hester] on their heads'. This was an expression indicating absolute devotion to the service of another, and Hester was touched and delighted. It was confirmation of what she had already realized: she was probably the only person in the Levant, or indeed the world, who could go anywhere in the deserts of the Near East not only with safety, but with veneration.

She had no wish to risk the lives of Nasar and his men, however, even if she herself was in no danger, so the party left for Hamah as planned, and had an exciting ride back through the desert, anticipating ambush around every hill.

All the Bedouin tribes of the desert knew by now that Lady Hester had been to Palmyra, and those that were friendly to the Anizis gathered along her route to meet her and pay their respects. She was regally entertained by so many sheiks that she quite lost count. The Beni Khalids, the Hadidiens, 'the Melhem, the Beni Hez, the Beni something else,' she wrote to General Oakes – the list was endless. Her first impressions of the Bedu were totally reinforced. 'They are the most singular and wonderfully clever people I ever saw,' she declared, 'but require a great deal of management for they are more desperate and more deep than you can possibly have an idea of. . . . Respecting etiquette and politeness, these people certainly far exceed even the Turks, but for eloquence and beauty of ideas (though one can hardly be a judge of it) they undoubtedly are beyond any other people in the world.' Praise indeed, and small wonder that she was content to be called their Queen.

The party returned to a massive welcome in Hamah where vast crowds that she estimated to be 10,000-strong gave Lady Hester a hero's reception. She and her party had spent thirty days alone with the Bedu in the desert, a feat that 'not a pasha in all Turkey durst venture to do with all his troops at his heels'. It was a real triumph, and perhaps the single most easily identifiable achievement of Lady Hester's life in the East.

No sooner had they reached Hamah, however, than their elation was eclipsed by an ominous and deadly cloud. Everywhere people were dying. Since Lady Hester had left Damascus, 100,000 people had perished in that city alone. No one knew what caused the disease, how it was spread or how to cure it. They only knew what it was called. *La peste* – the plague. It was raging all over the country and was totally out of control.

CHAPTER FOURTEEN

Plague and the parting

According to Meryon, Lady Hester was still not a healthy woman. Although everyone in the party had been complimented on their 'improved good looks' when they returned from Palmyra, the journey had required a lot of stamina, and Meryon wrote of Hester that 'her spirit rather than her physical powers helped her to surmount so much fatigue and to endure so many privations. Her pursuit was indeed health, but the phantom fled before her.'

As soon as they had returned to Hamah the doctor was besieged by the sick: although the plague had not yet been identified in the town, there was an epidemic of 'bilious remittent fever' and everyone wanted to be cured by the English doctor. Michael's dragoman, M. Beaudin, gave everyone, including himself, a nasty fright by suddenly becoming ill after receiving some unfumigated letters from plague-ridden Acre. He was lucky – it was not the plague – and he recovered, but perhaps it helped Lady Hester to make up her mind to leave Hamah. She decided they would go to Latakia, a small town on the coast. There was no plague there, and they would be able to wait in comparative safety for a vessel to take them on either to Malta or Russia, depending on their plans.

On 10 May they set out for the coast. Taking the main part of their former entourage with them, they travelled in the cool of the evening, and rested during the heat of the day. The two guides that Lady Hester had employed were not happy with this arrangement; they had rather she journeyed in the early morning, reaching their destination by midday, for it was much easier to put up a tent in daylight. Dr Meryon watched indulgently as they tried to change her mind. They were unsuccessful of course, but it was good entertainment to see them try. Their route took them along a chain of mountains inhabited by the fierce Ansari Bedu who came down to meet Lady Hester one night. On another evening they made camp near the ruins of Apamea, a town nearly as ancient as Palmyra. As Meryon scrambled casually over the rocky hillside to wander among the ruins he had no idea that he was the first modern traveller to see them, and later regretted that he 'did not make so correct an account of them as I otherwise should have done'.

They travelled on, tormented by swarms of mosquitoes, until after twelve days they arrived at Latakia. Lady Hester and Michael settled into a 'spacious mansion' with high-vaulted rooms and enough stabling for fifty horses, whilst Dr Meryon found himself a more modest house nearby. When they ventured out, they were disappointed to see that Latakia was a dirty town and the inhabitants seemed to be more ragged and poor than in any other place they had visited. It was hard to understand why this should be when the immediate surroundings were so bountiful and pleasant. To the west lay the glittering Mediterranean with all its richness of harvest and trade, whilst the land that bounded Latakia on all other sides was unbelievably fertile and productive. The mountains were clothed with trees – sycamore, jujube and ancient, gnarled olive trees covered with fruit larger then they had seen anywhere else on their travels. The valleys were cultivated and filled with every kind of fruit and vegetable known to Europeans – and several more besides. The anomaly between the richness of the land and the apparent poverty of the inhabitants was one they were unable to solve.

The town consisted of three or four thousand people, of whom the Muslim majority seemed devout to the point of eccentricity. 'Every night several individuals might be seen parading the streets, bawling in a dissonant tone – "There is no other God but God",' shuddered Meryon, whilst others 'formed themselves into a ring, and imitated the cries and impassioned gestures of the howling dervishes'. This mystery was easier to unravel: an extremely zealous religious leader had recently arrived in town and professed himself shocked at the spiritual laxity he had found. In their keenness to make amends the bawlers and the howlers had simply overcooked it.

It soon became clear to Lady Hester that they would have to stay in Latakia until the plague that surrounded them died down. She wrote to Lord Sligo that 'to expect a frigate upon this coast till the plague is quite gone is out of the question, and to pop into a nasty infected ship would be folly'.

There was quite a lot of general illness in the town, and Dr Meryon was kept busy. Hester had an inflamed eye and was suffering from pains in her face, and the doctor himself had toothache. Any fevers were instantly suspect. Hester said, rather disparagingly, 'All these little ills are magnified into the plague . . . certainly people ought to be very careful, but that is quite a different thing from frightening themselves to death.'

It was difficult to know when the plague claimed its first victim in Latakia. Accurate diagnosis was not made any easier by the fatalistic attitude of the Muslims that not only inhibited them from disclosing the cause of any recent deaths, but also prevented them from taking any overt precautions against catching the disease. As spring lengthened into summer, however, it became evident that plague had indeed crept in. People were dying, and the bubonic swellings under their arms told their own story. Meryon wrote bleakly, 'it was not extraordinary that the plague should be in the town, but only that its presence could have been for a moment doubted.' Small boats and fishing craft from further along the coast had been entering harbour not only to trade but also to bury their dead. Warehousemen in the port were among the first to die, and from there the plague spread into the town.

The terrifying spectre that had swept over nearly all of Syria had cast its shadow over Latakia: the swiftly fatal plague for which there was no cure and whose mode of transmission was unknown. Amazingly, people seemed to get used to the idea that they could fall ill and die at any time, and apart from some local Christians shutting up their businesses, life went on much as usual. Those whose religious laws did not forbid it, practised what precautions they could, and a few were probably quite helpful. Some people shut themselves away and hoisted food in through an upstairs window. Others felt it safe to go out as long as they were not touched by anyone. Any sealed letters that passed hands were carefully slit through and fumigated, or scorched nearly to illegibility in an open flame. Some of the local traditions, however, seemed calculated to help the spread of any disease. Syrian

Christians believed that the underclothes of a sick person should not be changed from the onset of illness right through to recuperation or death, whilst the fatalistic Muslims regarded it as their duty to congregate around the sickbed, thus enabling any plague-carrying fleas to hop smartly onto a choice of new hosts.

For whatever reason, the dreaded disease did not get such a stranglehold on Latakia as it had on most other towns in Syria, but anyway, Lady Hester carried on with her life as if nothing were wrong. She rode out nearly every day on one of her horses, supervised her household and as always, wrote letters. In June Michael went to Aleppo to see his old friend Mr Barker, the consul of the town. He had been ill of a recurring fever, and while Michael was there, Hester wrote to him with medical advice for the invalid. The advice was sound, but the letter is of more interest as it is one of the first from Hester to Michael that has survived. It gives glimpses of the vast well of affection there was between the two of them: 'Pray take care of yourself and take medicine if you want it on the road and repose a day under a tree . . . Pray be careful on the road.' It also shows the humour and love: 'The poor sick horse is much better, but so thin and ugly. I think upon the whole vastly like me. God bless you dear love.'

Acting on Lady Hester's advice, Michael helped Mr Barker and his family to move out of Aleppo, to rest and recuperate in a small village called Phidio, a few hours' ride from Latakia. There he would have peace and quiet and clean air, and Dr Meryon would be able to attend to him if necessary.

Lady Hester wrote to many other friends that summer: Henry Williams Wynn in England, Stratford Canning in Constantinople, and General Oakes in Malta. Several letters went to Ibn Saud, the leader of the Wahabees. Hester was flirting with the idea of travelling down into the Arabian peninsula to visit him and his tribes. She had heard stories of the magnificence of his life at Dariya, of his dromedaries that could outrace any horse and of his legendary power in the vast desert once called Arabia Felix. It was just the kind of adventure that she loved to plan, but it would have needed more money than she had available: even as she wrote she knew it was impossible.

By now Lady Hester had been away from England for nearly three and a half years. It was eighteen months since she had left Constantinople to travel down to Cairo and only just over a year since she had landed in Jaffa. Her reputation in the Levant as a great and brave English milady had now reached new heights. The journey to Palmyra had proved her courage beyond all doubt, and the respect and honour she was paid by men of power wherever she went had led to a mantle of power settling around her shoulders. It was not at all an idle notion that she was now a woman of considerable influence. All through her journeys she had met and charmed the most powerful men in every town and city, and the network she had built up was one into which, if she wished, she could tap at any time. Her independence of spirit meant that she had no need of help on her own account, but now other people started to approach her to help them. One illustration of this is shown by some correspondence from M. Catafago, the consul she had met in Acre. He was having some trouble with the English agent there and had written to Constantinople for help, quoting Hester's name. Mr Pisani, the interpreter and Lady Hester's friend, had replied, and M. Catafago then wrote to Lady Hester asking for a letter of recommendation, and rejoicing in her 'generous protection'.

Requests for her to use her influence on other people's behalf became more and more frequent, and when the cause was just or Hester deemed the supplicant worthy enough, she did what she could.

This was a strange period for her. She was suffering a little from the anti-climax of having completed the Palmyran trip: it had shaped and dominated her life for so many months that it probably felt strange to be without an immediate goal. Superimposed on this was the strain of living in a town where there was plague, but there was something even more important than this playing on her mind. Dominating everything was the knowledge that soon Michael and she must part.

Some time in the previous months, she and Michael had received at least three letters from Craufurd Bruce. The letters have not survived, but it is obvious from subsequent correspondence that they urged Michael to return to Europe. Maybe Craufurd felt that Michael had been under Hester's sway for long enough, or perhaps he was frightened of his son catching the plague. Hester was unhappy to think that Craufurd wished Michael 'to scamper about the continent alone', but was prepared to go along with his wishes. In her first ever letter to Craufurd she had promised that she would let Michael go when the time came, and that time was now. 'It is your wish,' she wrote to

Craufurd in July, 'his duty to comply with it if possible, and mine to resign my own opinions.' Michael had no particular wish to go but he was torn. He was still in love with Hester, but he also loved and respected his father, besides which he was entirely financially dependent upon him. Hester, for her part, still loved Michael very much, but was certainly exasperated by his many annoying habits such as making silly faces and always slouching down in chairs with his feet up on the table.

Michael knew it was impossible to change Hester's mind once it was made up, and he realized, albeit rather grudgingly, that he owed a duty to his father, so he accepted the fact that he would have to return to England. Knowing they were soon to be parted, their love for each other became rejuvenated, and all minor irritations forgotten. They waited for a suitable ship to call to take Michael to Constantinople, but none came, for the plague was still present along the coast. Finally, in October, they had word from England that Craufurd's health was failing, and he was desperate to see his son. Now there could be no more waiting. Hester decided that Michael must leave overland for England and hope to avoid the plague on his travels. There was no other alternative. On 7 October 1813 he left, and they never saw each other again.

CHAPTER FIFTEEN

'Farewell, my once dearest B.'

'Nothing could have induced Mr. Bruce to have gone but his implicit obedience to [Hester's] wishes,' Meryon wrote to Lord Sligo. 'He was so amazingly affected at taking leave that I was afraid he would have retracted his intentions at the last moment.' There can be absolutely no doubt that had she pressed Michael to stay then he would have done so gladly. With her he was strong, and he trusted her sense of honour absolutely, but it was precisely this sense of honour that forced her to make him go. Hester was also very distressed at the parting – far more than she had anticipated. With Michael's departure she had lost more than just a lover. Michael had also been an intellectual sparring partner, an emotional security, a companion, a social equal, a friend. Hester's stubborn, Pitt-like determination to keep her promise to Craufurd, and her usual disregard for the outcome of her actions meant the depth of loss she felt was a horrible revelation to her.

It is usually easier to be the one who leaves rather than the one who is left, and so it was in this case. Michael was utterly miserable at the prospect of leaving and quite distraught when the time came to go, but it is probably fair to speculate that he was also excited at the prospect of returning to England. Hester, being by far the stronger character of the two, was the instigator, the organizer, and could not allow herself the luxury of indulging in emotional outbursts lest the whole departure degenerate into a bog of tears and passionate declarations. It was only after Michael had finally gone that she allowed her self-control to slip and her loss to overwhelm her. Perhaps the knowledge that she had done the right thing was a consolation to her, and perhaps it was not. It made little immediate difference: for a long time she was desolate.

Lady Hester's initial reaction to Michael's departure was a truly female one, but revealingly mother-like in tone: there had been strong maternal elements in this affair, as in all the close relationships she had ever had. Convinced that he would be unable to manage on his own, she bombarded him with great, long letters full of loving, detailed and probably unwelcome advice.

'Be sure dearest Love to wear a little red fezz (a shallow one) under a large red fezz in case it should rain very hard. You ought to have two large fezzes certainly and two travelling turbans for they may get so wet as not to be dry the next day. . . . Remember also never to cover yr saddle with an oil cloth, unless it is lined, as the wax will stick and make you ride very uncomfortably when it is taken off, a skin is a much better thing.'

She was anxious about his health, particularly his stomach, which had always been delicate:

'After the great heat you have been used to, cold will be really quite dangerous, for the first year you must absolutely take every kind of precaution or your headaches will return, yr stomach will be affected, and perhaps from lack of usual perspiration you will be covered with boils, like many of the officers after their return from Sicily . . . remember if you sd. be constipated with hard indigestible food, 2 spoonfuls of castor oil when going to bed, or very early in the morning wd. be the best medicine for you.'

Sources do not relate Michael's reaction to this distinctly unglamorous advice, but had Hester known how he was amusing himself in Constantinople – the very place where he had proposed to her such a short time before – she might have wished him to be covered in boils, constipated and irrevocably stuck to his saddle. He had scarcely arrived there before he met a woman called Theophanie with whom he began a passionate affair. He later wrote to her:

'You are the only woman worthy of replacing my guardian angel. . . . From the first moment of my arrival in Constantinople . . . I told myself that here was a person to inspire great interest at first sight. . . . I cultivated your acquaintance . . . at last you had so much gained my affection that I declared my feelings to you.'

Theophanie was loved and left, as was another woman in Vienna on the next stage of his journey. Michael certainly did not deserve the loving messages so trustingly sent by Hester: 'Were I to tell you all I feel dearest Creature it wd. only make you low,' she wrote, 'so I will only say I am tolerably well and will do all I can to be better. Take care of yourself for my sake, I shall never cease to pray for you, and as loving you cannot be a sin God never will be deaf to my prayers.'

It is a telling reflection on Michael that he could become emotionally involved with another woman so soon after a passionate parting which in his own words did 'great violence' to his feelings. There is little doubt that he was sincere in his love for Hester, but his sincerity sprang from a shallow base. He dallied in Constantinople until the end of March under the pretext of concern for Lady Hester's health, and only continued on his journey to England when finally forced by imploring letters from his father.

One can only hope that Lady Hester never knew how quickly Michael was faithless to her, but reading a letter she wrote to Thomas Coutts, her banker and an old family friend in London, it is possible that she suspected and forgave in advance. She spoke of having allowed Michael to believe she would come with him to England:

'If I deceived him, it was only to render parting less painful and to do the thing by degrees, for, after he had opportunities of forming other intimacies upon the Continent or elsewhere, what he would have considered at one moment with agony of mind, at another he might have considered as a release. I know the human heart too well not to know also how to foresee and tolerate all its changes.'

With those she loved Lady Hester could be extraordinarily kind and wise.

No sooner had Michael left than Lady Hester decided she too would leave Latakia to spend the winter at a small place called Mar Elias at the foot of Mount Lebanon, near Sayda. It was called a monastery but in fact was the house of the patriarch of the local Greek Catholic community, who agreed to let Lady Hester have the house. All non-essential luggage was packed up and sent ahead, and Lady Hester and Dr Meryon were preparing to follow when illness struck. First one of Hester's janissaries died, then two of Mr Barker's young children, Harissa and Zabetta, were taken ill with a 'malignant fever'. Tragically, despite the most careful nursing, they too died within five hours of each other on 31 October.

Lady Hester was the next to succumb. Her usual strength and vitality had been drastically lowered by Michael's departure, and on 15 November, just as she was about to set out for Sayda, she collapsed with a high temperature. By the evening, Dr Meryon was also ill.

Hester was delirious for five days. For three of those days Meryon managed to crawl from his bed to attend to her, but then he too became delirious and bedridden. Mr Barker, still recovering from the loss of his daughters, managed to find an Italian and a French doctor to tend his friends, but they were not much use. On 27 November, twelve days after he and Hester had first become ill, Dr Meryon was practically dragged from his bed by a desperate Mr Barker. Lady Hester was becoming even worse.

'For fifteen days after this I did not quit her day or night, never undressing the whole of that time,' Dr Meryon wrote, 'and during this period, for twelve hours, I despaired of her life, and a communication was made to her by Mr. Barker to that effect.'

John Barker was so impressed by Hester's courage and fortitude in the face of death that the following August he wrote to Sir Sidney Smith about her bravery.

'Her disorder was an epidemical putrid fever, in which the paroxysms were so violent each night as to render her continually delirious, but in the day, although the fever never left her, she was generally quite composed and gave me orders for her funeral and the disposal of her effects with a calmness and resignation that was truly edifying.'

Finally the crisis passed and her life was no longer considered to be in danger, but the illness had been so violent that she was profoundly weakened. Months afterwards she wrote to Michael 'just after my illness I was a monster larger at my knee joints than in the leg or thigh and my arm was enough to frighten anyone. You could see the large and small bone and I looked altogether like a spectre.' Unable even to sit up in bed, she decided to try three experiments to see if one might help her recovery. The doctors in attendance said she was risking her life.

'The first was the application of a great number of Leaches to her side,' Mr Barker wrote, 'the next to drink every hour or two a goblet of asses milk, so that for several days four Asses could hardly afford a sufficient supply, and the last to have herself carried into a hot bath (a Turkish bagnio) while her fever was still very high.'

Helped by the milk but hindered by the leeches, her recovery was very slow. In December it started to rain, and the roof of her house leaked appallingly. When the bedclothes became wet there was none to replace them because all had been sent to Sayda. Hester was 'seized with an ague' and became ill all over again. She was not able even to stand until 1 January, and a few days later she left Latakia for Mar Elias.

Hester was convinced she had had the plague, and Dr Meryon agreed that it could have been a variation of the disease. 'If there be,' he later wrote, 'as the native physicians say, a sporadic disease constantly remarked at the beginning and close of the first year in which plague appears, but which, alike in most of its symptoms, loses for a time its infectious powers and is not equally disposed to affect the glandular system, then had Lady Hester indeed the plague.' Whatever it was, it was a virulent disease: it had killed seven people on the 15 and 16 of November alone and as Meryon said, 'there might have been as many deaths on the subsequent days for aught I know.'

Ill fortune never seemed to come singly to Lady Hester. As in England when, in the space of two years, her uncle, her favourite brother and Sir John Moore had all died, this time within five weeks she lost her lover and nearly lost her life.

These most recent traumas heralded the start of an intensely difficult period for her. She no longer had the option of returning to England. She despised the current politicians there and disagreed with nearly everything they did; she could not afford to live there either, and knew that even if she did return she would be a social pariah. Her Stanhope pride would not have allowed it. Hester realized that she would live out the rest of her life abroad and probably alone, but it was not an easy prospect to accept. She was also extremely worried about Michael. He was passing through plague-infested country and she had not heard from him since he had left over three months before. The knowledge that she was now an exile, her loneliness and her worries about Michael all combined with the infuriating weakness that was the legacy of her illness to make her extremely irritable to everyone around her, even the faithful Meryon.

'I must not conceal from you,' he wrote to Michael, 'that an extraordinary sensibility and irritation of the brain, much tenderness in the chest and that debility in the knee which I mentioned in my last, still hang about her.'

The move to Mar Elias cheered her for a time. The Emir Beshyr near whose province she was staying, had been most welcoming. Both he and the Sheik Beshyr had given orders, she said, that 'all is to be at my feet', and the Emir had ordered glass for her windows from Damascus and given her 'oil that is like milk', and 'his own favourite ass'. The little convent was prettily sited at the base of Mount Lebanon with distant views of the sea. It was not very well appointed, however, and she spent some time having it renovated. Some chimneys, a bigger oven and a steam bath were constructed, together with a small 'gazelle yard' and 'a stone and mud wall round part of the Convent to keep out strangers and dogs'. There was a discolouration in one of the walls around which a horrible smell hung. A servant told them that the late patriarch had been buried there, sitting in an armchair, and the embalming procedure had gone a bit wrong. Meryon expected it 'would give rise to many ghost stories'.

Hester continued with her long letters to Michael. She knew that letters were subject to unpredictable delays, but grew increasingly anxious as she heard nothing from him in return. He finally managed to write on 11 January, well after his arrival in Constantinople. Hester received the letter on 26 February and wrote delightedly back with details of her new way of life. The clean air and good food had done much to repair her health. 'I toddle about upon a Ass and enjoy my ride,' she wrote. Less enjoyable were the servants: in her current frame of mind she found fault with nearly all of them. Worst of all was poor Ann Fry, who had apparently been 'noisy and disagreeable'. She had also been inconsiderate enough to be ill. 'Since she came here she has had a dissentry and I never set eyes upon her for three weeks,' Hester complained. Evidently the combination of 'dissentry' and an irate Lady Hester was too much for Mrs Fry to cope with: she had prudently absented herself from Hester's house. 'She is now in the town at Damiani's lodgings as I cannot trust her where a kitchen is,' Lady Hester continued. 'She will eat everything she sees and therefore falls ill again.' In Hester's defence however, Dr Meryon was later forced to write to Michael for help. 'Indeed Mr Bruce,' he wrote, 'Mrs Fry's ignorance and insolence are incorrigible ... the woman keeps her Ladyship's mind constantly agitated and does more harm than all the good effects of air, exercise and physic can rectify.'

Sadly, Michael was far too busy in his new life to pay much attention to letters and requests: he was quite caught up in the pleasures and excitements of life in Europe. Napoleon had abdicated and was exiled to Elba. Vienna was packed with heads of state discussing the future of Europe and the salons were full of glamorous women keen to meet the dashing young man about whom they had heard so much. It was all too easy for Michael to forget the woman he had left behind in Syria. When he did occasionally find time to write he contrived to sound sick with worry and love for her. As a device to keep himself uppermost in Lady Hester's mind it was very effective, but it was also very selfish. Lady Hester had always been totally honest and open with Michael: when they were together she had been the source of his happiness, but now they were apart she desperately needed to know that he could be happy without her. This was a certain sign of the depth of her love for him just as his spuriously emotional letters were a sign of his shallowness and immaturity.

Life continued to be very difficult for Lady Hester. Her thoughts were so often many thousands of miles away that she could not properly apply herself to life in Syria. She was distracted and depressed and longed constantly for letters from Michael, yet when they finally arrived they had inevitably crossed with several of her own, so she would shoot off another missive immediately. Her health waxed and waned. When she heard from Michael that he was tolerably happy she put on weight and felt well, but when no letters came or disturbing reports filtered through that he was making a fool of himself somewhere, she became gaunt and wan again.

In August 1814 she innocently read a letter from Craufurd Bruce intended for Michael in which he moaned that the affair with Hester meant his son was 'hampered for life' with all his brilliant prospects over. Furious and upset at being blamed for Michael's shortcomings when she felt she should have been praised for insisting on his return to Europe, Hester wrote an angry letter to Michael severing her connections with his father. Craufurd wrote an abject letter back, praising Hester's qualities and her contributions to Michael's life, but Hester could never bear dissimulation. She had prized her friendship with Craufurd and now felt it had all been false. She could not forgive him.

By June 1815, Lady Hester had reached a crisis point. She had not heard from Michael for over a year, and had received only three letters in the eighteen months that they had been apart. She could contain herself no longer.

'A year ago you wrote to me from Vienna and in England in October, these are all the letters I have recd. from you, is this kind?' she cried. 'I was sincere in my wish to give you up for yr. happiness and for yr. pleasure, but I expected I must confess to have ever found you an attentive, an affectionate friend, and one I cd. have relied upon.... You have pained me by this neglect.'

She was perfectly justified in writing such a letter, and she wrote another in December having heard from various friends in England how Michael had been behaving stupidly – quite what he was meant to have done not even Lady Hester knew, but she was alarmed by the reports.

'I have of late had an opportunity of hearing a great deal about you, and nothing to yr. advantage, so much so that a man whose character is irreproachable, and whom you were once very anxious to get acquainted with, gave as his opinion to a friend of his, that from what he could judge of yr. character, I must be too happy to have got rid of you!' What mortification for Lady Hester.

A letter from Michael finally arrived in March 1816, and when Hester realized that it had taken seven months to reach her she regretted her angry letters. She also heard from her brother James, who had become friends with Michael in England, that the rumours about Michael's bad conduct were untrue. 'I wish my tears could blot out what I have written,' she wrote contritely, 'it does not matter now what my fate is, if I can only reflect upon you with pleasure, that I can believe you honest, honourable and feeling. I cannot then be really unhappy, happen what may.'

The relationship continued its roller-coaster course for a few more months, but the disillusionments continued. At one stage she planned to go to France to meet her brother James. She was longing to see him again and to congratulate him on his recent appointment as ADC to the Duke of York. When she heard that Michael had been spreading rumours that she was coming to see him, not James, she decided to stay in Syria. She wrote saying it would probably be better if they never met again.

She had finally begun to realize that he was not to be relied on for much of anything, although she was still trusting him to sort out her financial affairs. Even that was a mistake. In 1814 he promised to give her half of his allowance, which would amount to the sum of one thousand pounds a year. She was unhappy about accepting any money at all from him, but accepted temporarily so that people would not be able to say that he had quite abandoned her. Taking his promise in good faith, she informed Mr Coutts, her banker in London, that he could expect this amount of money to be coming into her account, and she probably adjusted the standards of her life accordingly, but Michael behaved atrociously. First, although his allowance was increased to £2,500 he decided that he had been too generous and told Hester that he was reducing the amount to £600, then, after all his promises, he never gave her anything at all.

All Hester's financial problems stemmed from this time. She was plunged into debt, and was never able to extract herself.

The final and most shattering nail in the coffin of Michael's behaviour was contained in a letter he wrote to his father. Some large bills were coming through to London, and Mr Coutts had appealed to Michael to pay them, as he should have done had he honoured his promise to her. He refused to pay them, and wrote to the banker: 'I am afraid that from what I have heard myself, and from the accounts communicated to me by her brother that she is become rather flighty. She forms the most absurd plans and launches into the most extravagent expenses.' This is from the man who had shared many such 'absurd' plans with her and was frequently, and to no avail, castigated by his father in exactly the same way.

What he then wrote was even worse. Complaining that Hester had been abusive to him in her letters he said this: 'God knows that we do not deserve it, nor does it afflict one in the least, as I am perfectly convinced ... from my own observation ... that her mind is affected.'

It was the ultimate betrayal. His only motive can have been to wriggle out of having to honour his financial promises to her. Happily there is nothing in her letters to show that Lady Hester ever knew of Michael's treachery. Even she might have found it hard to forgive.

It all ended in January 1817. Hester read in a French paper that Michael was to be married, and she wrote him one last, generous and heartbreakingly dignified letter. 'May you be happy,' she wrote. 'Adieu! Farewell, my once dearest B! I must call you so no more – but I never shall cease to pray for your prosperity and your happiness.'

Had Michael been older or richer or stronger he would perhaps not have left Hester so obediently when he was told to, and the rest of their lives would have been very different. As it was, the personal sacrifice that Hester made when she compelled him to return to England was in vain. Michael never fulfilled the promise he had shown as a child and young man. He remained an essentially superficial person – charming and handsome, but petulant and sullen when he did not get his own way. Apart from one dashing episode when he helped rescue Count Lavalette from a French prison, he accomplished nothing outstanding in his life.

Lady Charlotte Bury, in the original edition of her *Diary* said: 'If ever there was a person to whom the Scotch proverb of "Great cry and little wool" is applicable, it was so to Mr. Bruce. He began his career as a spoilt child, he pursued it as a spoilt youth, and after having become an Eastern Dandy, returned to enact the part of a hero in a Parisian melodrama. Mr. Bruce,' she continued caustically, 'would have been a very harmless and rather ornamental member of society in his youth had not an overweening vanity rendered him the dupe of flattery and froth.'

This particular judgement seems almost too vitriolic to have been purely the outcome of dispassionate observation, but it echoes Dr Meryon's scathing remark. 'With too little knowledge of the world to enable him to conduct himself like a great man,' the doctor said, 'he makes continual strides towards becoming a little one.'

Lady Hester was perhaps the person most entitled to pronounce judgement on Michael, and she wrote of him in 1814, 'I fear Bruce will turn out idle, though it is his ambition to be great and I lament that his father changes his plans about him every day, and wishing him to be everything is the sure means of making him turn out nothing at last.'

Sadly it seemed that everyone was right when they forecast a life of mediocrity for him. He had many affairs, including one with Marshal

Ney's widow, before he finally settled down. In August 1818 he married a rich widow with several children – a woman, like Hester, many years older than himself.

Although everyone felt entitled to state their own opinion, a few vital facts remain indisputable. Michael Bruce was a man of great charm who for a while had adored Lady Hester as she adored him. Although their conduct shocked a great many people, they hurt no one, and for the few years they were together, they made each other happy. Whether or not those times made up for the years of sad disillusion that followed their parting, perhaps only Lady Hester herself could say. She never referred to it in any later correspondence, or if she did, her letters have not survived.

CHAPTER SIXTEEN

'Honoured with distinctions'

The late winter of 1815 was a depressing time for Lady Hester. Apart from Mrs Fry's 'dissentry', M. Beaudin the dragoman had become partially paralysed and Lady Hester had a recurrence of ague. Owing to lack of space at Mar Elias, Meryon had taken up lodgings in the nearby village of Abra. It was a small, rough place, but the villagers, whose chief livelihood was the breeding of silkworms, were friendly to the Doctor, which was quite a consolation to him. There were rumours of plague once more, and everyone stocked up with as many provisions as they could afford.

Sheik Beshyr, chief of the Druses, was in the habit of making an annual circuit of all the villages in his province to collect rents and hear any grievances. He usually combined business with pleasure, and hunted as he travelled from village to village. This year when he came to Abra, he was most careful not to allow Lady Hester to feel she had to entertain him: he arranged his own food and lodgings. 'It cannot be denied that the Orientals are well bred,' admired Meryon. But even the Sheik was wary of plague. He dispensed with the usual custom of having his hand or the hem of his robe kissed by all who approached him, and he was right to be cautious: within weeks a man in the village had contracted plague and was dead. Following the local custom, the dead man's family and all who had been in contact with him were turned out of the village, and were forced to take shelter in some nearby caves. This was not quite the hardship it would seem, because as Meryon said, 'A fine climate renders the shade of a tree more agreeable than the most commodious apartment.'

Although Lady Hester had no wish to become ill again, she could not bear the thought of people starving, and bravely went in person to the caves with medicines and money for provisions, but to no avail – they all died.

More than half the village died in this new epidemic, but luckily there was no illness at Mar Elias, and the plague seemed to go as quickly as it had come. The long weeks of isolation had been very wearing for everybody, but the tedium of being confined to her house was magnificently relieved for Lady Hester on 14 June by the arrival of His Majesty's sloop of war, *Kite*, commanded by Captain T. Forster. Dr Meryon, marooned in his village, was aware of the excitement but in total ignorance as to what was going on. It was not yet safe to venture out, so he had to contain his curiosity as well as he could. After being in 'long and private conversation' with Lady Hester, Captain Forster boarded his ship and sailed south, only to return again a week later on 24 June, which coincided with the easing of plague restrictions – 'the Franks of Sayda opened their houses' – and Dr Meryon was able to satisfy his curiosity.

Lady Hester had been planning a new adventure. She had come across an old manuscript describing the exact spot where a vast hoard of treasure had been buried in the ancient and ruined city of Ascalon. It was not as far-fetched an idea as it might have seemed. In the days before paper money or banks existed the accumulated wealth of rich merchants or rulers was very vulnerable to theft, and burying chests of money for safe-keeping was commonplace. This practice had led to European archaeologists being regarded with the deepest suspicion. What other reason could there be for digging in ruins other than that of looking for treasure? Finding treasure was also fraught with difficulty. There was only one explanation for a peasant becoming rich overnight, but if the man were to declare his findings to the authorities, he would automatically be suspected of having declared only half, and would be whipped or bastinadoed until he had confessed his misdeed, even if he was entirely innocent.

Lady Hester had no wish to be accused of theft, yet she could not quite resist the excitement of a treasure hunt. She decided to get official sanction for her search and wrote to Mr Liston, Stratford Canning's successor at Constantinople, for help and advice. She proposed to give all of the treasure to the authorities, taking for herself only the credit of the find. Mr Liston, not yet become Sir Robert, knew all about Lady Hester, and it is a mark of the respect in which she was held at the Porte that he had immediately despatched HMS *Kite* to be at her disposal.

The plan to sail to Ascalon was doomed however. After his exploratory sail down the coast, Captain Forster reported back to Lady Hester that there was no suitable anchorage: the trip would have to be made overland. This required further planning and correspondence, which Hester set in motion before retreating from the July heat to the cool of Meshmûshy high up in the mountains.

Meshmûshy was a beautiful place, all the more so for being nearly inaccessible. 'Few places which are at all accessible to beasts of burden can be more rugged and steep than this,' Meryon wrote of the early stages of the ascent. After the unpromising start though, the village was charming. Set in a vast mulberry orchard, the house in which Lady Hester stayed was shaded by plane and walnut trees and had a cooling fountain, fed by a nearby stream. The local monastery made great quantities of wine every year from the twenty-one sorts of grapes that Meryon counted in the steep terraced vineyards. He was scandalized at the lack of hygiene they tolerated 'particularly in what regards the feet of the persons who tread it, generally peasants'. It seemed they were filthy. It did not, however, seem to affect his enjoyment of the wine.

After ten weeks the heat of the summer was gone and Lady Hester decided to go north to visit Baalbek before returning to Mar Elias. She decided that the trip would be a more ascetic one than usual. She had enjoyed the simplicity of her stay at Meshmûshy and besides she was feeling neglected by her friends and relations. Perhaps she hoped that by travelling as the poorest of pilgrims, word would filter back to England and make people there feel guilty at their negligence.

Apart from Dr Meryon she took only three servants with her: a maid, an 'outdoor man' and a sturdy, brave old lady cook called Um Risk. Meryon was in the kitchen one day when a snake slithered in and wrapped itself around Um Risk's bare leg. 'I had seen other proofs of courage in this withered old woman, but was astonished most by this,' he said. Far from panicking 'she felt the serpent, and, looking down, calmly seized it by the neck, held it so until she had unwound the tail, and then killed it.' She was obviously just the calibre of cook best suited to a modest trek through the mountains of Syria.

On 18 October they set out for Baalbek, which lay to the north-west and high in the mountains of Ante-Lebanon. Also known as Helio-polis, Baalbek was another ancient city that, by AD 700, had estab-lished itself as a centre of piety, learning and land ownership. As their departure date drew near, it became evident that there were still pockets of plague to be found in isolated villages in the interior, so, rather than risk infection, Lady Hester decided they would travel as a self-contained unit. They took tents and enough provisions for the journey, and increased the number of servants to help guard against robbers. Apart from enough minced meat dumplings to last for a week they took 'kitchen utensils, beds, coffee, rice, burgol or malted wheat, soup, candles, oil, wine, vinegar, vermicelli, macaroni, cheese, tea and sugar, syrups for sherbets and fuel for Lady Hester'.

Having been so efficient and thorough, Dr Meryon then rather spoilt the record by becoming separated from the rest of the party and getting thoroughly lost. He was on foot, and, weighed down by his heavy riding breeches and brace of pistols, he toiled along until it got too dark for him to see where he was going. He finally stopped for the night at the top of a precipice. He was quite lost and very frightened. 'The jackals howled around me,' he recalled with a shudder, and – worse – 'I was not sure that there were not leopards near the spot where I was.' He survived the night, but by the time he found the rest of the party his feet were so itchy and hot he had to sit with his feet in an icy stream: 'a dangerous mode of cure', he observed.

By the end of the week the minced meat dumplings were like rocks, but Lady Hester insisted they be eaten. 'The maids cried, the men grumbled and rebelled . . . but no one fell ill.' It was unlike Hester to be so intransigent, but it was a sign of things to come.

When they finally reached Baalbek, they thought it a wretched town. The Governor's house was poor and the ruins of the old city were covered with rubbish. There was no sign of its illustrious past and it was not until ninety years later that the vast Roman Temples to Jupiter and Bacchus would be excavated. To crown it all the weather was appalling, so they left as soon as they could to go over the Lebanon mountains to take the coastal route home to Mar Elias. It was a possibly disgruntled Meryon who said of the famous Cedars of

Lebanon, 'These Cedars have a very dubious reputation and no great beauty to recommend them. Those which grow in the grounds of Warwick Castle are almost equally worth seeing.'

Then followed an episode which was much discussed in later years. Some people criticized Lady Hester for it, others admired her. It was in a nearby monastery, Mar Antonius, which was famous for two things. The first was that miracle cures were said to take place there, and the second was the last word in misogyny: nothing female whatsoever could be tolerated within the monastery grounds. If, by mistake, something female were to enter the monastery, divine interception would see that the female thing was overtaken by some ghastly accident shortly afterwards. Even the hens were cooped up in case one should stray, whilst the cocks were allowed to roam free.

Lady Hester had her own unique ideas on where to draw the line on other people's beliefs. She was quite prepared to defend the right to religious freedom, but equally ready to trample all over beliefs that she thought ridiculous. This was one of the latter.

Mounted deliberately on a she-ass, she rode right into the hall of the monastery. She visited the refectory, the cells – she went everywhere. Calm and imperturbable, she was like the eye of a storm. In front of her was the frenzied flapping of the Maronite monks, half of whom expected the ground beneath her to open and swallow her up. Behind her, the anxious Meryon and other members of her party followed closely, watching out in case some of the more level-headed monks played a trick on Hester in order to preserve the miraculous consistency of the legend.

Nothing happened. After presenting handsome gifts to the monks to calm their frayed nerves, Lady Hester departed for Tripoli. All round the area people talked of nothing else for months. Some called it bravado and others called it sacrilege. Whatever it was it showed one thing: Hester was in no mood to be crossed. But although her motives were occasionally suspect one could never doubt her courage. She was, after all, a lone 'infidel' woman in a Muslim country.

She arrived in Tripoli in the middle of a tremendous thunder storm, but the streets were lined with people waiting to see her. Once more her reputation had travelled before her, and she was the centre of attention.

The Governor of Tripoli was a man called Mustapha Aga. He was the son of a muleteer and had risen to his present position by extremely devious means. He was unpopular and greatly feared, but nevertheless gave Lady Hester a 'frank and hearty welcome'. They got on well. After staying there for several weeks, Lady Hester and Meryon started off down the coast towards Mar Elias. She had adopted the habit of breaking a day's journey mid-way for an hour's rest. Since it was now winter some kind of shelter was needed, and they usually managed to appropriate a 'peasant's cabin' for the purpose. There was one major flaw in this habit – fleas. They were sometimes so numerous that they decided to appoint a servant to be on 'flea duty'.

'On these occasions the practice of the servant employed on this duty was to go into the middle of the room, bare his leg, and watch how many fleas jumped on him from the floor,' Meryon wrote. 'Sometimes they might be seen like iron filings drawn to a magnet, blackening the skin.' It was probably not a very popular job.

By the end of January they had reached Chouifat, a small town just south of Beirut. Lady Hester was visiting a famous Druse lady there when M. Beaudin returned from a ride into Beirut with alarming news. A Capugi Bashi had arrived from Constantinople on his way to Sayda to see Lady Hester. As everyone knew, these frighteningly important officials only ever emerged from the Porte on serious and nasty business. Stranglings, confiscation of property and strippings of title were the usual result of a visit from a Capugi Bashi, or Zaim, as they were also known. The servants were terrified, but Lady Hester had been expecting his arrival. Summoning a scribe she wrote to him, to arrange a meeting at Mar Elias.

Not even Dr Meryon knew what she was planning this time, and no sooner had they arrived back at Mar Elias than a messenger arrived with word from the Capugi. He was at the Governor's house in Sayda and wished to see her immediately. Typically, Hester decided that the Capugi should come to her, and told the messenger so. It worked. 'Our dinner was just over,' Meryon wrote, 'when a great bustle was heard in the courtyard, with the trampling of horses' feet and the voices of the servants.' The Capugi Bashi had arrived.

Meryon and Beaudin were taking no chances. They primed their pistols and slipped them into their belts. 'If we saw the bowstring dangling from under the Capugi's robe,' they declared stoutly, 'no use should be made of it whilst we were there.'

They need not have worried. Far from posing a threat to Lady Hester, Derwish Aga, as the Capugi Bashi was called, had come bearing three firmans – documents – from the Sultan. These orders bestowed upon her more power over the Turks than had ever been granted to any European before. One was addressed to the Pasha of Damascus, the second to the Pasha of Acre, and the third to the remaining Governors in Syria. They were all commanded to help Lady Hester in whatever way she needed during the search for the buried gold at Ascalon. The Capugi himself was to be placed completely at her disposal: he was to do nothing without her authority. She had been handed power of breathtaking dimensions. She was elated.

Preparations for the journey to Ascalon began immediately. Meryon was despatched to Damascus, where he bought horses and donkeys and a tempered Damascus sword for himself. Lady Hester had decided on Acre as being a good place from which to start the expedition. Derwish Aga and Giorgio the steward were sent there to give letters to the Pasha and to prepare lodgings for Lady Hester. Mr Catafago, the Austrian consul at Acre, was invited to join them, an offer he accepted with alacrity.

In Acre Hester was treated like royalty. She was received by the Pasha with 'peculiar affability' and as Meryon observed, 'honoured with distinctions usually paid to princes only'. The trappings of a great expedition rapidly assembled, and by 18 March they were ready to go.

There were twenty-six tents of which Hester's was by far the largest and quite the most magnificent. It was double, 'like the calix and corolla of a flower inverted . . . a green colour on the outside, studded with yellow flowers and stars. In the centre of the inner tent was placed a sofa behind which, and bisecting the tent, was suspended a curtain made of broad bands of satin of the most vivid colours.' It more than satisfied Meryon's aspirations to grandeur. 'Nothing could be more showy or more elegant,' he breathed ecstatically.

The cavalcade itself was just as grand. Twelve camels carried the tents, and twelve mules the luggage. Among the scores of attendants there was a torch bearer, a water bearer and twenty-two tent pitchers. Mr Catafago, Dr Meryon and the dragomen rode on horses as did the Capugi Bashi and his entourage; the column was preceded by three messengers to make necessary arrangements and the whole was escorted by a hundred Hawary horsemen from Barbary.

As the magnificent procession left the thronged streets of Acre, the focus of everyone's attention was, of course, on Lady Hester. She had been provided with a gorgeous tartaravan in which to recline: 'A tilted palanquin, covered with crimson cloth, and having in front six large gilded balls, glittering in the sun.' She had scorned a tartaravan once before, and was no more inclined to ride in one now, but for a different reason. It was fitting to her rank that one should be provided, but the vast crowds were amazed and impressed to see that she rode, not her favourite horse or even a camel. She rode a humble ass.

It was a stroke of intuitive genius. She now had such power and fame that it was unnecessary to underline it with ostentation. She could afford to enhance it with modesty. Perhaps now that she was shown such respect, she was unconsciously seeking approval. If so, it worked. The crowd loved it, and her.

After the glories of their departure from Acre came a night of unparalleled drama and discomfort. A massive storm broke over them as they encamped for the night and all the tents either blew down on their inhabitants or blew up like umbrellas. One dignitary was entirely buried by his tent and lay roaring for help. Lady Hester opted for the safety of a much smaller tent pinned down with large stones, but was still nearly smothered twice. Mr Catafago, the Capugi and all the Hawary soldiers showed common sense but a distinct lack of gallantry by taking refuge in a nearby Carmelite monastery.

Everything was totally chaotic and things got worse as the night wore on. In the middle of all this confusion two quite separate strangers arrived in the camp to see Lady Hester. The messages of one of them took up the rest of the night for Lady Hester, but the introduction of the other was to have a considerable effect on the rest of her life.

CHAPTER SEVENTEEN

Ascalon

The first stranger to battle his way through the storm was an old tramp-like man wearing a threadbare Spanish cloak. He clutched a Bible under his arm and spoke fluent French. His name was General Lousteneau and he informed a bemused Lady Hester that at that very moment Bonaparte was escaping from exile in Elba.

Even she thought that he must simply be mad. She gave him supper and listened to him quote from the Bible before he vanished into the night once more. Weeks later, when Lady Hester received confirmation of Bonaparte's dramatic escape, she thought back to General Lousteneau's words. Napoleon had landed in Cannes on 1 March; for the news to have reached Syria in seventeen days was possible but not likely, so she decided to believe that he had psychic powers. Later, more startling predictions that he was to make only confirmed this opinion, and it made her think long and hard about many things quite new to her. Metaphysics, the nature of reality – a whole new world presented itself to her active mind. She later invited the destitute Lousteneau to live at Mar Elias, and together with him and a mystic called Metta she began an investigation into the world of astrology that became increasingly important to her as her physically active life declined.

For the time being, however, she was very much involved in the here and now. The second visitor to brave the elements that night was a moustachioed Italian dressed in British naval uniform who introduced himself as Tomaso Coschich, in the service of Sir Sidney Smith. He strutted in and informed a rather startled Lady Hester that after she had performed some errands for Sir Sidney, he was empowered to escort her back to Europe. His arrogance and presumption galvanized Lady Hester into action. Although it was the middle of the night she read the despatches immediately. They were 'very voluminous'.

Sir Sidney was famous throughout Lebanon for his gallant defence of Acre when Napoleon had laid siege to the city after the French fleet had been defeated by Nelson in the Battle of the Nile. Sir Sidney's fortunes had recently taken a turn for the worse, however, and having been unable to meet his debts in England he had decamped to Vienna where all the heads of state had been meeting. He had formulated a plan to rout the Algerian pirates who were wreaking havoc in the southern Mediterranean. They were ruining trade and dealing in slaves; most of Europe wanted to see an end to them, but no one was prepared to back Sir Sidney's scheme financially. He needed money, and any reflected glory from his scheme would not come amiss either. His message to Lady Hester was that he wanted her friend the Emir Beshyr to provide 1,500 soldiers to enable him to carry out his plan, and that she was to arrange it.

Apart from being outraged at his presumption that she would be willing to act as an intermediary, Lady Hester thoroughly disapproved of the whole plan and refused to be associated with it. She knew it was unthinkable that the ruler of one province of the Ottoman Empire should provide men to attack another province without direct instruction from the Porte. The Emir Beshyr would be risking his life were he to agree. She was also horrified at the meanness of the presents that Sir Sidney had sent for the various people involved. A set of flags under which the Emir Beshyr's men were supposed to rally proved the final straw. They were small and cheap and Lady Hester, with a flash of her old humour, named Sir Sidney the 'King of pocket-handkerchiefs'.

She wrote to him, detailing why she would not help him in his plan. She explained in her letter that in order for a scheme like this to succeed and not be misinterpreted by anyone he ought to go straight to the Sultan at Constantinople and be completely open about his plans. This of course was exactly what she had done with regard to the treasure hunt. Careful copies of Sir Sidney's letter and her reply to him were then sent to Mr Liston at Constantinople. Mr Barker at Acre was told of the situation and asked to intercept any more letters arriving from Sir Sidney and hold them for Lady Hester pending her return from Ascalon. Finally, Signor Coschich was politely but firmly invited to leave the country and the journey to Ascalon continued. She never heard anything more about it.

Ascalon had been one of the major cities of Palestine as far back as 1900 BC. For centuries more it had stood against the waves of invaders that swept across the Holy Lands, but now there was nothing left of it at all. Unlike Palmyra, which was deliberately destroyed by the Roman Emperor Aurelian, Ascalon seemed merely to have drifted into decay, aided perhaps by the fact that it had no harbour or safe anchorage for boats. Most of the marble blocks and pillars had been dragged away and used to rebuild Jaffa and Acre. There was nothing left to see except for the city walls and one wall of the mosque where the treasure was supposed to be buried.

On 1 April camp was struck. The tents that sprang up all over the ruins made a glorious sight. They were brightly coloured – most were green and blue – and the biggest of them were embroidered with glorious motifs of flowers and stars and flaming swords. Scurrying servants bustled to and fro preparing three meals a day not only for the two hundred members of the expedition, but also for the same number of workers who had been seconded from nearby villages to dig. The ruins of Ascalon had been transformed according to Meryon into 'a scene of showy gaiety almost as lively as a racecourse'.

The digging began, to the sound of pipes and tabors, and a large 'fort' was confidently constructed to hold the vast amount of gold that was going to be found. Everyone was in great good humour, even the diggers, and the unearthing of piles of entablatures and other bits of masonry, together with fragments of pottery, lamps and lapis specularis, kept the level of enthusiasm high. After a few days digging they discovered two pavements, one four feet above the other, made of fine marble slabs, which the Aga of Jaffa promptly loaded onto three boats and bore away, and on the fourth day a vast and magnificent marble statue was found eighteen feet under the surface. It appeared to be of a Roman Emperor and was larger than life size – although its head was missing it was still nearly seven foot tall. To an archaeologist this was treasure enough on its own, but the excitement at the discovery soon changed to dismay when Lady Hester commanded that the statue be broken up. Dr Meryon was scandalized at this decision, but try as he would to change her mind, she was adamant, and it was done. She said in her defence: 'I ordered it to be broken into a thousand pieces that malicious persons might not say I came to look for statues for my countrymen and not for treasures for the Porte.' No doubt she was influenced by the recent criticism of Lord Elgin for having removed the now famous 'marbles' from Greece.

It was the only treasure they were to find. They dug for ten more days and found nothing more. It was a huge anti-climax. Greatly dispirited, they packed up and left Ascalon. The Capugi Bashi returned to Constantinople well pleased with his gifts of a black slave and a cashmere shawl, and Lady Hester submitted a detailed account of all her expenses to Mr Liston. She had always been confident that they would be paid: the finding of a treasure trove for the Turkish Government by an English woman would have greatly enhanced diplomatic relations between the two countries. 'If Sir A. Paget put down the cost of his servants' liveries after his Embassy to Vienna and made Mr. Pitt pay him,' she reasoned, 'I cannot see why I should not do the same.'

She was never paid, and the extra expenses she was obliged to cover coincided with Michael's renege on his promise of a share of his allowance. She was forced to ask Mr Barker for an advance on her allowance. She sank deeper into debt.

Lady Hester was nearly forty years old. For the last five years, since she had first left England, she had been almost constantly on the move and was beginning to feel the need to settle down. The monastery of Mar Elias suited her very well and she decided to make it her home for the foreseeable future. From there she could make expeditions and forays to visit her friends, and when it became too hot in the summer she could retire to the cool heights of Meshmûshy. The letter-writing continued unabated and now that she was no longer moving around the country so much, people knew where to find her so she received replies to her letters much more quickly. There were still many major expeditions that she would have liked to have made which her money problems made impossible, but she had a constant stream of visitors and no one was ever turned away empty-handed.

Powerful people came – grand dignitaries with their large retinues wound up the mountain path to call on her. They were entertained in style, and their servants, slaves, camels, horses and mules were all fed and sheltered.

Poor people came – beggars, outcasts, orphaned children. She helped them all, and found increasing pleasure in doing so. Apart from providing food and clothing, she tried to find work and accommodation for them in the local villages. For those who seemed suited she would offer work and a home at Mar Elias, especially the homeless children. These she looked after with extra care, making sure they were taught skills that would be useful to them as they grew, and ensuring that they had continued instruction in whatever religion they believed in. She had always regarded it as a privilege to help those less fortunate than herself, but had rarely had the opportunity to practise it before.

It was around this time that she wrote to her friend Colonel Anderson, now a general: 'I should not, I imagine, be answering that for which I was created were I to become a grub on the face of the earth and make no exertion to be useful to my country and my friends.'

People with grievances came to her to have their arguments resolved and she rapidly became the pivot of the local community, but her power and influence stretched far wider than that. The network of contacts that she had built up over the years provided her with a power structure that was quite unique, and it was one that she was not afraid to use, although her final loyalty always lay to the Sultan in Constantinople.

People soon discovered that being helped by Lady Hester was not to be regarded as a soft option. She was sometimes a demanding benefactor. 'I am not an angel of kindness like Mr Pitt,' she once wrote. She demanded loyalty and honesty from those she helped and quite liked them to be grateful too. Anyone caught stealing or lying was thrown out and people who complained or were lazy were briskly dealt with. When people did not do their best she would scold and berate them, but, as she sometimes pointed out, she would treat a servant-boy or a great Pasha in exactly the same way. 'It has ever been my custom to use strong language, that I might not be misunderstood,' she said, 'without meaning the least disrespect towards the person addressed.' Indeed it was often a curious mark of esteem to be scolded by her. She never wasted her breath on anyone she considered to be beyond redemption, and Dr Meryon, deemed to be someone worth saving, was frequently on the receiving end of her lectures.

The third group of people who came to visit Lady Hester at Mar Elias were the European travellers. With the end of the Napoleonic Wars it was now far safer to journey abroad, and of course the French themselves were now able to travel more freely too. Lady Hester had always loved the French and it was with particular enjoyment that she entertained M. Boutin. She and Michael had met him several times before and had nicknamed him 'le boutonne', 'the button'. They had thought him most agreeable – 'in points of talent and integrity he was a man of ten thousand,' Hester wrote of him. He had been made Consul General of Egypt but had been instructed by his Government to learn Arabic and to make a secret survey of Egypt and Syria. He was travelling quietly through Lebanon when he visited Hester at Mar Elias. After staying for a few days he left to travel through the Ansari mountains, although Hester tried to dissuade him because the Bedu tribes in that area were known to be particularly fierce. Her fears for him were well founded. When his watch was discovered in a Damascus souk they knew that he had been robbed and murdered.

'A horrid, too horrid, story,' Lady Hester wrote, 'it affected me vastly.' What was worse was that no one seemed to care. 'Had a dog been massacred, all the European Consuls could not have shewn more apathy than they did,' she cried.

She waited for an official enquiry to be made into his death, but months went by and none was made. She was so appalled by the indifference of those in power that she decided to take action herself. 'In me and me only rested the power of revenge,' she wrote, and observed with some justification that if nothing was done, no European could hope to be safe anywhere in the country.

She sent 'four villainous-looking fellows, very ill-dressed, to shuffle themselves into the different villages and to pick up some just information'. No French consul would help her – they were all too frightened of the murderous Ansaris – and the Ambassadors at the Porte would not respond either. Finally the Pasha of Acre agreed to help, and, ordering the Governor of Tripoli to assist Lady Hester, troops were sent into the mountains under her direction. They found the murderers, cut off their heads and burnt their villages. It was a bloody revenge.

Lady Hester's sense of honour was satisfied, and strangely, the

Ansari Arabs bore her no ill will. She was extremely gratified when France acknowledged her actions in a vote of thanks from the Chamber of Deputies, proposed by Count Delaborde.

Thankfully not all her European visitors came to such a violent end. In 1816 Lady Hester received two Englishmen – friends who had been travelling together but who had become parted. William Bankes, who afterwards became MP for Cambridge University, arrived first. He was a young man with a rather high opinion of himself, but he brought news of Hester's friends in England, and she was glad to see him. After resting for a few days at Mar Elias he told Lady Hester that he wanted to go to Palmyra, so she gave him letters to enable him to get through the desert.

Months before, Hester had agreed with Mahannah, King of the Desert, that he should accept no one as her friend unless they carried a letter of recommendation from her. The letter was to be marked with seals: one seal would indicate to Mahannah that he should allow safe conduct, but two seals would tell him that this was a great friend of Lady Hester's, a person for whom camels could be killed and roasted.

Rather unwisely, Hester told Bankes about this arrangement, and after he had set out with his letter he opened it to see what rank he had been awarded. Disgusted to see that he had only merited one seal, he threw the letter away, deciding that he could do perfectly well without Lady Hester's help, but he was wrong. Without her patronage he had appalling difficulties getting across the desert. On his first attempt he was simply thrown out by Mahannah's tribe and the next time he tried he was held prisoner by them for quite a while before being ejected. The third attempt was successful, but only after he had paid Mahannah a lot of money. He was so enraged by the whole experience that when he returned to England he devoted a great deal of time to slandering and ridiculing Lady Hester to anyone who would listen. Unfortunately a lot of people did.

Mr Silk Buckingham, who arrived only days after Bankes's departure, reacted entirely differently. He arrived at Mar Elias dirty, tired and ill, and was nursed back to 'freshness and vigour' by Lady Hester. When he returned to England he published an account of his travels in Syria and had nothing but praise for Lady Hester's kindness and hospitality. 'When the period approached for my quitting Mar Elias,' he wrote, 'I felt extreme regret, for I had scarcely ever before concentrated so much of highly intellectual pleasure in so short a space of time.' He went on, 'I had regained much of my former health and strength in a surprising manner . . . and I was now better prepared for my future journey than I had ever been before.'

He also concluded, contrary to what many people liked to think, that Lady Hester was both fortunate and happy.

'If to be sincerely and generally beloved by those among whom we reside,' he wrote, 'to possess power and influence with those who govern, and to have abundant opportunities of exercising these for the weak and helpless be sources of delight, it may be safely concluded that Lady Hester Stanhope is one of the happiest of human beings.'

It was extraordinary that two friends visiting Lady Hester almost simultaneously should have formed such wildly differing opinions of their hostess, but it seemed that Lady Hester often had the effect of inspiring people to extremes of either admiration or dislike. Unhappily, people in England preferred to listen to Bankes's poisonous words than read Buckingham's praise. Lady Hester was so saddened and hurt when she heard how Bankes was vilifying her that she decided never to entertain any other strangers from England. It was a rule she was seldom to break. Her horizons were drawing in.

Buckingham was not entirely right when he said that Hester was happy. Although she was moderately content with her life she was extremely lonely. If the definition of a friend is an intimate acquaintance, Lady Hester had none except for a faithful few two thousand miles away in England. Her tiny entourage provided company for her, but Dr Meryon and Elizabeth Williams, who had recently rejoined Lady Hester from Malta, were basically her employees and neither was her social or intellectual equal. Mrs Fry had left, much to everyone's satisfaction. John Barker was perhaps the closest thing to a friend that she had. She had a deep dislike of all consuls and he was the one exception. They wrote to each other regularly; she called him a 'thoroughbred John Bull' – ('liberality and sincerity without parade') and he was flattered by her attention and always did everything he could for her.

At one stage she had talked about establishing an association of literary, scientific and artistic men around her with the aim of making

new discoveries and of exploring and quantifying little-known countries in the Middle East. When she realized how she was being
maligned in England she abandoned the idea. She had no wish to
become a peep-show for inquisitive travellers who had listened to
scurrilous stories about her.

Her financial problems were a continual background worry to her.
Although she had not made any more expeditions since Ascalon, her
charitable works were a constant drain on her pocket. Visitors had to
be looked after, servants and messengers paid, so although she had
curtailed nearly all of her previous extravagant ways, she was still
living beyond her means. When her allowance was late in arriving, she
was obliged to borrow from moneylenders, and the high interest rate
they charged only served to compound her problems. She managed to
remain fairly optimistic however, and the fatalistic attitude towards
money that she had inherited from the Pitts helped her in this. Life had
to go on, and she was confident that all would be well.

CHAPTER EIGHTEEN

'Left to my fate and faith alone'

Dr Meryon had been feeling homesick for eighteen months or more. He was tired of being scolded by Lady Hester, and she was weary of his little pomposities and sulks. Now that she was settled and her health was fairly stable, they agreed that he could go as soon as a replacement could be found for him. In June 1815, Giorgio, a young man who worked for Hester, was sent to England to look for another doctor. It took a long time.

'My last, dated Christmas Day 1815, was sent in the hope that it would be the last I should have occasion to write from this country,' Meryon wrote wearily to his sister in England, on 6 September 1816. 'But nearly another year has past over my head and I am still here, languishing for home like a mother-sick boy, as I believe I always was, and feel I ever shall be.'

Charles Meryon and Lady Hester had travelled together for nearly seven years. It was inevitable that they should have had disagreements from time to time, but they had had frequent breaks from each other's company which had helped. They had both always scrupulously maintained their employer/employee relationship, but Meryon's respect for Lady Hester had amounted nearly to hero-worship. Lady Hester was more prosaic about Meryon. He had always been loyal to her, which she appreciated, and his usefulness was beyond doubt. What she had perhaps failed to appreciate was quite how sensible and open-minded a man he was in many ways.

Although he had quailed slightly when Lady Hester started openly living with Michael, he soon rallied, and in his professional life he was liberal enough to question accepted medical practice. He had recently developed, for example, quite radical ideas about diet. He experimented on himself and decided that too much meat and wine was a bad thing, and that fresh fruit, milk and water was healthier. He was also intrigued by the different traditions in childbirth between 'people styled uncivilized ... and other so called polished nations'. He realized that women in less sophisticated cultures had a much easier time of things. 'Ought it not at least to awake some doubts in our mind,' he pondered, 'as to which party pursues the right method, and whether over-officious zeal in some and mercenary motives in others have not tended to make of a natural act a very complicated and artificial one?' That same argument still goes on today.

Giorgio finally returned from England in November, bringing a new doctor, a sheaf of letters for Hester and twenty-seven packing-cases of household items, gifts and other things she had told him to bring back. Dr Meryon was free to go.

He wrote forlornly in his diary: 'It was not without great melancholy that I beheld the day arrive which was to separate me from a country where I had seen so many strange things, and from a person whose exalted courage, talents and character had gained an entire ascendancy over my mind.'

Despite his sadness, Meryon left Mar Elias in January 1817. Lady Hester and Miss Williams packed his bags with special provisions: gazelle pasties, tarts, plum cake and 'cold fowls'. He also took with him Lady Hester's final letter to Michael, so his departure was a double melancholy for her. It was, or seemed to be, the ending of two quite different relationships at the same time.

This was not the only loss that Lady Hester sustained in 1817. As before, misfortunes never came singly to her. There were two more to come. Firstly she heard that her father had died, and then she quarrelled irreconcilably with the new Lord Stanhope, Philip, her once 'incomparable Mahon'.

The death of her father was not a great blow to Lady Hester because she had been completely estranged from him for years, ever since she arranged Philip's dramatic escape from Chevening. The quarrel with Philip was a bitter disillusionment, however, although it was one that she initiated herself. After years of silence on both sides, she wrote him a furious letter in which she accused him of ingratitude, the one fault she could never tolerate. It was understandable. Hester had literally rescued Philip from their father, securing his inheritance and enabling him to lead a proper and full life. The years of silence that had stretched between them had hurt Lady Hester badly. It was he, as a man, financially comfortable and living in the safety of the English countryside, who should have extended a helping hand to his sister, living alone and so far away. She would not have rejected his friendship even though she might have been too proud to accept financial help. It is always sad when pride and stubbornness blight a loving friendship, and doubly so when it is within a family. They were both the losers.

In the same month that Meryon left, a handsome young man arrived at Mar Elias. His name was Captain Lousteneau and he was looking for his father, the half-crazy general who had foretold Napoleon's escape from Elba. The general had been nearly destitute when he wandered in to Lady Hester's camp that night, nearly two years before, and was now living at Mar Elias, but he was unsurprised to see his son, for he had apparently foreseen his arrival. What happened over the next few months is shrouded in mystery but Captain Lousteneau evidently became very important to Lady Hester in a very short time. Dr Meryon had gone, and Lady Hester never referred to the Captain in her letters to England, but it seems likely that they had a brief but intense affair. From what little information there is to be found about him he appeared to have been a rather cocksure, unlikeable person, so perhaps it was as well that his reign was short-lived. He contracted food poisoning and died within a few months of his arrival at Mar Elias. Lady Hester had him buried in the garden, and issued orders that she was to be buried with him. When she decided to move from Mar Elias a few months after his death, she had his body disinterred and moved to the garden of her new home.

The reason for the move was that Mar Elias was getting too small. Sometimes there was simply not enough room to house all the people who came to Lady Hester for help, so she decided to move to another former monastery a few miles inland from Sayda, called Djoun. It was beautifully situated on top of a hill that was in a valley surrounded on three sides by the Lebanon mountains. On the fourth side the land ran away to a view of the sparkling blue Mediterranean.

As always, Lady Hester knew exactly what she wanted and despite

Mehemet Ali, Ruler of Egypt.

The Tombs of the Mamelukes, Cairo.

Lady Hester Stanhope, a portrait from memory.

Lady Hester in conversation with Dr Meryon. They are smoking their tchibouques whilst a black servant, possibly Zezefoon, brings them coffee.

Dr Charles Meryon, Lady Hester's physician.

Emir Beshyr, the infamous Prince of the Druses.

Lady Hester's entry into Palmyra in March 1813.

Palmyra.

Arabs of the Beni Said by David Roberts.

Cairo by David Roberts.

Arrival of the Caravan, Khan Asad Pasha, Damascus by Charles Robertson.

Detail from *Ascent of the Lower Range of Mount Sinai* by David Roberts.

Djoun, Lady Hester's final home.

her lack of money, work on the house started immediately. She drew up her plans and supervised the builders. It was to be not only a home for herself but a place of safety and refuge for anyone who was in real need. Copying the simple style of the single-storey buildings, she created what was almost a tiny village surrounded by a stout wall with a strong, well-guarded gate. There were about forty rooms in the different buildings and each was designed for a specific use. Some connected with each other, others were quite self-contained, and at least one had a secret passage to the outside, to allow for private departures. Between the various buildings there was a network of courtyards and passages designed so that no one could enter or leave unseen unless Lady Hester wished it. In the south-west corner of the residence was Lady Hester's apartment. She had a bedroom, a drawing room and a small kitchen used for the preparation of her food. Another more Eastern-style room was the divan, an open-air courtyard with seating, where she would sometimes entertain visitors.

There was one crowning glory to Djoun, however, the only luxury that Lady Hester allowed herself, and one that only the most favoured visitors were allowed to see. From the barren, stony soil of the foot-hills of Lebanon she created a garden – a wonderful, scented triumph of a garden that made an indelible impression on all who saw it.

There were pergolas and arbours smothered with fragrant tumbling profusions of jasmine and honeysuckle. Gloriously perfumed roses clambered over walls and filled the marble-edged beds. Winding paths lined with banks of brilliant blue periwinkles led to an emerald green lawn where a delicate fountain played.

'We descended into it by a flight of steps,' one privileged visitor wrote, 'and I followed her in a perfect state of enchantment through one of the most beautiful gardens I had yet seen in the East. Trellises from whose green vaults, like millions of fairy lamps, hung clusters of the sparkling grapes of the Promised Land; kiosks and sculptured arabesques interlaced with jasmine and other climbing plants ... alleys planted with all the fruit trees of England, of Europe ... green lawns studded with flowering shrubs ... marble borders enclosing masses of flowers which I never saw before – such is this garden!'

She had created a place of beauty and life that became a refuge to her, a place of comfort and inspiration as the rest of the world began to desert her. It was a joy to her and to everyone who saw it.

Lady Hester's growing fascination with astrology was beginning to make itself felt in her life. She started to draw up horoscopes for her visitors, and she only allowed herself to become friendly with those people whose stars were sympathetic to her own. Only when the stars were exceptionally compatible were people allowed into her garden and into another enclosure beyond. This was a courtyard and stables where she kept two very special horses. One was a beautiful grey mare called Lulu that had been given to Lady Hester by the Emir Beshyr. The other was its foal, an equally beautiful but deformed chestnut that Hester named Laila. The foal apparently had a double backbone, and such a hollow back that it appeared already saddled.

Lulu and Laila were kept like royalty and had their own special grooms. One visitor compared the horses to two rather portly and elderly princesses that were 'obliged to grant an audience that bored them to death. Very slowly and indifferently they turned their heads,' he reported, 'and looked at us with an air of haughty repose.' Lady Hester was devoted to the two horses however, for they held a special significance for her. She thought they could be part of the prophecy of the fortune-teller Brothers. She had often thought about his works. He had told her that she would be crowned Queen in the East and that she would enter Jerusalem at the head of the chosen people. For years she had laughed about it with her friends, but after her visit to Palmyra when she had been ritually crowned, she had begun to think of it as more than just a joke. Recently two more prophecies had echoed Brothers's words with uncanny precision. The first was made by General Lousteneau, who tried to persuade her that her arrival as Queen had been foretold in the scriptures. He was probably just a rogue who knew a good thing when he saw one, but he seemed to have certain powers: not only had he foretold Napoleon's escape from Elba with startling accuracy, but he predicted the 1822 earthquake in Aleppo.

The second corroboration of Hester's apparent destiny in the East was made by one of her servants, an old man called Metta. He was a spiritualist and astrologer and he translated a passage for her from an ancient book of prophecies. 'A European woman will come and live on Mount Lebanon at a certain epoch,' the prophecy said. 'She will build a house there and obtain power and influence greater than a Sultan's. A boy without a father will join her and his destiny will be fulfilled under her wing. The coming of the Mahdi [Messiah] will follow, but be preceded by war, pestilence, famine and other calamities. The Mahdi will ride a horse born saddled,' it continued, 'and a woman will come from a far country to partake in the mission.'

The Turkish Christians, unlike their European counterparts, believed the second coming of Christ to be imminent. It all seemed to fit; she found it fascinating.

As a child Hester had always been asking questions, never taking things at their face value. Her years in the East had rekindled that habit in her and made her question all her basic beliefs. She had never been actively religious, but by now she had studied and compared Christianity, Islam and the Jewish faith and understood the different strengths and virtues of each. It was a natural extension for her to be interested in spiritualism, astrology and magic, especially in a country where such things had been an accepted part of life for centuries. She began to study these things, seeking out dervishes and prophets to be her teachers. She was an apt pupil and learned quickly. As she learned she began to wonder. Could it not be, she asked herself, that there was some truth in these prophecies? She had been crowned Queen of Palmyra already, had come to live on Mount Lebanon and built a house there. Her power was indisputable. The foal, Laila, had been born 'saddled', – was it possible that the Messiah would ride Laila into Jerusalem at his second coming?

It was tempting to believe it all. There was only one problem. Hester had always been far too sensible to believe in humbug. She despised affectation in others and would have been mortified to discover it in herself. Yet the truth remains that as she grew older she came to believe in the prophecy. For some of the visitors in whom she confided it was proof of the rumours they had heard – that she was mad. Others were more generous and put it down, correctly, I believe, to a strong individualism which sometimes bordered on harmless eccentricity. This independent streak was a characteristic without which she would never have travelled as far and as long as she did, and it was one she shared with all the Victorian lady travellers of whom she was the forerunner.

The naturally intuitive side of her nature and her enjoyment of power made her want to believe that the prophecy would come true, and that she still had a glorious role to play in history, but her logical, realistic side told her she was being foolish, so she could only partly allow herself to accept it. By the time she came to believe it, she had been living in isolation at Djoun for many years. It was hardly surprising that she should have developed some strange ideas. One eminently sensible visitor said compassionately, 'I fancied that I could distinguish the brief moments during which she contrived to believe in herself, from those long and less happy intervals in which her own reason was too strong for her.'

As the years passed she became very skilled at reading the stars, and at reading people's faces – the art of physiognomy. Her intuitive understanding of people was enhanced by these skills, and a new reputation began to spread across the country – she was not only a Queen, but a prophet and a mystic. If it was possible for people to respect her more, they did. 'All the learned of the East pronounce me to be an Ulema min Allah – a heaven-born Sage,' she told Mr Madden, a visitor.

She accepted increasingly few visitors to Djoun. People interpreted her refusal to see them as another sign of madness or as inhospitality at the very least. The truth was very different. Her health was beginning to deteriorate and often she was simply too ill to entertain, and her other problem was poverty. Arabic custom and her Stanhope pride would not allow her to welcome people without giving refreshment to them, their servants and horses. 'How many times have I been abused by the English when I did not deserve it, and for nothing so much as for not seeing people, when perhaps it was quite out of my power,' she wrote sadly after she had received a rude letter from two Englishmen she had turned away. 'Little did they know that I had not a bit of barley in the house for their horses, and nothing for their dinner. I could not tell them so. . . .'

One visitor that she was able to entertain was Captain Yorke, afterwards Earl of Hardwicke. It was in 1825 and he was entranced by her. 'She received me as an English lady of fashion would have done,' he wrote to his father. 'I at once became delighted with her wit, her knowledge and, I must say, her beauty, for she is still one of the finest specimens of woman I saw.' Lady Hester was then forty-nine. 'Her conversation animated beyond any person I ever met; she was in great spirits; her dress . . . very rich.'

They talked all night of 'histories of marvels and wonders, manners and customs of the people, plague, pestilence and famine etc. etc.', but when he returned the following evening she was not the same – 'she talked wildly, and was much distressed in mind.' Hester knew that she could quickly become ill when she was overtired, and this is what had happened. She had confided all of her worries to him. She was being threatened with eviction from Djoun unless she bought the place for £500. She had no money at all, and no 'good people about her'.

In a kind and thoughtful act he wrote to the second Lord Chatham, Hester's uncle. 'She is very forlorn,' he said, 'nothing will ever induce her to return to her native land . . . but what would make her comfortable and as happy as she can be made in this world, would be to purchase Djoun for her and send such people as I have described out to her.' He thought she needed a dependable manservant and a maid.

'PS' he wrote, 'I do sincerely hope some measures will be taken to make her comfortable. She has not very long to live, depend upon it. C.Y.'

Nothing was done.

Civil war broke out in Lebanon that same summer. Sheik Beshyr and the Druses sided with the Pasha of Damascus against the Emir Beshyr and the Pasha of Acre. 'The whole mountain is in a flame,' Lady Hester wrote to Dr Meryon. 'All the villages about me are deserted except one, which remains trembling between the troops on one side and the mountaineers on the other.' She was not frightened, but admitted 'my situation is not a very agreeable one . . . the great number of miserable people who have announced their intention of taking refuge here . . . presents me with the prospect of starvation if this business lasts long, for these poor people are destitute of everything.'

Luckily for Lady Hester the war was soon over, but the repercussions were to go on for a long time for her. The hostilities ended when the Sheik was tricked into surrendering to the Emir, who strangled and beheaded him, and had his body cut up and thrown to the dogs. The Emir then castrated the Sheik's three sons, burnt out their eyes, cut out their tongues and threw them out of the country. Lady Hester's erstwhile friend and close neighbour had revealed himself as a man capable of atrocious cruelty, and although by now she had become used to the cruelties of the East, she was totally appalled by this display and denounced the Emir as 'a dog and a monster', and in so doing declared herself the enemy of one of the most ruthless men in Syria.

To be openly defiant in this way was totally unprecedented for the simple reason that the Emir had all his enemies killed. As Meryon said: 'All those who were obnoxious to him, high or low, were sure, in the course of his protracted despotism, to be removed, either by secret machinations or overt acts.' Hester was protected only by her connections with the Porte and the fact that she was a high-born foreigner, but the Emir became her most bitter enemy.

There was one final blow to fall that summer. Hester heard from England that her dear brother James had killed himself. His beloved wife, Frederica, had died in childbirth two years before and he had never got over her loss. Lady Hester was bereft.

James had not only been a much-loved brother, he had been a symbol to Hester of what good there was left in the world. He had brought her Sir John Moore's dying message, they had travelled to Gibraltar together, he had offered her his savings when she was shipwrecked in order that she could buy new clothes, he had been the only person left in the world whom she loved wholeheartedly. When Frederica died Hester had not heard about it until six months later, and had decided not to write to James in case she caused him further grief. It was not a decision she had taken lightly: 'to write, not to write – no proper conveyance – what to say – after a year perhaps to open the wounds of his heart without being able to pour in one drop of the balm of consolation! What I say would be vain.' It was a decision she now bitterly regretted and her grief was compounded by guilt, for she felt that her silence might have been misunderstood by James.

No one can say how she coped, for she was quite alone except for the faithful Miss Williams. We only know that she was utterly overwhelmed with grief – 'her weeping was not woman-like, it had a wild howl that was painful to hear.' James's death was a blow which struck at the already weakened foundations of her life. She never left Djoun again.

By 1826 Lady Hester was beginning to be seriously concerned about her debts. The outrageous amount of interest that she was being charged on amounts borrowed from moneylenders meant that things were spiralling out of control. 'It is not, as you think, 25 per cent yearly that I have to pay,' she wrote to Meryon, 'but 50 and 95; and in one instance I have suffered more loss still. Gold of 28 and a half piastres they counted to me here at 45, which I spent at 28 and a half and am to repay at Beirut at the rate of 45 – calculate that!'

Late in the year a visitor came to Djoun, claiming to be the representative of the Dukes of Sussex and Bedford and of other individuals who were concerned for her. He told her that they intended to sort out her affairs and arrange for her debts to be paid. Lady Hester had been very ill with fever and convulsions and the promises that the man made seemed to her like the answer to a prayer, but although she could see no reason for him to be lying she could not quite bring herself to believe him. She decided to ask for Dr Meryon's help. The doctor who had replaced him had long since left, and Lady Hester had been treating herself but with singular lack of success. Her sight was affected and she could hardly read or write. She had weakened herself by regular bleedings and had diagnosed her illness as asthma, which it certainly wasn't. She had written to Dr Meryon asking him to come out to her again. Although he had married shortly after his return to England, he had never stopped worrying about Lady Hester, and he agreed to come. She wrote to him again after the messenger had visited her.

'I will not afflict you by drawing a picture of my situation or of the scare-crow grief and sickness have reduced me to, but I must tell you that I am nearly blind, and this is probably the last letter I shall be able to write to you.' Luckily this turned out to be untrue, but no doubt she believed it at the time. She outlined two courses of action he was to take – one if the man's promises turned out to be true, and another in case they were false. If they were false she said she wished to be publicly disowned and 'left to my fate and faith alone'. If her finances were to be sorted out then she wanted Meryon to bring some servants for her. Her hopes came to nothing, for there was no plan to help her, – no money, no servants and no reprieve. The man was an impostor and it had all been a cruel and inexplicable trick. Her opinion of the British sank even lower.

It must have seemed to her that there was to be no Meryon either. He and his wife set out from England in January of 1827. Bad weather and bad luck delayed them at every point. Eight months later they were still on their way, sailing in an Italian brig off Crete, when they were attacked by pirates. The Italian captain, encouraged by the terrified Mrs Meryon, took them back to Italy where they stayed until November. Mrs Meryon refused to carry on with the journey, but would not let the doctor go without her, so they returned to England in June of the next year.

All this time Lady Hester was awaiting their arrival. By the late autumn of 1827, she had pawned most of her possessions and been forced to borrow from scurrilous moneylenders once again to cope with a new influx of needy people. Djoun had been inundated with all the 'Franks of Sayda', who had heard news of the Battle of Navarino. The plans that Mehemet Ali, the ruler of Egypt had made to annihilate the Greeks had been thwarted by the British Navy and the Europeans in the coastal towns feared reprisals. Somehow Lady Hester found the necessary money and energy to cope with the refugees. 'I shall never want courage or forget the duty I owe to my fellow-creatures,' she said. But she sank further into debt.

Ever since his triumph over the Sheik, the wicked and unrepentant Emir Beshyr had been trying to terrorize Lady Hester. He had not forgiven her for denouncing him after his ruthless treatment of the Sheik and his sons and was doing all he could to make her life a misery. He told the local villagers that he would kill them if they helped her, and he did, sometimes laying the corpses outside the gate of Djoun.

On one occasion, the Emir sent a messenger to Lady Hester ostensibly on some errand but really to try to intimidate her. She was absolutely outraged. 'Do not think I am afraid of you or your master,' she stormed at him, 'you may tell him I don't care a fig for his poisons – I know not what fear is. It is for him and those who serve him to tremble.' By this time the unfortunate man was shaking 'like an aspen leaf'. 'And tell the Emir Khalyl,' she continued, referring to the Beshyr's son, 'that if he enters my doors I'll stab him – my people will not shoot him, but I will stab him – I, with my own hand.'

She really did not know what fear was, especially when she was roused over someone as iniquitous as the Emir Beshyr. Later, when she had calmed down, she told Dr Meryon about the visit. 'The man almost fainted away before I had done with him,' she said scornfully. 'I was not afraid of them, and even now, weak as I am, I do believe I could strangle the strongest of them.'

The only precaution she would take against the Emir was to hide a dagger under her pillow at night, but poor Miss Williams was terrified. Finally, word of the Emir's threatening behaviour towards Lady Hester reached Constantinople, and Mr Canning, who was once again in residence, put a stop to it all. She was jubilant. 'The Emir Bechyr with all the art and meanness well known to him has now become abjectly humble,' she wrote triumphantly to Meryon. 'Finding he had made a false calculation and displeased the great and small in the country by his vile conduct, he ... repents having given me the opportunity of showing what I am. I am thus become more popular than ever, having shown an example of firmness and courage no one could calculate upon.'

She was always at her best when under pressure, but her health and spirits continued to fluctuate. Worry about money and the strain of looking after the refugees from Sayda finally took their toll. Both she and Miss Williams fell gravely ill with yellow fever. With no one to stop them, the servants looted Hester's rooms of what little there was left to steal. Two black servants and an eight-year-old girl were the only ones who remained. They did their best but sadly the poor, faithful Miss Williams died. Lady Hester's life was saved only by chance. A rich Syrian, passing through the village, heard of Hester's illness and called to see if there was anything he could do. Shown to Lady Hester's room by the eight-year-old, he found her 'stiff and cold, in the state of one dying of hunger'. He gave her food, organized proper care for her, and she recovered.

Her powers of recuperation were phenomenal. Within weeks she was quite better and attributing her well-being to God. 'One feels much more elevated when God has been one's physician,' she wrote airily to a friend; 'It is the Supreme Being alone who has saved me in all my difficulties for these last twenty years, and who has given me strength to support what others would have sunk under.' One hopes she also thanked her good samaritan.

After the euphoria of recovery she felt the loss of Miss Williams badly. From being a maid she had become Lady Hester's secretary and friend – without her she had no one even to talk to. She closed up Miss Williams's room without touching anything, and buried her under a tamarisk tree in the Catholic cemetery in Sayda.

She began to look forward to Meryon's arrival with almost pathetic anticipation. When he finally came she astounded him by kissing him on both cheeks. He was overwhelmed. They stayed up half the night, talking, but when Meryon finally returned to his house in the village it was to a hysterical wife who thought he'd been eaten by wild animals.

Lady Hester had advised Meryon not to bring his wife, but Mrs Meryon had insisted on joining him. She was undoubtedly curious to meet the woman who had dominated so much of her husband's life. When they met, Lady Hester was exceedingly kind to her, but they were destined never to get on, because, for different reasons, they both wanted the complete attention of the same man. Meryon was evidently attracted to strong women, for his wife was not the meek little soul one might have expected him to marry. She proved to be just as intractable as Lady Hester on occasion, and Dr Meryon was frequently caught in the middle.

Lady Hester was now living in conditions of extreme poverty. She was still receiving her allowance from England, but a great deal of it went towards paying off the moneylenders to whom she resorted when her money ran out, as it frequently did. When she was well enough she took great pleasure in walking in her garden and visiting her horses, Lulu and Laila. When she was ill, however, she remained in her bedroom which was, as Meryon noted, 'hardly better than a common peasant's'.

Her bed was a rough affair, made of planks nailed onto trestles. She had a mattress and silk pillow-cases, but no sheets. A knotted rope hung down beside the bed and went, through a pulley on the ceiling, to a 'powerful bell' that she would clang imperiously at all times of the day and night. She was very demanding of her servants: when she was ill nothing seemed right. Her bed would have to be made over and over again, while she stood on a rough felt mat giving instructions and smoking a pipe. Even when she had finally gone to bed she slept so poorly that the servants would hardly have time to rest. 'Ding ding goes the bell again,' Meryon recalled with a sigh, 'Dar Djoun was in a state of incessant agitation all night.'

A black slave called Zezefoon slept, when she was able, on a thick cushion beside Lady Hester's bed, and the whole room was strewn with dust-covered paraphernalia. Two deep niches in the wall held 'a few books, some bundles tied up in handkerchiefs, writing paper – all in confusion with sundry other things of daily use'. Scissors, spectacles, pins and sealing wax were piled on white china plates, and there was an 'old parchment cover of some merchant's day-book with blotting paper inside . . . in which, spread on her lap as she sat up in bed, she generally wrote her letters.'

There were no curtains at the windows, just pieces of felt propped up with sticks. A wooden stool beside her bed served as a table. Lemonade, chamomile tea, ipecacuanha lozenges and a bottle of water jostled for space with 'a bottle of wine, or of violet syrup, aniseeds . . . cloves, quince preserve, orgeat, a cup of cold tea covered over by the saucer, a pill-box etc.' It was almost impossible to pick anything up without knocking over the rest.

Meryon's sense of propriety was affronted. 'Such was the chamber of Lord Chatham's grand-daughter! Diogenes himself could not have found fault with its appointments!'

Now that Meryon had returned Lady Hester expected him to be as constantly available to her as he had always been, but his wife would not stand for it. Hester's favourite occupation was to spend endless hours talking and smoking her tchibouque, and she never seemed to tire. 'Talking, with her, appeared to be as involuntary and unavoidable as respiration,' the doctor once observed, and he some-times sat with her for ten or twelve hours, listening and learning until the room was wreathed in smoke and dawn had come. One unfor-tunate visitor actually fainted from exhaustion during one of her sessions, but Meryon was like a sponge, absorbing everything she said.

'There was no secret of the human heart, however carefully con-cealed, that she could not discover;' he wrote in admiration, 'no workings in the listener's mind that she could not penetrate; no in-trigue, from the low cunning of vulgar intrigue to the vast combina-tions of politics, that she could not unravel; no labyrinth, however tortuous that she could not thread.'

She was able to make people most uncomfortable with her powers of perception: 'It was this comprehensiveness and searching faculty, this intuitive penetration, which made her so formidable,' Dr Meryon wrote, 'for, under imaginary names, when she wished to show a person that his character and course of life were unmasked to her view, she would, in his very presence, paint him such a picture of himself, in drawing the portrait of another, that you might see the individual writhing on his chair, unable to conceal the effect her words had on his conscience.'

Unfortunately for Meryon he could not please both Lady Hester and his wife at the same time. When he was spending hours enthralled at his mentor's words, Mrs Meryon was building up a head of steam at home. What pleased one infuriated the other: it was an impossible situation.

The climax came when the Pasha of Damascus asked Dr Meryon to visit a friend of his who was ill. Lady Hester wanted him to go, but Mrs Meryon said he could not. Hester tried every persuasion she knew to get her to change her mind, but she was adamant, and Lady Hester was thwarted. She quarrelled bitterly with the doctor and wrote him a letter: 'You are the last of my disciples whom I thought I could make something of,' she accused, 'but it is like cutting the hair off the legs of half-bred horses; it grows again, and you may often get a kick in the face for your pains . . . when a man gives his beard to a woman,' she finished, 'it is all over with him.'

The doctor and his wife left, but not before Lady Hester had made him feel thoroughly guilty by 'painting him a picture of himself'. It came in the form of a story of a faithful servant.

'I was so touched by her eloquent and forcible manner of recounting the story,' he confessed, 'and with the self-application that I made of it to my own tardiness in going to her in her distress, together with my intention of leaving her owing to our recent differences, that I burst into tears and wept, as the expression is, bitterly.'

Perhaps when Meryon had left, Lady Hester wept a few bitter tears as well: after he and his wife had gone she was, once more, quite alone.

CHAPTER NINETEEN

'Alone in such a storm'

The horizons of Lady Hester's life, once so limitless, continued to draw in. She had not stepped outside the walls of Djoun since she had heard of her brother James's death in 1825, nor did she ever leave it again. Gradually a type of daily routine evolved in her life. Having kept her servants up for half the night she would fall into a fitful sleep for a few hours, awaking again soon after sunrise. Rousing the household with an imperious clanging on the dreaded bell, she would spend most of the day in bed, issuing orders and directions with endless vigour. One of the few European habits she had clung to was having a bedroom with a permanent bed in it: the Eastern habit was to unroll a mattress in the living room, or simply to sleep on a sofa covered with a quilt. She had adopted the Syrian habit of sleeping almost fully dressed however, so she was quite decently clad at all times, and able to have even her male servants come and go quite happily. She kept about thirty servants, most of whom were moderately incompetent. She would see them all in the morning, one after the other, and occasionally, on especially awful occasions, all together. She was in charge of every detail of everything that went on both in the monastery and further afield.

Dr Meryon had been amazed at the energy she still had in spite of her failing health. 'In the same day I have frequently known her to dictate with the most enlarged political views, papers that concerned the welfare of a pashalik [a pasha's area of jurisdiction], and the next moment she would descend, with wondrous facility, to some trivial details about the composition of a house-paint, the making of butter, the drenching of a sick horse, the choosing of lambs, or the cutting-out of a maid's apron. She had a finger in everything, and in everything was an adept,' he continued. 'Her intelligence really seemed to have no limits.' She involved herself closely in the machinations of the local Pashas and Emirs, sending scouts out into the souks to glean information for her. She devoted just as much energy, however, to foiling the plots of servants who were trying to cheat her, and sadly there were many. A few were loyal to her and these she rewarded handsomely. General Lousteneau was still living at Mar Elias supported entirely by Lady Hester, indeed, she frequently sent money she could ill-afford to his family in France. The clairvoyant Metta had died, leaving his two nearly adult sons to Lady Hester's care, and the faithful service of her steward and general factotum, a man called Logmagi, was amply rewarded with a house and gifts of money.

Having written her letters and dealt with the servants and life in general, she would rise at four or five in the afternoon to wash and change. In keeping with her much reduced circumstances her clothes were not nearly so magnificent as they had once been, indeed, she designed and made most of them herself. She had taken to shaving her head for comfort, and wore a red fez covered with a *keffiyeh* – a pale striped silk handkerchief that draped either side of her face or was tied under her chin. Coiled over this as a turban was a cream-coloured Barbary shawl. Her habit of having herself bled regularly had combined with her poverty to make her extremely thin by now, but this was disguised by the elegantly draped gowns and cloaks she wore. She presented a gracious and imposing figure to the few strangers she consented to see, but her health continued to deteriorate. Her chest gave her trouble every winter and she began to cough up blood. 'I am very thin,' she wrote to Meryon, 'but contented about my health, as this gives proof of my natural strength.'

It was quite true that she had a remarkably strong constitution – she had needed it on many occasions –and it was about to be tested again, for in 1832 war erupted once more in Lebanon. Mehemet Ali's son, Ibrahim Pasha, armed with the might of the Egyptian Army, invaded Lebanon and laid siege to Acre. The city was well-armed and manned, but after seven months it fell to the invaders and the Egyptian forces marched into Syria and Lebanon, creating terror and havoc wherever they went.

Lady Hester now found herself in an awkward situation. She had always liked and respected Mehemet Ali, the ruler of Egypt. He had been courteous and hospitable to her in Cairo, but she could not condone his invasion and his insubordination to the Porte. Her loyalty lay with the Sultan in Constantinople. Knowing what Lady Hester was like, Mehemet Ali had instructed his Minister Boghos Bey to write to her, warning her not to interfere with his plans. The very idea that a lone English woman could make things awkward for the invading army of a nation as powerful as Egypt gives an idea of what a formidable reputation she had. She wrote back disdainfully to the Minister. She showed her utter disapproval by declining to address him directly.

'Sir,' she wrote, 'I once knew when I was in Egypt a Mr Boghoz, a polite and accomplished gentleman, who left every agreeable impression of himself in my memory. I hear now there is a Boghoz Bey, the minister of His Highness the Viceroy of Egypt, and that he has joined in a revolution with his master against his legitimate sovereign. If Boghoz Bey would listen to me, I would tell him that partial revolutions never succeed, and that I never thought well of them. The lot of those who rise against their lawful sovereign has always been unfortunate.'

Survivors from Acre flooded into Djoun seeking protection from Lady Hester and she took in all she could. 'After the siege all that remained of the wretched population fled here,' she wrote to Dr Meryon, 'and my house and the village were, for the space of three years, the Tower of Babel. . . . I had at one time, seventy-five coverlets out for strangers, chiefly soldiers – the village full of families – and those at Sayda and other places coming and going for a little money to buy their daily bread.'

She had declared herself against the invading forces of Egypt, and throughout the coming years she never deviated from that commitment, even though she was surrounded by hostile troops. She enrolled the remnants of the Albanian soldiers from Acre to act as an armed guard for Djoun, but they were never needed. They spent their time lounging around in the courtyards, for Lady Hester's name and reputation was enough to keep the Egyptians away.

Mehemet Ali tried all he could to win her over, using every technique from direct threats to offers of friendship and patronage, but she was adamant in her stand against him. Even the Consul-General for Egypt and Syria, Colonel Campbell, was thwarted in his attempt to mediate. She would have no dealings whatsoever with what she saw as an illegal government. It was to have dire consequences for her.

No sooner had the last refugee from Acre left Djoun than Ibrahim Pasha started a merciless campaign of conscription for his Egyptian armies. His troops had always been formed out of mercenaries before, but he needed more men, and decided to take them by force. It was well-known that service in the Egyptian Army was for life: Syrian soldiers served in Egypt, and only escaped through death or desertion. It was not a prospect that appealed to many.

Press-ganging was entirely unknown in Syria, and its start was sudden, violent and premeditated. Late one evening, as men were making their way home from the Mosques and coffee-houses, they were seized by ruthless gangs of soldiers. The city gates had been closed to prevent their escape; many were taken but some managed to hide or take shelter in Consulates. Their reprieve was short-lived, for when their fathers were dragged out and beaten, and their mothers hung up by their hair and whipped, the poor young men soon gave themselves up to save their parents. Many who escaped over the city walls made their way to Djoun, to beg protection from Lady Hester once again. She hid whom she could.

Soon even the ferocious Druses were under the Egyptian rule. Their leader, the infamous Emir Beshyr, preferred to be on the winning side, so, waiting until he saw the Egyptians gain control of first Lebanon then Syria, he tricked his Druse tribesmen into giving up without a struggle.

Ibrahim Pasha was astounded that the Emir Beshyr and his men had given in without firing a single shot. 'What, didn't those dogs of Druses have a single bullet for us?' he was reputed to have cried. Lady Hester had worked unceasingly to rouse the Druses and local Bedu against the occupying forces and when she heard of Ibrahim Pasha's words she saw them as ammunition. Whenever a Druse came to her stronghold she would greet them with the same taunt: 'Dog of a Druse, why hadn't you a single bullet for Ibrahim Pasha?'

Her challenging words, her refusal to bow to the invading powers, and the refuge she gave to all who opposed Mehemet Ali, all helped to keep an independent spirit alive in the local tribesmen. And in 1837 the Bedu and Druse together formed a massive uprising which marked the beginning of the end of Egyptian rule in Palestine. It is very probable, knowing Hester's love of intrigue and her loyalty to the Porte, that she also played an active part in the revolt: Djoun was ideally placed to act as a centre and a 'safe house' for those involved in planning the uprising.

Not for nothing did Mehemet Ali say 'the Englishwoman has caused me more trouble than all the insurgent people of Syria and Palestine.' For six years she provided help, shelter and hope for hundreds of Syrian and Lebanese people who would otherwise have been killed. When the last refugee had finally gone, she was exhausted and desperately in debt. 'From the time the Egyptian troops entered this county until now I have been in hot water,' she wrote to Meryon. It was a wonderful understatement. 'I went through fatigue enough to kill a boatswain,' she recalled, 'but whatever sacrifices I may have made of money or health, I do not regret it, and I should do the same thing tomorrow if circumstances called for such exertions.'

She had housed, clothed and fed most of the refugees entirely at her own expense, and had continued to borrow from moneylenders at exorbitant rates of interest because there was no other choice. Owing to the great unrest in the country it was difficult to get her pension from England, and when it arrived it was not enough. She was even forced to borrow money to repay her most pressing creditors, but she kept throughout a most scrupulous account of all her debts. This was quite an achievement, not least because so many currencies were in circulation in the country. Piastres, Spanish dollars, and pounds all appear in her list of creditors and she was determined that all her debts would be repaid. 'I shall pay them all just double what they lent me,' she wrote to Meryon, 'and I think nobody can say that is unjust.'

She was rightfully proud of the help she had given to so many. 'I have saved many lives by my energy and determination,' she wrote, 'and have stood alone in such a storm! All trembled, but ... I have treated [the usurpers] without mercy and carried all before me. God helped me in all, for otherwise I never could have got through with it.' What she had achieved was scarcely credible. She was sixty years old.

For many years people in Britain had been avid for information about Lady Hester. Michael's return had titillated their appetite for gossip. Pampered ladies in perfumed salons continued to spread the gloating rumours that she had spent all Michael's money on luxuries and extravagances and now had gone mad.

Most of the people who came to see Lady Hester came out of curiosity, to see if the rumours were true. Those she turned away either because she was ill or because she had no food in the house were only too happy to confirm that she was mad: they had no other story to tell. During the years that Djoun was filled with refugees she accepted only a handful of European visitors. Two of them were writers and both, in their very different styles, confirmed her sanity to anyone who cared to listen.

The first was the French poet called Lamartine who was a quite outrageously affected man. He had a habit of constantly turning his feet this way and that to admire their long, elegant line, and he dandled a little pet dog on his knee and showered it with kisses. His description of Lady Hester was gallant and admiring. 'The lady appears to be about fifty years of age,' he wrote – she was fifty-six – 'but possesses those peculiar features which years cannot alter: freshness, colour and grace depart with youth, but when beauty resides in the form itself, in purity of expression, in dignity, in majesty, in a thoughtful countenance, whether in man or woman, beauty may change with the different periods of life, but it does not pass away; such is the person of Lady Hester Stanhope.'

They talked long into the night, with Lady Hester expounding her theories of the stars, the future and the coming of the Messiah: all the topics that had led people to say she was mad. Lamartine was much more shrewd than his dandyish exterior threatened. He knew that the people of Syria and Lebanon had strong beliefs in the supernatural and guessed that Hester's beliefs were a 'policy' she had adopted to gain credence with the Syrians, and that she had, over the years, half come to believe them herself. 'The men inhabiting this country . . . require a commerce with the stars, with prophecies, miracles and the second sight of genius: Lady Hester understood this, first by the exalted views of her truly superior intelligence, and in the sequel, perhaps . . . she deceives herself as well as others, and is become a convert to that faith she creates in them.'

He was quite emphatic on the question of her sanity. 'Lady Hester is not mad. Madness which is written so strongly in the eyes is not expressed in her beautiful and amiable look. Folly, which always betrays itself in conversation, interrupting the sequence by irregular, eccentric and sudden departures from the subject is in no way to be perceived in the elevated, mystic and cloudy, but well-sustained and connected conversation of her Ladyship.'

They parted friends, and he wrote a glowing tribute to her in his book *Souvenirs de l'Orient,* which was published in Lady Hester's lifetime. She was sent a copy of it, but dismissed his descriptions of her 'one half invented and the other half incorrect. Some of it made me angry,' she said, 'and some of it made me laugh very heartily.' It was very flattering however, and she was probably not unpleased.

The second visitor to Djoun was a very different kind of writer. It was Alexander Kinglake, and he wrote of their meeting in his book *Eothen.* Kinglake's mother had known Lady Hester during her years at Burton Pynsent and he said 'her name was made almost as familiar to me in my childhood as the name of Robinson Crusoe; both were associated with the spirit of adventure.'

Kinglake saw in Lady Hester 'exactly the person of a prophetess not, indeed, of the divine sybil imagined by Domenichino, so sweetly distracted betwixt love and mystery, a good business-like practical prophetess, long used to the exercise of her sacred calling.' They smoked, and Lady Hester talked, all night.

'For hours and hours this wondrous white woman poured forth her speech, for the most part concerning sacred and profane mysteries; but every now and then she would stay her lofty flight and swoop down upon the world again: whenever this happened, I was interested in her conversation.' At these times she was 'cool, decisive in manner, unsparing of enemies, full of audacious fun, and saying the downright things that the sheepish society around her is afraid to utter'.

Kinglake was unimpressed with her 'lofty' side but had to admit that a prophesy she made for him came true. She foretold that after leaving her he would go to Egypt and then return to Lebanon. 'I secretly smiled at this last prophecy as a "bad shot",' he wrote, 'because I had fully determined, after visiting the Pyramids to take ship from Alexandria to Greece.' The plague came to Egypt however, and he was forced to alter his plans – 'the unbelieved Cassandra was right after all.'

Whilst he remained sceptical about her mystical ability he freely acknowledged her more temporal powers. 'In truth,' he wrote, 'this half-ruined convent, guarded by the proud heart of an English gentle-woman, was the only spot throughout all Syria and Palestine in which the will of Mehemet Ali and his fierce lieutenant was not the law . . . and so long as Chatham's grand-daughter breathed a breath of life, there was always one hillock, and that too in the midst of a most populous district, which stood out and kept its freedom.'

All the years of defiance, hard work and poor nutrition were taking their toll. Her health was slowly deteriorating. It is probable that she had tuberculosis. She got thinner and weaker and her gaunt frame was racked by the dreadful cough that at times threatened to suffocate her. Her eyesight weakened – though probably only as a natural result of age – and she began to find her favourite occupations of reading and writing very difficult. She remained grimly determined not to succumb to illness, but everything seemed to be against her.

In the midst of all her worries about money there came a sudden ray of hope. She received a letter from England telling her of an inheritance in Ireland that had been concealed from her by her family. Like the impostor who had made promises that her debts would be paid, the news seemed almost too good to be true. She wrote eagerly to friends in England requesting details. Many years before, a land-owning colonel in Ireland had bequeathed his estates to Pitt as a token of esteem for his services to the country. When Pitt predeceased him the estates reverted to the colonel's next-of-kin, Lord Kilmorey. After the childless Kilmorey died, someone had the idea that the inheritance should revert to Hester, as Pitt's niece. It was a tenuous link at best, but Lady Hester convinced herself that she should inherit.

She wrote to the kind Captain Yorke, now Lord Hardwicke, asking him to assist her in claiming what was rightfully hers. He wanted to help, but had to tell her that he thought she had no claim on the inheritance. She then turned to her childhood friend, Sir Francis Burdett, and while she was waiting for his reply she also wrote to Dr Meryon, asking if he would return to Syria to help her sort out her financial affairs.

Meryon and his family had been living in Nice for several years. He was not doing very well. 'I have heard of your situation, and it pains me beyond description,' Lady Hester wrote to him. 'I hope I shall not claim in vain the assistance of an old friend, at the moment I most require one I can depend upon, to settle the business of my debts etc. now made public. Money has been left to me which has been concealed from me. . . . I should wish you to come as soon as you can possibly make it convenient to yourself, and return when the business is over.'

She gave him a list of commissions to bring over from France. Compared to her previous orders, their modesty is pathetic. 'I want for myself six cups and saucers. . . . I had a cup I was so fond of, for tea and coffee tasted so good out of it. It was strong and good china, but it is gone, and one cup held enough for my breakfast – a moderate cup and a half . . . a few common candlesticks (brass or something strong), a few common entangling combs, a few scrubbing brushes for the kitchen – that is all.' A request for her twelve-year-old maid shows she was not always a dragon to her servants – 'as an encouragement, a pair of earrings, a string of beads, a pair of bracelets and a thimble'.

Meryon arrived in July 1837 bringing with him his wife, his daughter Eugenia and a governess. Arriving in Sayda they found that so many houses had been damaged by a recent earthquake that they were forced to camp in a 'handsome green double marquee' in the garden of the French Consulate. The same earthquake had damaged Djoun badly, so that even if Lady Hester had been willing to accommodate Meryon's family, there would not have been enough room. Predict-ably, Mrs Meryon was not happy. After she had been reduced to hysterics by the unexpected appearance of an extremely meek Syrian deserter in the entrance to her tent, Dr Meryon moved his family to the old convent of Mar Elias. Here they were very comfortable, and Meryon was able to divide his time between the two women in his life in a way that was moderately acceptable to all parties.

It was now many months since Lady Hester had written to Sir Francis Burdett about her Irish inheritance, and she was getting des-perate for an answer. Her creditors were constantly pressing her for repayment of her debts; it was a continuous source of anxiety to her. It seemed that life was in a downward spiral for her, and that things were slipping out of her control.

Her servants were driving her to distraction. They were increasingly lazy, sloppy and rude, and they cheated and stole from her whenever they could. She reacted by becoming ever more strict with them, but nothing seemed to help. When Meryon saw what she had to cope with he was entirely sympathetic. 'The endless trifling acts of ignorance, awkwardness, carelessness, forgetfulness, falsehood and impudence which she used to relate to me were quite sufficient ... to justify the severe control she found it necessary to exercise over them.' Another problem was that the female servants kept on getting pregnant. When this happened Lady Hester 'obliged the man to marry [the girl] and gave them both their freedom'. She was not always a tyrant.

One day the doctor found her in tears. It was the first time he had ever seen any sign of weakness in her. 'Doctor, I am very poorly today,' she wept, 'and I was still worse in the night. I was within that,' – holding up her finger – 'of death's door and I find nothing now will relieve me.' She had spent the night convulsed with spasms, unable to breathe properly. 'A little while ago I could depend on something or other when seized with these spasmodic attacks, but now everything fails! How can I get better when I can't have a moment's repose from morning till night?'

The doctor was so upset that he burst into tears himself, and Lady Hester was forced to pull herself together and restore him with coffee and little pats on his back.

The weeks passed. Due to her ill health, Lady Hester was often confined to her bedroom where the squalor shocked Meryon. 'Such dust!, such confusion!, such cobwebs!' On New Year's Eve, 1837, she was once again reduced to utmost misery, remembering some of the few happy evenings of her childhood. 'Doctor,' she said, 'tonight in my father's house there used to be a hundred tenants and servants sitting down to a good dinner and dancing and making merry. I see their happy faces now before my eyes, and when I think of that and how I am surrounded here it is too much for me. When you left me this morning, things of former times came over my mind, and I could not bear to sit here, so I went out to break the chain of my thoughts. I would have gone into the garden, but it rained.'

Finally, on 27 January, a letter arrived for Lady Hester. It was brought by the English agent at Sayda, but she would not see him. Over the years she had become completely disillusioned with most consuls and agents; they always seemed to be too full of their own importance, yet useless in a crisis. 'If anything in the shape of a consul sets his foot within my doors, I'll have him shot, and if nobody else will do it, I'll do it myself,' she raged from her bed. The agent was finally persuaded to allow Dr Meryon to take the letter in to her.

She thought the letter was from Sir Francis Burdett with news of her inheritance, and 'her agitation and impatience arose to such a degree that I thought she would have gone frantic,' Dr Meryon wrote, anxiously. Lady Hester opened it eagerly with thin, trembling fingers. Perhaps this was to be the end of all her worries. With enough money all her problems would be solved, the creditors paid, the cracked walls of Djoun repaired, and perhaps some nourishing food would even help to make her healthy once again.

It was not from Sir Francis and it was not good news. It was a letter from Colonel Campbell, the Consul-General of Syria and Egypt and Mehemet Ali's confidant. He informed Lady Hester that, acting on instructions from the British Government, he was empowered to stop her pension until she repaid a debt that was outstanding with a Cairo moneylender. It was the cruellest blow she could possibly have received.

CHAPTER TWENTY

'A stab to the heart'

As soon as Lady Hester understood the content of the letter she grew almost frighteningly calm. Gently placing the letter on the bed, she read it slowly. It was marked from Cairo and dated 10 January 1838.

'Madam,
'I trust that your ladyship will believe my sincerity, when I assure you with how much reluctance and pain it is that I feel myself again imperatively called upon to address you upon the subject of the debt so long due by you to Mr Homsy.

'The Government of the Viceroy has addressed that of Her Majesty upon the subject, and, by a despatch which I have received from Her Majesty's Principal Secretary of State for Foreign Affairs, I am led to believe that a confidential friend of your ladyship will have already written to you to entreat you to settle this affair.

'Your ladyship must be aware that in order to procure your pension from Her Majesty's Government, it is necessary to sign a declaration and to have the consular certificate at the end of each quarter.

'I know that this certificate has hitherto been signed by M. Guys, the Consul of France at Beyrout; but, in strict legality, it ought to be certified by the British, and not by any foreign Consul; and, should your ladyship absolutely refuse the payment of this just claim, I should feel myself, however deeply I may regret it, forced to take measures to prevent the signature of the French or any other Consul but the British being considered as valid, and consequently your bill for your pension will not be paid at home. I shall communicate this, if your ladyship's conduct should oblige me so to do, to M. Guys and the other foreign Consuls of Beyrout, in order that your certificate may not be signed – and also send this under flying seal to Mr. Moore, Her Majesty's Consul at Beyrout in order that he may take the necessary steps to make this known to those consuls, if your ladyship should call on them to sign the quarterly certificate for your pension.

'I trust that your ladyship will be pleased to favour me with a reply, informing me of your intentions, and which reply will be forwarded to me by Mr. Moore.

'I beg your ladyship will be assured of the pain which I experience in being obliged to discharge this truly unpleasant duty, as well as of the respect with which I have the honour to remain, your ladyship's most obedient humble servant,

'P. Campbell

'Her Majesty's Agent for Egypt and Syria'

There can be no doubt that he was acting on instructions from Lord Palmerston and the British Government. It seemed that Royal consent must also have been obtained to rescind a pension given by Royal decree.

To have her life-long pension taken away was a mortal blow. It was also a morally and legally reprehensible act, and to someone of Lady Hester's heritage, integrity and pride, a slap in the face. The doctor was worried about her calmness – it seemed totally unnatural, especially for Lady Hester – but she was, quite simply, stunned at what had been done.

Slowly she started to analyse the situation to herself and Dr Meryon. The word 'again' in the first sentence bothered her – she had never before been addressed on the subject of debts by Mr Campbell. Similarly no 'confidential friend' had ever asked her to settle her affairs with Mr Homsy. The young Queen Victoria had just acceded to the throne the year before – what could she be thinking of? Was it not her own grandfather, George III, who had said that Lady Hester should have 'the greatest pension that can be granted to a woman'?

'My grandfather and Mr Pitt,' Hester pondered slowly, 'did something, I think, to keep the Brunswick family on the throne, and yet the grand-daughter of the old King, without hearing the circumstances of my getting into debt, or whether the story is true (for it might be false), sends to deprive me of my pension in a foreign country, where I may remain and starve. If it had not been for my brother Charles, and General Barnard, the only two who knew what they were about when the mutiny took place against the Duke of Kent at Gibraltar, she would not be where she is now, for her father would have been killed to a certainty.'

Even after the initial shock had worn off, Hester could think of nothing else than the letter. It totally refocused her mind. The daily irritations and worries about servants and health, though very real, were forgotten as the magnitude of what had happened to her sank in. If she were to believe what the letter said, it meant that what little income she had was now drastically reduced and once the confiscation of her pension became public knowledge, as it would through the consuls, not only would she be unable to borrow any more money, but her creditors would move in like vultures.

She was still very ill, and was having convulsive attacks every day. At one stage she came close to breaking down completely. 'She worked herself up into a state of madness,' the doctor recalled fearfully, 'I was afraid she would rupture a blood-vessel.' Unable to calm her, he left the room only to be called back immediately by her – 'Don't leave me,' she cried, 'I am much obliged to you, very much obliged to you, for the trouble you take on my account, but you must not be angry with me.' Poor Lady Hester. She had no one but Meryon now.

It was true that Lady Hester owed money to Mr Homsy. According to her accounts it was in the sum of 5,250 Spanish dollars, and had been contracted in September 1825. Unknown to Lady Hester, Mr Homsy had decided he could wait no longer for repayment. He had appealed to Mehemet Ali for help, saying his entire livelihood depended on the sum being repaid. It was extremely unusual for the Viceroy of Egypt to involve himself in a civil matter, but perhaps the fact that the debtor was his old adversary Lady Hester made a difference. He sent Homsy to Colonel Campbell for action. Campbell too had felt himself to have been humiliated by Lady Hester, so he was energetic in pursuing justice for Mr Homsy. On 22 October 1834, he wrote for advice to the Duke of Wellington at the Foreign Office. The Duke, who knew Lady Hester and her family, refused to let Campbell interfere.

'Her Majesty's Government have no control over Lady Hester Stanhope which could be exercised in favour of her creditors,' the Foreign Office wrote, 'and as the pecuniary transactions referred to appear to be entirely of a private nature, his Grace does not conceive that you can interfere in any official or authoritative manner with respect to them.'

Nothing could be clearer than that, but in 1835 Campbell applied again to the Duke. This time the Attorney-General was consulted and he confirmed the Duke's decision. He said that British consuls had no right to interfere in disputes between Turkish and British subjects unless both parties consented. 'Lady Hester must be asked to submit to his jurisdiction,' he wrote, but as she had been known to call all consuls reptiles it was hardly likely that she would.

The matter had rested for two more years until the tireless Homsy, egged on perhaps by Mehemet Ali, pressed for repayment again. By this time the Duke of Wellington had been replaced at the Foreign Office by Lord Palmerston, who appeared only too ready to help. Without referring to the Attorney-General, Palmerston advised Campbell that he might 'confidentially' inform her that her pension would be stopped for repayment of debts. He knew perfectly well that he was exceeding his powers by doing this, indeed there was no legal way for it to be done. Only by forbidding the consuls in Syria to sign Lady Hester's quarterly life certificate could he stop her from claiming what was rightfully hers. It remains a mystery how Lord Palmerston thought that Homsy might subsequently extract the debt from her pension, and indeed, if it was ever done.

Not once was any independent enquiry made into the validity of Homsy's claim on Lady Hester. No investigation was made as to why she had fallen into debt. The fact that she had been a magnificent ambassador for her country and deeply involved in philanthropic works was ignored, as was the fact that she was old, ill and alone. It was an outrage: it should never have been allowed to happen on humanitarian, moral, political or legal grounds.

By early February Lady Hester had determined what she would do. She decided that since the subject of her debts had been brought out into the open in this way, that it should be made as public as possible. She felt that since most of her debts had been incurred in helping others less fortunate than herself that she should not be portrayed as a criminal or even as a spendthrift. 'Perhaps it is better for me that this should have happened,' she said to Dr Meryon, 'it brings me at once before the world and let them judge the matter. It would have looked too much like shucklaban [charlatanism] if I had to go and tell everybody my own story, without a reason for it. But now, since they have chosen to make a bankrupt of me, I shall out with a few things that will make them ashamed.'

She decided to write to all her old friends asking them to help her in her fight for justice, and to try and get her letters published in the British press. She felt sure that public opinion would be on her side, and that this would force the Government's hand.

Having made the decision to fight, she felt mentally rejuvenated; all her old energy and vigour came flooding back. 'My body is nothing,' she told Meryon, 'the heart is as full of fire as ever.' She had always been incensed at injustices of any kind and this was the very apex of them all. She was still too weak, and her eyesight too poor to write the letters herself, so she dictated them to Meryon. First she wrote to Colonel Campbell and Mr Moore, the British consul. She had lost none of her skill at letter-writing. They were short and to the point.

'Sir,' she wrote to Campbell, 'I shall give no sort of answer to your letter of the 10th January until I have seen a copy of her Majesty's commands respecting my debt to Mr Homsy, or of the official orders from her Majesty's Secretary of State for Foreign Affairs, as also of Mr Homsy's claims, as well as of the statement sent to England – to whom and through whom – in order that I may know whom I have to deal with, as well as be able to judge the accuracy of the documents.

'I hope in future you will not think it necessary to make any apologies for the execution of your duty; on the contrary, I should wish to recommend you all to put on large Brutus wigs when you sit on the woolsack at Alexandria or at Beyrout.'

He deserved no better. The letter to Mr Moore was kinder.

'Sir, the sacrifice which I have made of your acquaintance and your society, that you might stand quite clear of everything that affects me, appears to be to little purpose. You will have some very disagreeable business to go through, as you will be made Colonel Campbell's honourable agent, and he the agent of the wise Lord Palmerston, and he the agent of your magnificent Queen.

'If in the end I find that you deserve the name of a true Scotchman, I shall never take ill the part that you may have to take against me, as it appears consistent with your duty in these dirty times.

'I remain with truth and regard,

'Yours,

'Hester Lucy Stanhope'

Having dealt with the local letters she then composed the ones to go to England. 'I should like to see that person come forward who dares to threaten a Pitt,' she said in one of them. All of her old fire and brimstone was back again. She wrote to Lord Palmerston, the Duke of Wellington, Mr Speaker Abercrombie, Sir Edward Sugden and Queen Victoria herself.

The letter to the Queen speaks for itself.

'Madam,' she wrote, 'Your Majesty must allow me to say that few things are more disgraceful and inimical to Royalty than giving commands without examining all their different bearings, and to cast without reason an aspersion upon the integrity of any branch of a family who has faithfully served their country and the House of Hanover.

'As no inquiries have been made of me what circumstances induced me to incur the debts alluded to by Y.M.'s Secretary of State for Foreign Affairs, I deem it unnecessary to enter into any details or explanations upon the subject. But I shall not allow the pension given by your Royal grandfather to be stopped by force: I shall resign it for the payment of my debts, and with it the name of an English subject and the slavery at present annexed to it. And as Y.M. has given publicity to this business, by Y.M.'s orders to consular agents, I surely cannot be blamed for following your Royal example.'

It was magnificent. It was a letter from one Queen to another and the resignation of her pension and her nationality was no less regal. It has never been established exactly how much Queen Victoria had to do with the decision to rescind Lady Hester's pension. Probably not much at all. What is known, however, is that she did nothing to change the situation after she became aware of it.

Lady Hester wrote to the Duke of Wellington, telling him of her refugees. 'Can you, as a soldier, blame me for what I have done? I should have acted the same way, before your eyes, to the victims of your own sword. Then the host of orphans, and widows, and little children, whom to feed and clothe for nearly two years took away all the ready money with which I ought in part to have paid my debts, and caused new ones. Yet I am no swindler, and will not appear like one ... all that I have to entreat of your Grace is to allow me to appear in the light in which I really stand – attached to humanity, and attached to royalty, and attached to the claims that one human being has upon another.' She appealed to him to talk to the Queen: 'There is nobody more capable of making the Queen understand that a Pitt is a unique race than your Grace: there is no trifling with them.'

She wrote to Sir Edward Sugden in a similar vein: 'The revolutions and public calamities which often take place in what is called a semi-barbarous country, call for great presence of mind and energy, and a degree of humanity and liberality unknown in Europe. To leave unfortunate sufferers starving at your gate until you have had an opportunity of inquiring into their private character, and investigating how far it is likely to endanger your own life or risk your property in receiving them – these reflections are not made in the East.'

She also pointed out an important fact to him perhaps not made before. 'I owe [not] a farthing to a poor peasant or a tradesman, but all to usurers and rascals that have lent their money out at an exorbitant interest. You may judge of their conscience,' she continued, 'in their last levy of troops, made about two months ago by Ibrahim Pasha, some rich peasants gave one hundred per cent for six months for money to buy off their sons who were conscripts.'

To Mr Speaker Abercrombie, with whom she used to play as a child, she wrote 'probably the wheel horse has forgotten his driver, but the latter has not forgotten him. I am told that the chief weight of the carriage of state bears upon you; if so it must be a ponderous one indeed, if I can judge by a specimen of the talent of those who guide it.' She continued, 'Your magnificent Queen has made me appear like a bankrupt in the world, and partly like a swindler. . . . Her Majesty has not thrown the gauntlet before a driveller or a coward.'

Sadly, her letter to Lord Palmerston has not survived. Judging from her form, it would have been a masterpiece of scathing but polite vituperation.

When all these letters had been sent there was nothing for her to do but wait. The longed-for letter from Sir Francis Burdett about her Irish inheritance had still not arrived and the enforced inactivity and feelings of helplessness were hard for her to bear. Occasionally she was overwhelmed by a black depression. An entry in Dr Meryon's memoirs tells of one such occasion.

'Lady Hester was in very low spirits this evening, and as night advanced, she had a paroxysm of grief which quite terrified me. With a ghastly and frenzied look, she kept crying until my heart was rent with her wretchedness. When I left her for the night, although she was somewhat composed, her image haunted me, even when sleep had closed my eyes.'

As spring approached, the weather improved and so did Lady Hester's health and spirits. She managed to get out into her garden, and Meryon recalled seeing her in one of her favourite alcoves.

'A sofa, covered with maroon-coloured cloth with flowered chintz cushions, ran across the back of the alcove. On this she was leaning, and being dressed in her white abah, with its large folds, she looked exactly like the statue of an antique Roman matron. ... As I advanced towards her, between two hedges – the one of double jessamine in full bud, and the other of the bright green periwinkle plant with its blue flowers forming an azure band from one end to the other – I was struck with the magical illusion which she ever contrived to throw around herself in the commonest circumstances of life.'

Even though she was ill and irascible she still had the power to charm and enchant – it was not something she tried to do, it was simply the way she was. She once said to Meryon late one evening, 'When I was young people might say there was something brilliant about me which caught everybody's attention. Now my looks are gone, but if I had not a tooth in my head, which will very soon be the case, I shall go on in my old way and change for nobody; so do not think with your grumpiness that I shall alter – and now go to bed.'

She made one last conquest that spring. She received a delightful letter from Prince Pückler-Muskau who was travelling in Egypt and Syria and wished to call upon Lady Hester to pay his respects. After first declining to see him, she finally agreed, persuaded by the charm of his letters. 'I find your highness to be a great philosopher but nevertheless a very unreasonable man,' she wrote flirtatiously. 'Is your object in coming here to laugh at a poor creature reduced by sickness to skin and bone, who has lost half her sight and all her teeth?'

Having agreed to entertain him, Lady Hester was thrown into a panic. She wanted to give a good impression and wished the Prince to be comfortable but she was well aware of the shortcomings of her monastery. There was nothing she could do about the cracks in the masonry and the fallen walls, but she found some old paint and had the doors repainted. She ordered the servants to lay out all her crockery on a courtyard floor, and pointing her stick at first one piece then another, she managed to muster some semblance of a tea and dinner service. Meryon offered his own crockery to her, but she refused. 'Let him see what I am reduced to,' she muttered. Paths were swept and linen sorted out. Her last few silver knives were taken out from under a cushion where she had put them for safety and counted out to the servants in the kitchen. All that could be done, was done.

The Prince arrived on Easter Sunday, 15 April, and stayed for six days. He was a dashing man of about fifty, stylishly dressed with an 'immense Leghorn hat, lined under the brim with green taffeta' to shade his fair complexion. With an Arab *keffiyah* thrown over his shoulders as a scarf, 'blue pantaloons of ample proportions' and Parisian boots, he cut quite a figure. When Meryon had first met him, to deliver Lady Hester's replies to his letters, he had had two chameleons crawling about him. *'Où sont mes petits bijoux?'* he had been heard to cry as he looked for them among his clothing. He had sensibly left his little jewels behind, and Lady Hester was charmed by him. Every night she and the Prince talked together for hours. 'What a handsome man the Prince has been, and is still, doctor, don't you think so?' she asked. He was one of those rare men who liked women enough to make even the old and toothless feel witty and attractive. It was the last time in her life that she was able to feel that way.

She confided in him about her pension being stopped and he agreed to help get the letters published when he returned to Europe, but months later he wrote to her that he had not felt the time was right to publish. She had been let down again.

In July, at long last, she received the long-awaited letter from Sir Francis Burdett. It was as she had feared: she had no legal claim on the Irish inheritance, and there was nothing he could do to help. She began, finally, to despair of everything and everyone. The recurring weakness in her chest had now become chronic: it was difficult for her to walk, even, at times, to breathe. She began to realize that her glorious dreams of riding into Jerusalem at the side of the Messiah were no more than empty illusions. Her bouts of depression became more frequent, and it was only her extraordinary strength of spirit that prevented her from giving up completely.

She began to face the possibility – and it was only that – of her own mortality. She had been near death several times before but only now, with her strength and health failing her, did it seem a reality. 'I have had a very bad night, and whether I shall live or die I don't know,' she told Meryon one morning, 'but this I tell you beforehand,' she continued, 'if I do die, I wish to be buried like a dog, in a bit of earth just big enough to hold this miserable skin, or else to be burnt, or thrown into the sea. And, as I am no longer an English subject, no consuls nor any English of any sort shall approach me in my last moments; for if they do I will have them shot.'

She was quite indomitable: being shot at from Lady Hester's death-bed was a threat any consul would be a fool to ignore. It was exactly the kind of dramatic and glorious gesture that she would have loved to make.

CHAPTER TWENTY-ONE

'There is my crime, to be independent'

Lady Hester decided that Meryon and his family should go back to England. Now there was to be no inheritance there was nothing for him to do and no money to pay him. He agreed to go, and started to wind up his affairs, but he had very mixed feelings about leaving Lady Hester. The truth was that he knew he would never see her again: it was clear to him that she was dying, and he knew that he was risking severe criticism if he left her to die alone. On the other hand, she had told him that she did not want him with her at the end. 'The day before I die, if know it, I shall order you away,' she told him severely, 'and not only you but everything English.' When she had made up her mind about something she was quite intractable, as Meryon well knew. 'Opposition to her will was altogether out of the question,' he had written once, wanly, and it was true. The doctor had always been a man of great common sense, and he decided the only thing to do was obey her as he almost always had, and leave.

In the middle of all the preparations, Lady Hester received another letter from Lord Palmerston in which he tried to excuse his confiscating of her pension as being in her own best interests.

'Any communications,' he wrote, 'have been suggested by nothing but a desire to save your ladyship from the embarrassments which might arise if the parties who have claims upon you were to call upon the consul-general to act according to the strict line of his duty, under the capitulations between Great Britain and the Porte.'

It was an extremely precarious piece of reckoning and it incensed Lady Hester. He knew perfectly well that the Consul-General had no power to act in any dispute between a Turkish national and a British citizen, and it was naive of him to think that Lady Hester would not know as well. He deserved the reply she sent.

'If your diplomatic despatches are as obscure as the one which now lies before me,' she wrote scathingly, 'it is no wonder that England should cease to have that proud preponderance in her foreign relations which she once could boast of.

'Your lordship gives me to understand that the insult which I have received was considerately bestowed upon me to avoid some dreadful, unnameable misfortune which was pending over my head.' She continued, 'I am ready to meet with courage and resignation every misfortune it may please God to visit me with, but certainly not insult from man. If I can be accused of high crimes and misdemeanours, and that I am to stand in dread of the punishment thereof, let me be tried as I believe I have a right to be, by my peers; if not, then by the voice of the people.'

Receiving Palmerston's letter had decided Lady Hester on a plan of action that was both dramatic and tragic.

'It is but fair to make your Lordship aware that, if by the next packet there is nothing definitively settled respecting my affairs, and that I am not cleared in the eyes of the world of aspersions, intentionally or unintentionally cast upon me, I shall break up my household, and build up the entrance gate to my premises, there remaining, as if I were in a tomb, till my character has been done justice to, and a public acknowledgement put in the papers, signed and sealed by those who have aspersed me. There is no trifling with those who have Pitt blood in their veins upon the subject of integrity.'

She did not hear from him again, and she remained true to her word. Before Meryon left she dismissed most of her servants and set the stonemasons to work, walling up the entrance to Djoun. Since she was a practical woman, she had them leave a little gap to allow her cows out to pasture, but it was a tragic gesture all the same. She felt, with considerable justification, that she had been betrayed by Britain, the country to whom so many of her family had dedicated their lives in outstanding political service, and in whose defence her brother, fiancé and many other close relatives had died. She felt, also with justification, that her former lover, her friends and her family had all deserted her too. The decision to have herself walled in symbolized her positive rejection of all those who had rejected her. It took just two days.

On 6 August, Meryon left for England for the last time. Both he and Hester were greatly saddened by his departure. She hated endings of any kind, and in the typical way she had of adding postscripts to all her letters she sent a servant racing after the doctor with a Persian rug to make the cabin on the steamer more comfortable for him and his family.

Meryon's feelings of sadness were compounded by a complex mixture of guilt and relief. His only consolation was that he knew that he could be of use to her in England, and so he was. He took with him a complete set of all the correspondence to do with her pension, and firm instructions that it was all to be made public. He managed to get all her letters published and an appeal on her behalf was printed in *The Times*. Despite his efforts, however, it all came to nothing.

Hester's belief in the intrinsic good of her peers and 'the people' was touching, but misplaced. The whole sad story was met with nothing but humiliating indifference and a degree of cruel amusement. Only one man stood up in her defence: her old friend Sir William Napier. To his everlasting credit he risked ridicule and ostracism by writing a dignified but impassioned letter to *The Times* defending his old friend.

'Sir,' he wrote, 'This "crack-brained lady", as some of your contemporaries – falling, with the true instinct of baseness, upon what appeared to them a helpless and afflicted woman – have called her, may appear, judged by English customs, somewhat wild in her views and expressions; but in the East she is, as she well deserves to be, for her nobleness and virtues revered.

'Her influence is vast with the Arab tribes,' he continued, 'and with all those who have suffered from Ibrahim's army, or who sigh over the tottering condition of the Turkish Empire. She, more than any person, can secure to England the friendship of nations whose goodwill must be vitally essential to our interests, when – and the time must soon come – we have to contend with Russia for the independence of the Porte. And if her disposition was not too noble, too magnanimous, to seek such revenge, English travellers in the East might bitterly rue the insults offered to Lady Hester Stanhope.

'It is no idle vaunt, no "crack-brained" threat for her to say "the gauntlet has been thrown down before no driveller or coward." To more than woman's quickness of perception, intuitive judgement and fortitude, she adds more than man's sagacity, intrepidity and daring. The extent of her power and resolution may be understood too late. If driven, by insult, to active enmity, she can and will do more of hurt to the interests of England in the East – aye, more of hurt than the pitiful policy of Lord Palmerston has already done in that quarter.'

He then gave his credentials for delivering such testimony.

'In early life I was an inmate of Mr Pitt's house, when Lady Hester Stanhope was the mistress of it, and when those who now insult her would have been too happy to lick the dust from her shoes. The hospitality, the kindness, the friendship I then experienced from Lady Hester did not cease with Mr Pitt's death, nor by me are they forgotten.'

He had remembered her well, and repaid her in full with this glowing tribute. It gave her immense pleasure and she wrote to him in buoyant mood: 'Good cometh out of evil. Who would have imagined that this disagreeable business would have been the means of my finding out and trying the friendship of one whom I always thought well of but from whom I could hardly expect after so many years so manly, so kind a demonstration of interest in my welfare?'

She knew that the letter had not been enough to sway public opinion, however, and continued sadly, 'There is my crime, to be independent. . . . It is a strange thing to have singled out one poor woman to abuse and be hard upon in every way, when so many women of fashion spend fortunes in dress and folly and run into debt without any reason whatever.' She still had her pride though: 'I am a mite, a very mite in my own eyes before men I have met with from the extremity of the East, but a giant before Lord Palmerston and his squad.'

She wrote to Meryon every month, and one letter in particular showed how much she had absorbed the Eastern attitude to life. 'Remember! All is written: we can change nothing of our fate by lamenting and grumbling,' she wrote. 'Therefore it is better to be like a true Turk and do our duty to the last and then beg of the believers in one God a bit of daily bread, and if it comes not, die of want, which perhaps is as good a death as any other, and less painful. But never act contrary to the dictates of conscience, of honour, of nature, or of humanity.'

She was grateful for all he had done for her in England, and anxious that he felt guilty about returning to England. 'Do not keep reproaching yourself about leaving me; it did not depend on you to stay,' she told him, kindly. It was the last letter she ever wrote to him.

Realizing that her pension was not going to be reinstated, she made one last attempt to get hold of some money to repay her debts. She wrote to Lord Hardwicke asking him if he would sell her pension and the annuity her brother James had left her in his will. It took several months for his reply to arrive.

'Were you in England,' he wrote, 'you could then manage to make terms with the creditors, so as to make you comfortable for life; and knowing, as I well do, that these debts were contracted chiefly to assist others, your conscience need not, I think, feel too acutely if, after your best exertions and your surrender of nearly all you have, your property will not cover the whole of your debts . . . but then you must be *seen* and *known,* and in *England* to produce this sum from your income. In the present state of affairs [with] yourself in Syria, it will fetch nothing; *they will not buy it.'*

Realizing that he had made great efforts to help her, she wrote back affectionately: 'What you say about my coming to England I understand, and appears very reasonable, but I cannot, will never, go there but in chains, therefore that subject must never more be mentioned.'

What she then wrote revealed that she knew herself very well. 'Do not be unhappy about my future fate,' she continued. 'I have done what I believe my duty, the duty of everyone of every religion; I have no reproaches to make of myself but that I went rather too far; but such is my nature, and a happy nature too, who can make up its mind to everything but insult.'

There was nothing more she could do, and two weeks later, on 23 June 1839, she died.

She died alone, except for the few servants she had retained, and we can only hope that she met her death with as much courage and cheerfulness as she had led her life. When the news finally reached England it provoked the same extremes of reaction to which she had been accustomed during her life. The following extraordinary obituary appeared in edition no. 1486 of *The Literary Gazette.*

'All the miseries to which she was subjected, or subjected herself, were the just and too light punishment for her utter want of feeling and savage barbarity towards every soul within the scope of her crazy vagaries and remorseless selfishness. She died as such a person ought to die, neglected and forsaken; for those who have no sympathies for their fellow-creatures deserve neither sympathy nor succour – as they have existed for themselves, let them perish by themselves and rot by themselves.'

Lady Hester had been quite unknown to that writer, and it is hard to imagine what fuelled such powerful vitriol.

The feelings of her friends, and all those who had known her were reflected in a brief letter that Sir Francis Burdett wrote to Philip: 'The death of so highly-gifted and honourable-minded and extraordinary a person as was Lady Hester . . . fills my heart with a sadness I could not have anticipated and can scarcely account for.'

When news of her death reached Beirut, Mr Moore, the British consul, set out for Djoun accompanied by the Reverend Thompson, an American missionary. They arrived late in the evening, and found Djoun apparently deserted, and Lady Hester's body lying in her bed, quite unattended. Since the weather was so hot, they decided she must be buried immediately and, finding some servants, placed her body in a plain deal box which they covered with a Union Jack. The tiny cortège wound its way through the paths of Lady Hester's garden by the light of flickering torches and lanterns until they came to the place where Captain Lousteneau was buried. Reverend Thompson managed to get lost in the winding alleys, and when he finally found the arbour, he saw a macabre scene. The captain's bones had been dug up and placed in a pile with his skull on the top. The servants had stuck a candle in each of his eye-sockets, a 'hideous, grinning spectacle'.

They buried her according to the Church of England service, and placed Captain Lousteneau's bones beside her. The presence of a despised consul, albeit Mr Moore, and the fact that her coffin was draped in the British flag would have had her reaching for her rifle.

Reverend Thompson was greatly affected by her burial, and made great efforts to find out all he could about her. What he wrote does not make a bad obituary.

'She was not merely sane, but sensible, well-informed and extremely shrewd. She possessed extraordinary powers of conversation, and was perfectly fascinating to all with whom she chose to make herself agreeable. She was, however, whimsical, imperious, tyrannical and at times, revengeful to a degree. Bold as a lion, she wore the dress of an Emir, weapons, pipe and all; nor did she fail to rule her Albanian guards and her servants with absolute authority.'

She was also unfailingly loyal and honourable. Strangely, for a clergyman, Thompson omitted to mention her charity and kindness to those in need, a continuing generosity that contributed to the sadness and poverty of her death, but his final observation was apposite:

'She was wholly and magnificently unique.'

Bibliography

Armstrong, M., *Lady Hester Stanhope*, Gerald Howe, 1927

Bruce, Ian, *The Nun of Lebanon*, Collins, 1951

Bury, Lady Charlotte, *Diary Illustrative of the Times of George IV*, 1838

Byron, Lord, *Letters and Journals*, 1898

Carick Moore, James, *Life of Sir John Moore*, 2 vols, 1834

Cleveland, Duchess of, *Life and Letters of Lady Hester Stanhope*, John Murray, 1897

Ehrmann, John, *The Younger Pitt*, Constable, 1969

Fox, Caroline, *Memoirs of Old Friends*, 1882

Gordon Hughes, Jean, *Queen of the Desert*, Macmillan, 1967

Hamel, Frank, *Lady Hester Lucy Stanhope: A New Light on her Life and Love Affairs*, Cassell, 1913

Haslip, Joan, *Lady Hester Stanhope: A Biography*, Cobden Sanderson, 1934

Hutton, W.H., *Constantinople*, Dent, 1900

Kinglake, Sir Alexander, *Eothen*, 1906

Meryon, Dr Charles (ed.), *Memoirs of Lady Hester Stanhope*, 3 vols, Henry Colburn, 1845

Meryon, Dr Charles (ed.), *Travels of Lady Hester Stanhope*, 3 vols, Henry Colburn, 1846

Newman, A., *The Stanhopes of Chevening*, Macmillan, 1969

Reilly, Robin, *Pitt the Younger*, Cassell, 1978

Selley, W.T., *England in the Eighteenth Century: 1689–1815*, A. & C. Black, 1934

Stanhope, G. and Gooch, G.P., *The Life of Charles, 3rd Earl of Stanhope*, Longmans, 1914

Thompson, Reverend W.M., *The Land and the Book*, Nelson and Sons, 1898

Archives

Letters between LHS and Thomas Coutts by kind permission of Coutts Bank, The Strand, London.

Letters and general correspondence between LHS and her family at Maidstone County Records Office.

Letters and papers in the Victoria and Albert Special Collections Department.

Index

Index

Index